THE GERMAN IMMIGRATION INTO PENNSYLVANIA

Through the Port of Philadelphia
from 1700 to 1775

AND

THE REDEMPTIONERS

ಐಐಐಐ

By

Frank Ried Diffenderffer

GENEALOGICAL PUBLISHING CO., INC.

Baltimore   *1988*

Originally Published as Part VII of
Pennsylvania: The German Influence in its
Settlement and Development; A Narrative and
Critical History in The Pennsylvania-German Society
Proceedings and Addresses, Vol. X, 1900
Reprinted: Genealogical Publishing Co., Inc.
Baltimore, 1977, 1979, 1988
Reprinted from a volume in the George Peabody Department
Enoch Pratt Free Library
Baltimore, Maryland
Library of Congress Catalogue Card Number 77-77782
International Standard Book Number 0-8063-0776-5
Made in the United States of America

TABLE OF CONTENTS.

THE REDEMPTIONERS.

CHAPTER VI.

CHAPTER VII.

CHAPTER VIII.

CHAPTER IX.

CHAPTER X.

INDEX TO FULL-PAGE INSETS.

ILLUSTRATIONS IN TEXT.

PREFATORY.

 THE story of the German immigration to Pennsylvania in the 17th and 18th centuries, and since, forms one of the most interesting and notable chapters in the history of the colonization of the New World. For many decades its importance and significance was not recognized or understood even by those who formed part and parcel of it. It is only within a recent period that it has received the attention it deserves. During the past few years a dozen books on this and germane subjects have been written and published and several more will be issued before the year's close.

Perhaps the main factor in directing attention to this needed work was the organization of the Pennsylvania-German Society in 1891. The enterprise of a few enthusiastic men resulted in arousing an interest in the subject unknown before. Their action met with a hearty response from Pennsylvanians of German descent in all

(5)

parts of the country, and while to-day it may not stand first in actual membership, the Society is certainly far in advance of every similar organization in the land in the amount of excellent work it has done towards carrying out the purposes of its organization, and in placing the German element in the colonization of Pennsylvania in its proper light before the world. Its contributions to the literature of the subject have received recognition and praise on two continents. The "Slumbering Giant," as the German element in Pennsylvania has been aptly called, has at last been aroused to a consciousness of his might and importance, his birthright and inheritance, and manifests a determination to assert his claims to the same.

The question of the German influence in the physical, political and intellectual upbuilding of this Commonwealth is of special interest to those of German ancestry. It has not yet been fully worked out but the present day is radiant with promise. The following chapters are offered as presenting some of the "lights and shadows" accompanying this immigration least familiar to the general reader.

It affords me much pleasure and satisfaction to make grateful acknowledgment to Julius F. Sachse, Esq., for the excellent original illustrations he has prepared to accompany this volume; they not only add much to its attractiveness, but have, in addition, an historical value all their own.

F. R. D.

LANCASTER, October, 1900.

CHAPTER I.

> "I hear the tread of pioneers,
>   Of nations yet to be ;
> The first low wash of waves where soon
>   Shall roll a human sea.
>
> "The rudiments of empire here,
>   Are plastic yet and warm ;
> The chaos of a mighty world
>   Is rounding into form."

IT must be conceded that the materials, both written and traditional, along many lines of the history of the Commonwealth of Pennsylvania are abundant and, for the most part, thoroughly reliable. Its founder was himself a university man, ready with tongue and pen, and the writer of many pamphlets, and his selection of agents, assistants and advisers proves him to have had a natural preference for cultured and scholarly men to aid him in carrying out his views for the advancement of his province. His

(7)

selection of the youthful but scholarly Logan, for more
than a generation his tried and trusty Secretary, Griffith
Owen, Samuel Carpenter and others, seems to show the
importance he attached to having men of culture about
him to forward his wise and enlightened schemes of government and commonwealth-building.   It was in a large
measure due to these men, along with himself, that the
mass of written material at the command of the diligent
historian of to-day is so full and so accessible.

Then, too, time has dealt kindly with our early records.
Much has undoubtedly been lost or destroyed, or, mayhap,
is still buried in unsuspected and neglected depositories;
but that which has disappeared or failed to appear must
of necessity be only a fractional part of the whole.   We
have no reason to believe that any material of supreme
importance to a reasonably full record of our provincial
period—any lost books of Livy, so to speak—has perished from our annals.   The chain of evidence along most
lines of investigation is as complete and unbroken as we
have a right to expect.   It is not to be expected that there
should not be a hiatus here and there, something to be
wished for, something that seems to be needed along a
stretch of time covering more than two hundred years of
the fortunes, the trials and triumphs of the most conglom-
erate people that ever built up a free and independent State
in modern times.   But we may congratulate ourselves that
our records, even back to our beginnings, are so full, and
that with them as faithful guides we can sit down and build
up anew upon the printed page the continuous story of the
men who laid deep and strong the civil, social, religious
and political foundations of Pennsylvania.

And yet there is one chapter, and that a very important
one, from which we turn with regret, because while it

deeply concerns all men of German, Swiss and Huguenot ancestry, it is the one most needed to throw light on the arrival of the first comers, the men who came here from the Rhine provinces during the first quarter of the eighteenth century. Of the many thousands that found their way across the broad Atlantic to Pennsylvania during that period, only a small portion brought written records with them, or took measures to prepare and preserve them after their arrival. The more highly educated did not neglect this obligation to posterity. Still others brought with them that most precious of all their household treasures, the heavy, oak-lidded German Bible, wherein the Old World pastor had with scrupulous care recorded the brief life and death record of the family. Most precious heirlooms are these household treasures to-day to the few so fortunate as to have them. But an infinitely greater number, descendants of those who had not the learning of the schools and who were incapable of preparing such memorials for themselves, left no such records for their descendants to fall back upon, and the latter have in consequence been left to sail about upon the broad sea of doubt and uncertainty, unable to obtain their bearings or find their moorings.

It is here that the historiographer of the "Immigration of the Germans through the port of Philadelphia" finds himself confronted with almost insuperable difficulties. During the period between 1683 and 1727, the landmarks that could and should guide him are not to be found. They have not been obliterated; they were never erected, and the perplexed chronicler sails to and fro over that unknown and uncharted sea of our provincial history, vainly endeavoring to pick up and preserve the flotsam which accident, rather than design, may have cast into his pathway. No wonder that to-day ten thousand men and women of

German ancestry are tireless in their search for the floating threads, the missing links that are needed to bind them to the unknown kindred in the Fatherland, but which in many instances have seemingly been lost forever.

When the first German settlers came to Pennsylvania, and in what numbers, and under what circumstances, are questions more easily asked than answered. Besides, it would perhaps be more interesting than profitable, for they left no permanent settlements, left no impress upon the future of the Province and may therefore be dismissed

ARMS OF SWEDEN.

with a mere allusion. The settlements planted by Gustavus Adolphus and his illustrious minister Oxensteirna on the Delaware in 1638, and later, although under the auspices of the Swedish king, contained a large infusion of Germans, to whom unusual inducements were offered. The second Governor of that little colony, Johannes Printz, was a Holsteiner, and brought with him a considerable number of Pommeranian families. These facts are ample to establish the presence of German settlers in Pennsylvania long before Pastorius led his colony of Crefelders to Germantown. Even as these pages are running through the press a letter has been found in Germany, through the efforts of a member of the Pennsylvania-German Society,[1] written from Germantown itself by one of the Op den Graeff brothers, dated February 12, 1684, in which the presence of a German Reformed congregation in that lo-

[1] Julius F. Sachse, Esq.

cality is announced at the time when the Pastorius colony was established. Who these were, whence they came, how long they had been there, and kindred questions may perhaps never be revealed, but the general subject is nevertheless a most interesting one.

The story of the first strictly German settlement in Pennsylvania, and of the men and women who composed it, has recently been so fully and so ably written as to leave nothing further to be desired.[2] Owing to circumstances which it is not necessary to recount in this place, the existing records were ample to prepare the story of the beginnings of that mighty Teutonic wave of immigration which, commencing with that colony of less than two score members in 1683, continued to come in an ever-increasing volume until it has outgrown and in a measure displaced some of the other nationalities which preceded it, and which was destined eventually to outnumber all the rest, a preëminence it has never lost, but which is to-day as marked and lasting as at any previous period in our history. Well have the results of the past two hundred years fulfilled the promise of that earlier day when Francis Daniel Pastorius and his earnest compatriots established their thriving settlement upon the verdant slopes of Germantown.

At the beginning of the German immigration, the wonderful dimensions it was destined to attain in the course of time seem not to have dawned upon anyone either in the Old World or the New. It was of gradual growth and it was not until nearly two score years after the founding of the Province that even an organized effort was made to

---

[2] See the splendid contribution to the Provincial history of Pennsylvania, *The Settlement of Germantown,* by JUDGE SAMUEL W. PENNYPACKER, published in Volume IX. of the *Proceedings of the Pennsylvania-German Society.*

take an account of the names and numbers of the Germans who landed on these shores. But although fear then did what should have been done from the beginning, the records made were far from complete. We have the names of most of the new comers, know the names of most of the vessels that brought them over, and in some instances the ages of the immigrants, but what to-day seems almost as essential as either of these, we cannot tell in the majority of cases the locality whence they came. They came from every portion of the German Empire; many from Switzerland; others were of French extraction, but who had for a generation or more been radicated in the cantons of Switzer-

SIGNATURE OF GUSTAVUS ADOLPHUS, KING OF SWEDEN.

land or in the Netherlands, whence, after acquiring the language of those countries, they finally made their way to the shores of the Delaware. In many instances family traditions preserved through after generations the precise name of the Old World home. Fortunate indeed are those who brought with them authenticating documents covering the birthplace, ancestry, age and other valuable items of family history. But the number of such is comparatively small when compared with the entire number of arrivals. How gratefully would such information be appreciated to-

GUSTAVUS ADOLPHUS, KING OF SWEDEN.

(BORN DEC. 9, 1594; DIED NOV. 16, 1632.)

FROM PAINTING AT HISTORICAL SOCIETY OF PENNSYLVANIA.

day by the thousands of German ancestry, who in their search for information covering these and other points find that their ancestors were among the ten or the fifty of the same name who came to America in the eighteenth century, but which they were or whence they came must ever remain a sealed book to them. Right here is where our historical annals are most defective. There should have been a complete registration from the beginning. Lacking that, ten thousand men and women of German lineage are to-day vainly longing for the information which in all human probability will ever remain irrecoverable.

ARMS OF THE HOLY ROMAN EMPIRE.

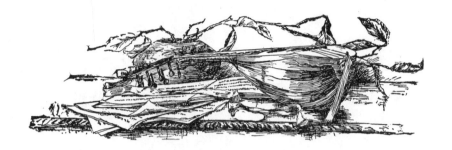

CHAPTER II.

Causes Leading to the Migration to Pennsylvania.—
Penn Favorably Known in Germany.—Descriptive
Accounts of the Province Published in Many Lan-
guages and Widely Circulated.

"There is nothing that solidifies and strengthens a nation like the reading of the nation's own history, whether that history is recorded or embodied in customs, institutions and monuments."

ALTHOUGH the causes responsible for the German immigration to Pennsylvania are to-day well understood, it will nevertheless be in order to refer to them briefly at the outset of this narrative. They were various and concurrent. There was a spirit of unrest and dissatisfaction throughout Europe and especially in Germany. That continent had been almost continuously torn by devastating wars for a hundred years previously. Destruction and desolation had been carried into millions of homes. In almost every kingdom and principality the tramp of the invader had been heard, and wherever he appeared ruin followed in his tracks by day,

(14)

and his incendiary torch marked his course by night. The peasant was no more considered in this clash of arms than the cattle in his fields. Like them he was valued only for what he was worth to his lord and master, whoever that might be. He was pressed into the ranks whenever his services were needed, while his substance was seized and converted to the public use. To eke out a scanty existence where the fates had located him without hope of betterment or material progression seemed the aim and end of his being. To rise from the plane of life to which he was born was a blessing vouchsafed to few. Generations of oppression and penury had in too many cases dwarfed the humanity within his soul, and he could only in exceptional cases look forward to anything better or higher.

But as the night of oppression and wrong was nearing its zenith, the light of a new and a better day was breaking. The fateful voyage of Columbus changed the fate and fortunes of two continents. It cleared the way for the era of maritime adventure which followed it at once. Western Europe arose and from the Iberian to the Scandinavian peninsulas the nations embarked upon a career of colonial enterprise. The marvellous tales told by the Genoese sailor of the new lands beyond the great ocean spread throughout the nations even more rapidly than the Fiery Cross among the ancient Highlanders of Scotland, and each one entered upon the game of seizing whatsoever it could of the spoils that seemed to await the earliest comer. England, Spain, The Netherlands, Sweden and France at once entered upon the work of seizure and division.

What a boundless field for enterprise, adventure and wealth was thus opened up to the cupidity of nations and of individuals, and how quickly they availed themselves of

the opportunity !   Colonists are needed to found colonies
and at once every available agency was employed to make
these new lands profitable to their new owners.   Government
companies were chartered, expeditions were authorized,
princely land grants were made to individuals and each
and all of these offered inducements to the lower ranks in
life, the husbandmen, the mechanics and men of all work
to enlist themselves in these new enterprises.   Of course the
most attractive inducements were held out to set this spirit
of emigration in motion.   The allurements of the pro-
moter of the present day hardly surpass, in their false attractiveness, the fairy tales held up before the starving
millions of the Old World by the Land Companies and
other schemers whose interests lay in the numbers they
could induce to cross the Atlantic and till their lands and
thus make them valuable.

It would require pages to tell this part of my subject in
all its fullness.   The printing press, that greatest of all
the agents in the world's civilization, was already held at
its true value.   The prospectus of to-day, it is true, was
not yet known, but in its stead the booklet was equally
effective.   Scores of small pamphlets of from ten to one
hundred or more pages each were written, printed and scattered throughout almost every country in Europe.[3]

CONCERNING PENNSYLVANIA.

To William Penn, and especially to his trusted agent
Benjamin Furly, must be credited the honor of diverting by
far the largest part of the German emigration to America,

---

[3] In Volume VII. of the *Proceedings of the Pennsylvania-German Society*
will be found the titles of more than two score of these booklets, all directing attention to the Province of Pennsylvania.   A few of the more important
ones will be found in this volume.

to his own Province. This fact has in recent years been so clearly demonstrated as to receive universal recognition. A chain of fortuitous circumstances seems to have been forged in the Divine workshop linking a series of events that finally culminated in the most remarkable, as it is also the most interesting, migration of a people from one country to another, although separated by thousands of miles of watery waste, which the world has ever seen.

Allusion has already been made to the crushed, oppressed and poverty-stricken character of the peasantry in certain parts of Germany, notably in the Rhine provinces, commonly known as the Palatinate. Religious persecutions were carried out against them even more relentlessly than the red hand of domestic and foreign wars. To a people ready to sacrifice and suffer all for conscience sake, the persecution by creed was as unbearable as that which despoiled them of their homes and their substance. Among these people thus affected, came in the year 1671 and again in 1677, a man of humble yet stately mien, one who preached the doctrines of peace and good will to men. He too had passed

ARMS OF PENN.

through the tribulations of persecution for conscience sake. He could enter into the true inwardness of the men of the Palatinate, condole, soothe and encourage. It was William Penn, the Quaker, whose religious tenets they found in comparison differed little from those held by the followers of Menno Simon, which was in itself a

strong bond of sympathy.   Penn's heart went out to these
resolute but amiable people.   Still another bond, one of
kinship, drew them to him.   His mother, Margaret Jasper,
was a Dutch woman and it has been alleged that Penn
spoke and wrote in Dutch and in German also, although
this is not certain.   There are few stronger ties than those
of language and this, perhaps, was not wanting.

At the period of his travels through Germany, Penn had
not yet acquired the ownership of Pennsylvania; it came
four years after his last visit.   Naturally, one of the first
things he undertook was to secure colonists for his newly-
acquired province.   The attention of Englishmen prior to
that period had been directed to New England, to Maryland, Virginia, and the young colonies to the south of her.
The Quakers, it is true, rallied around him and they were
his earliest adherents, and his was for a time a Quaker
colony.   But Penn was a man of broad and enlightened
views.   He cared little to what nationality his people belonged provided they were otherwise desirable.   Nor creed
nor birth nor color was excluded from the laws he formulated in 1682.[4]

A recent writer has referred to the influence exercised
by the personality of Penn upon the Germans in the Rhine
provinces in these words: " To all of them the news in
1681 that the tall young Englishman who four years before
had passed through the Rhine country, preaching a doctrine of religious life not very different from that of Menno
Simon, was now the proprietor in America of a vast region—greater than all Bavaria, Wurtemburg and Baden
together—and that he had invited them to come and live
there, without wars and persecutions, under laws which

---

[4] JOHN RUSSELL YOUNG'S *Memorial History of Philadelphia*, Vol. I., p.
62.

they should share in making—such news must indeed have roused and stirred many a discouraged peasant household." [5]

An earlier author wrote: "It has ever been the policy of our government (Pennsylvania), before and since the Revolution, and the disposition of our people to receive all sober emigrants with open arms, and to give them immediately the free exercise of their trades and occupations, and of their religion." [6]

It was this liberal spirit that at once induced him to turn towards his erstwhile friends in Germany. They, next to his own Quaker friends in England, were nearest his heart, and accordingly we find that among his first efforts to secure colonists were those directed towards Germany. He made them acquainted with his territory in America. He appointed agents to procure emigrants. Benjamin Furly,

an English Separatist, was perhaps the principal and most active of these and to him a large measure of credit is due for giving direction to the rising tide of Teutonic immigration. As early as March 10, 1682, he had sold several 5,000-acre tracts of land to merchants of Crefeld. This, it will be seen, was before Penn had himself visited his princely domain. In 1683 the elder Pastorius, as agent for a number of German friends, bought 25,000 acres, and on these the town of Germantown was soon after located.

That was the beginning, and thenceforward many

[5] JOHN RUSSELL YOUNG'S *Memorial History of Philadelphia*, Vol. I., p. 62.
[6] TENCH COXE, *A View of the United States of America*, p. 74.

other agencies were at work to increase the number of
German immigrants.   The Frankfort Land Company did
its utmost to attract settlers to its lands.   Such colonists as

were already here wrote home attractive accounts of the new home they
had found in the forests of Pennsylvania.   No one, however, was more
industriously engaged in this work
than Penn himself.   As early as 1681
he issued a pamphlet giving information concerning his province to
such as wished " to transport themselves or servants into those parts."
German and Dutch translations were
also printed and scattered broadcast
through the Low Countries and Germany.   In 1682 he sent out in English and German his *Brief Account
of the Province of Pennsylvania*.
Another description of his province
was issued in English, Dutch, German and French in 1684.   But his
were not the only pamphlets sent out.

FETT AMSEL.
(Blackbird) domestic fat
lamp, on stand.

Thomas Budd published an account in English in 1685 ;
Cornelius Bom one in Dutch in the same year ; Dr. Moore
one in English in 1687 ; the elder Pastorius one in German in 1692 ; Gabriel Thomas' well-known *Account* came
out in English and German in 1698 and had an excellent
effect, as had also Daniel Falkner's *Curiouse Information*,
published in Frankfort and Leipzig in 1702.[7]

---

[7] The above are only a small portion of this early Pennsylvania literature.
Fac-simile title pages of the above will be found in various places throughout
this volume.   For fuller details see JULIUS F. SACHSE's *Fatherland*, Volume
VII., *Proceedings of the Pennsylvania-German Society*.

CHAPTER III.

PENN'S OWN DESCRIPTION OF HIS PROVINCE, IN WHICH ITS
ADVANTAGES AND ATTRACTIONS ARE FULLY AND MINUTELY
SET FORTH FOR THE BENEFIT OF INTENDING EMIGRANTS.

"Bald zienen sie im fernen Westen
Des leichten Bretterhauses Wand ;
Bald reicht sie müden braunen Gästen,
Voll frischen Trunkes, eure Hand.

"Wie wird das Bild der alten Tage
Durch eure Träume glänzend weh'n !
Gleich einer Stillen, frommen Sage
Wird es euch vor der Seele steh'n."

IN the preceding chapter reference has been made to some of the early literature sent out by Penn and others concerning Pennsylvania. None is more attractive and interesting than the one entitled A Further Account of the Probince of Pennsylbania and its Inhabitants. For the Satisfaction of those that are (Abbenturers) and inclined to be so, written by Penn himself and published in 1685. It is full yet concise and, as will be seen, very fairly represents the actual con-

(21)

dition of things as they existed in the Province at that
time. As I know of no better account, I have reproduced
it almost in its entirety. There can be no manner of doubt
that, scattered throughout Central and Western Europe in
various languages, it was a mighty factor in directing immigration from the Fatherland towards Pennsylvania.

OF THE PRODUCE OF THE EARTH.

1. The EARTH, by God's blessing, has more than an-
swered our expectation; the poorest places in our Judg-
ment producing large Crops of Garden Stuff and Grain.
And though our Ground has not generally the symptoms
of the fat Necks that lie upon Salt Waters in Provinces
Southern of us, our Grain is thought to *Excell* and our
Crops to be as large. We have had the mark of the good
Ground amongst us from *Thirty* to *Sixty fold* of English
Corn.

2. The Land requires less seed: *Three pecks* of Wheat
sow an acre, a Bushel at most, and some have had the increase I have mention'd.

3. Upon Tryal we find that the Corn and Roots that
grow in *England* thrive very well there, as *Wheat, Barley,
Rye, Oats, Buck-Wheat, Pease, Beans, Cabbages, Turnips,
Carrots, Parsnups, Colleflowers, Asparagus, Onions, Char-
lots, Garlick*, and *Irish Potatoes;* we have also the *Spanish* and very good RICE, which do not grow here.

4. Our *low* lands are excellent for *Rape* and *Hemp* and
Flax. A Tryal has been made, and of the two last there
is a considerable quantity Dress'd Yearly.

5. The *Weeds* of our Woods feed our Cattle to the
Market as well as Dary. I have seen fat Bullocks
brought thence to Market before *Mid Summer*. Our
Swamps or Marshes yield us course Hay for the Winter.

A brief Account of the

Province of Pennsylvania,

Lately Granted by the

K I N G,

Under the GREAT

Seal of England,

T O

WILLIAM PENN

AND HIS

Heirs and Affigns.

Since (by the good Providence of *God*, and the Favour of the *King*) a Country in *America* is fallen to my Lot, I thought it not lefs my Duty, then my Honeft Intereft, to give fome publick notice of it to the World, that thofe of our own or other Nations, that are inclin'd to Tranfport Themfelves or Families beyond the Seas, may find another Country added to their Choice; that if they fhall happen to like the Place, Conditions, and Government, (fo far as the prefent Infancy of things will allow us any profpect) they may, if they pleafe, fix with me in the Province, hereafter defcribed.

I. *The* KING'S *Title to this Country before he granted it.*

It is the *Jus Gentium;* or Law of Nations, that what ever Wafte, or uncultted Country, is the Difcovery of any Prince, it is the right of that Prince that was at the Charge of the Difcovery: Now this *Province* is a Member of that part of *America*, which the King of *Englands* Anceftors have been at the Charge of Difcovering, and which they and he have taken great care to preferve and Improve.

                                          h   1 I. William

6. English GRASS SEED *takes well,* which will give us fatting Hay in time.   Of this I made an Experiment in my own Court Yard, upon sand that was dug out of my Cellar, with seed that had lain in a *Cask* open to the weather two Winters and a Summer; I caus'd it to be soun in the beginning of the month called *April,* and a fortnight before *Midsummer* it was fit to *Mow.*   It grew very thick: But I ordered it to be fed, being in the nature of a Grass Platt, on purpose to see if the roots lay firm: And though it had been meer sand, cast out of the Cellar but a Year before, the seed took such Root and held the earth so fast, and fastened itself so well in the Earth, that it held fast and fed like old English Ground.   I mention this, to confute the Objections that lie against those Parts, as that, first, English Grass would not grow; next, not enough to mow; and lastly, not firm enough to feed, from the Levity of the Mould.

7. All sorts of English fruits that have been tryed *take mighty well* for the time: The *Peach,* Excellent on standers, and in great quantities: They sun dry them, and lay them up in lofts, as we do roots here, and stew them with Meat in Winter time. *Mus Mellons* and *Water Mellons* are raised there, with as little care as Pumpkins in England.   The *Vine* especially, prevails, which grows everywhere; and upon experience of some *French People from Rochel* and the Isle of Rhee, GOOD WINE may be made there, especially when the Earth and Stem are fin'd and civiliz'd by culture.   We hope that good skill in our most Southern Parts will yield us several of the *Straights* Commodities, especially *Oyle, Dates, Figs, Almonds, Raisins* and *Currans.*

OF THE PRODUCE OF OUR WATERS.

1. Mighty WHALES roll upon the Coast, near the Mouth of the Bay of *Deleware.* Eleven caught and workt into Oyl one Season. We justly hope a considerable profit by a Whalery; they being so numerous and the Shore so suitable.

2. STURGEON play continually in our Rivers in Summer: And though the way of cureing them be not generally known, yet by a Reciept I had of one *Collins,* that related to the Company of the Royal Fishery, I did so well preserve some, that I had them good here three months of the Summer, and brought some of the same so for *England.*

3. ALLOES, as they call them in *France,* the Jews *Allice,* and our Ignorants, *Shads* are excellent Fish, and of the bigness of our largest *Carp*: They are so Plentiful, that Captain Smyth's Overseer at the *Skulkil,* drew 600 and odd at one Draught; 300 is no wonder; 100 familiarly. They are excellent Pickeled or Smok'd, as well as boyld fresh: They are caught by nets only.

4. ROCK are somewhat rounder and longer, also a whiter fish, little inferior in relish to our Mallet. We have them almost in the like plenty. These are often *Barrell'd like Cod,* and not much inferior for their spending. Of both these the Inhabitants increase their Winter Store: These are caught by Nets, Hooks and Speers. * * *

There are abundance of lesser fish to be caught of pleasure, but they gint not cost, as those I have mentioned, neither in Magnitude nor Number, except the *Herring,* which swarm in such Shoales that it is hardly Credible; in little Creeks they almost shovel them up in their tubs. There is the *Catfish* or *Flathead, Lampry, Eale, Trout, Perch, black* and *white Smelt, Sunfish,* etc.: also *Oysters, Cockles, Cunks, Crabs, Mussles, Mannanoses.*

OF PROVISION IN GENERAL.

1. It has been often said we were starv'd for want of food ; some were apt to suggest their fears, others to insinuate their prejudices, and when this was contradicted, and they assur'd we had plenty, both of Bread, Fish and Flesh, then 'twas objected that we were forc't to fetch it from other places at great Charges : but neither is all this true, tho all the World will think we must either carry Provision with us, or get it of the Neighborhood till we had gotten Houses over our heads and a little Land in tillage, we fetcht none, nor were we wholly helpt by Neighbors ; The *Old Inhabitants* supplied us with most of the Corn we wanted, and a good share of Pork and Beef : 'tis true *New York*, *New England* and *Road Island* did with their provisions fetch our Goods and Money, but at such Rates that some for almost what they gave, and others carried their provisions back, expecting a better Market neerer, which showed no scarcity, and that we were not totally destitute on our own River.   But if my advice be of any Value I would have them to buy still, and not weaken their Herds, by Killing their Young Stock *too soon*.

2. But the right measure of information must be the proportion of value of Provisions there, to what they are in more planted and mature Colonies.   Beef is commonly sold at the rate of *two pence per pound;* and *Pork* for *two* pence half penny ; Veal and Mutton at *three pence* or three pence half penny, that Country money ; an English shilling going for *fifteen pence*.   Grain sells by the *Bushel;* Wheat at four *shillings;* Rye, and excellent good, at *three shillings;* Barley *two shillings six pence; Indian Corn, two shillings six pence;* Oats, *two shillings,* in that money still, which in a new Country, where *Grain* is so much wanted for feed,

as for food, cannot be called dear, and especially if we consider the Consumption of many of the new Commers.

3. There is so great an increase of Grain by the dilligent application of People to Husbandry, that within three Years, some Plantations have got *Twenty* Acres in Corn, some *Forty*, some *Fifty*.

4. They are very careful to increase their stock, and get into *Daries* as fast as they can. They already make good *Butter* and *Cheese*. A good *Cow* and *Calf* by her side may be worth *three pounds* sterling, in goods at first Cost. A pare of Working *Oxen*, *eight pounds:* a pare of fat ones, *Little* more, and a plain Breeding *Mare* about *five pounds* sterl.

5. For *Fish*, it is brought to the Door, both fresh and salt. Six Alloes or Rocks for *twelve pence;'* and salt fish at *three fardings per pound*, Oysters at 2s per *bushel*.

6. Our DRINK has been *Beer* and *Punch*, made of Rum and *Water*: Our Beer was mostly made of molasses, which well boyld, with *Sassafras* or *Pine* infused into it, makes very tollerable drink; but now they make *Mault*, and Mault Drink begins to be common, especially at the Ordinaries and the Houses of the more substantial People. In our great Toun there is an *able Man*, that has set up a large *Brew House*, in order to furnish the People with good Drink, both there, and up and down the River."

This *Further Account* is too lengthy to be quoted in full here. He quotes a long letter written by one who had been in the Province and describes the existing conditions in the most favorable language. After this he resumes his own narrative, from which we make another extract.

" 1. It is agreed on all hands, that the *Poor* are the *Hands* and *Feet* of the Rich. It is their labour that Improves Countries; and to encourage them, is to promote the real benefit of the publick. Now as there are abundance of these people in many parts of *Europe*, extreamly desirous of going to *America;* so the way of helping them thither, or when there, and the return thereof to the Disbursers, will prove what I say to be true."

Then follow his several schemes for the settlement of immigrants upon his lands. The amount of lands to be allotted to each family; the improvements that will be built for them, the stock and farming tools that will be supplied, even their seed for the first year's harvest; this is followed by the easy terms upon which payment may be made, this for those who have the means to transport themselves thither, but no more. Still another plan provides for such as are destitute of any resources. To each family of such 100 acres are allotted, with £15 in hand before starting to provide adequately for the journey.

All in all, as we read over this scheme of colonization it appeals to our hearts and better natures as the wisest as well as most generous that had ever appeared among men. Plato's Republic, and Sir Thomas More's Utopia present nothing with all their wealth of ideal beneficence more striking than this practical, every-day humanitarianism of William Penn.

TIMES FOR MAKING THE VOYAGE.

While it was possible for ships to reach and leave Philadelphia during every month in the year, save occasionally during the inclement season of mid-winter, the late winter and autumn months were generally chosen for the departure from Europe. We accordingly find the ship arrivals were most numerous in early spring and late in the fall. April and May, September, October and November witnessed the largest influx of immigrants during the year.

Of such moment was this matter that Penn himself devotes a chapter in one of his various pamphlets, addressed to such as were casting their eyes across the Atlantic, to the proper season for the experiment. I quote what he says on this subject:

"Of the Seasons of Going, and Usual Time of Passage.

"1. Tho Ships go hence at all times of the Year, it must be acknowledged, that to go so as to arrive at *Spring* or *Fall*, is best. For the Summer may be of the hottest, for fresh Commers, and in the Winter, the wind that prevails, is the *North West*, and that blows off the Coast, so that sometimes it is difficult to enter the *Capes*.

"2. I propose, therefore, that Ships go hence (from Europe) about the middle of the moneths call'd *February* and *August*, which allowing two months for passage reaches in time enough to plant in the *Spring* such things as are carried hence to plant, and in the *Fall* to get a small Cottage, and clear some Land against next *Spring*. I have made a discovery of about a hundred Miles West, and find those back Lands richer in Soyl, Woods and Fountains, than that by Deleware; especially upon the *Susquehanna River*.

"3. I must confess I prefer the Fall to come thither, as believing it more healthy to be followed with Winter than Summer; tho, through the *great goodness and mercy of God* we have had an extraordinary portion of health, for so new and numerous a Colony, notwithstanding we have not been so regular in time.

"4. The *Passage* is not to be set by any man; for Ships will be quicker and slower, some have been *four* months, and some but *one* and as often. Generally between *six and nine weeks.* One year, of four and twenty Sayl, I think, there was not three above nine, and there was one or two under six weeks in the passage.

" 5. To render it more healthy, it is good to keep as much upon *Deck* as may be ; for the *Air* helps against the offensive smells of a *Crowd*, and a *close place.* Also to *Scrape* often the Cabbins, under the Beds ; and either carry store of *Rue* and *Wormwood ;* and some *Rosemary*, or often sprinkle *Vinegar* about the Cabbin. *Pitch* burnt, is not amiss sometimes against faintness and infectious scents. I speak my experience for the benefit and direction that may need it."[8]

The very minuteness with which every detail is given indicates the desire to leave no room for misunderstandings. He was anxious that there should be no cause for complaint. His very frankness must have convinced his readers and won them. All this became apparent to the new immigrant and this was no doubt one of the principal reasons why the reports sent back to Germany were almost universally favorable, and proved instrumental in keeping up the immigration movement so many years.

Peter Kalm, the Swedish botanist and traveller, who visited America in 1748, bears strong evidence to the fact that the large immigration of Germans was in a great measure due to the solicitation of those already here. He says : " The Germans wrote to their relatives and friends and advised them to come to America ; not to New York where the government had shown itself to be unjust. This advice had so much influence that the Germans who afterwards went in great numbers to North America constantly avoided New York, and always went to Philadelphia. It

---

[8] See PENN'S A Further Account of the Province of Pennsylvania and its Improvements. For the satisfaction of those that are adventurers and inclined to be so.

sometimes happened that they were forced to go on board such ships as were bound for New York, but they were scarcely got on shore before they hastened to Pennsylvania, in sight of all the inhabitants of New York." [9]

The historian Proud, writing in 1798, says that " William Penn, both in Person and writing, published in *Germany*, first gave them information that there was liberty of conscience in *Pennsylvania*, and that everyone might live there without molestation. Some of them about the year 1698, others in 1706, 1709 and 1711, partly for conscience sake, and partly for their temporal interests, removed thither, where they say they found their expectations fully answered, enjoying liberty of conscience according to their desire, with the benefits of a plentiful country. With this they acquainted their friends in *Germany ;* in consequence of which many of them in the year 1717, etc., removed to Pennsylvania." [10]

Another of our historians explicitly states that " from the writings and discourses of William Penn during his German travels they (the Germans) obtained a knowledge of Pennsylvania. Some of them removed to the Province in 1683, others in 1706–1709 and 1711. Their reports induced many to follow them in 1717." [11]

[9] KALM'S *Travels in North America*, p. 270.

[10] PROUD'S *History of Pennsylvania*, Vol. II., pp. 344-345.

[11] GORDON'S *History of Pennsylvania*, p. 573.

CHAPTER IV.

Efforts to Secure Colonists, Successful.— Alarm Created by their Great Numbers From Germany.— System of Registration Adopted.— Arrival of many Ships.— Their Names, Numbers and Places of Departure.

> "Vaterland! theurer Freund, lebt wohl!
> In dem es nach der Fremde soll:
> Ein anderes Land, eine and're Luft
> Die uns mit Ernst entgegen ruft;
> Kommt, kommt, hier solt ihr ruhig seyn
> Ungestört, frei von leibes Pein."

> "O Sprecht! warum zogt ihr von dannen?
> Das Neckarthal hat Wein und Korn;
> Der Schwarzwald steht voll finstrer Tannen?
> Im Spessart klingt des Älplers Horn."

WHILE the various measures put into operation by the proprietor to secure colonists were at once active and persistent, the results for a time were unimportant so far as immigration from Germany was concerned. The Crefeld colony under Francis Daniel Pastorius began its settlement at Germantown in 1683. The accessions to that early body were not numerous during the remainder of the seventeenth

century. Still, a few came each year. Johannes Kelpius
with his band of 40 pietists appears to have been among
the first to arrive after the Crefelders; he came in 1694.
Daniel Falkner brought additions in 1704. "In 1708–
1709–1710 to 1720 thousands of them emigrated. From
1720 to 1725 the number increased and settled principally
in Montgomery, Berks and Lancaster counties. In 1719
Jonathan Dickinson wrote, ' we are daily expecting ships
from London which bring over Palatines, in number about
six or seven thousand. We had a parcel who came out
about five years ago, who purchased land about sixty
miles west of Philadelphia, and proved quiet and industrious.' " [12]

This latter colony evidently refers to the little band of
Mennonites, perhaps I should say Swiss-Huguenots, who
came over in 1708 or 1709 and located themselves in the
Pequea Valley, Lancaster county, forming the first settlement of Europeans within that County.[13]   Some members
of that colony almost immediately returned to Germany to
bring over relatives and friends, and between the years
1711 and 1717, and for some years later there were large
accessions to the colony. It was one of the most substantial and successful settlements ever made in Pennsylvania.
Even then, as in later years, most of the colonists came
from the Palatinate, which sent forth her children from her
burned cities and devastated fields, their faces turned towards
the land of promise. Just how many Germans landed at
the port of Philadelphia prior to the passage of the registry law of 1727 is unknown, but the number was undoubtedly large as may be inferred from the quotation above from

---

[12] RUPP'S *Thirty Thousand Names,* p. 10.

[13] "Im Jahr 1709 Kamen etliche familien von der Pfalz welche von den
vertriebenen Schweizern abstamnten und liessen sich nieder in Lancaster
county." BENJAMIN EBY'S *Geschichte der Mennoniten,* p. 151.

Jonathan Dickinson. It was not until 1707 however that Germans in considerable numbers began arriving. From that time onward the number increased from year to year, and ten years later began to attract the attention of the Provincial Government.

The country seemed to be filling up with Germans, and as a result of the alarm that was caused thereby, Governor William Keith soon after his arrival, on September 7, 1717, observed to the Provincial Council sitting at Philadelphia " that great numbers of foreigners from Germany, strangers to our Languages and Constitutions, having lately been imported into this Province daily dispersed themselves immediately after Landing, without producing any Certificates, from whence they came or what they were; and as they seemed to have first Landed in Britain, and afterwards to have left it Without any License from the Government, or so much as their Knowledge, so in the same manner they behaved here, without making the least application to himself or to any of the magistrates; That as this Practice might be of very dangerous Consequence, since by the same method any number of foreigners from any nation whatever, as well Enemys as friends, might throw themselves upon us : The Governor, therefore, thought it requisite that this matter should be Considered, & 'tis ordered thereupon, that all the masters of vessels who have lately imported any of these fforeigners be summoned to appear at this Board, to Render an acct. of the number and Characters of the Passengers respectively from Britain; That all those who are already Landed be required by a Proclamation, to be issued for that purpose, to Repair within the space of one month to some Magistrate, particularly to the Recorder of this City (Philadelphia), to take such Oaths appointed by Law as are

Beschreibung

Der in AMERICA neu-erfundenen

PROVINZ

PENSYLVANIEN.

Derer Inwohner / Gesetz / Arth / Sitten und Gebrauch:

Auch sämtlicher Reviren des Landes /

Sonderlich der Haupt-Stadt

PHILA-DELPHIA

Alles glaubwürdigst

Auß des Gouverneurs darinnen erstatteten

Nachricht.

In Verlegung bey Henrich Heuß an der Banco / im Jahr 1684.

TITLE-PAGE OF THE GERMAN VERSION OF PENN'S LETTERS TO THE
Free Society of Traders.

necessary to give assurances of their being well affected to his Majesty and his Government; But because some of these foreigners are said to be Menonists, who cannot for Conscience sake take any Oaths, that those persons be admitted upon their giving any Equivalent assurances in their own way and manner, & that the Naval Officer of this Port be required not to admit any inward bound vessell to an Entry, until the master shall first give an exact List of all their passengers imported by them." [14]

The Provincial Council perhaps never did an act that so much deserves the thanks and the gratitude of those of German descent in the State of Pennsylvania to-day as in embodying the foregoing views in an Act of the Assembly a few years later. It resulted in the registration of the many thousands of German and other immigrants, and these ship masters' lists as we find them to-day in the *Colonial Records*, Rupp's *Thirty Thousand Names*, and *Volume XVII. of the Second Series of Pennsylvania Archives* are a priceless treasure, a veritable storehouse to which thousands of people of German ancestry have gone to find information concerning the names, ages and time of arrival of their ancestors. Never was a government scare so productive of good results.

GREAT SEAL OF THE PROVINCE.
(REVERSE).

The order was immediately acted upon. At the next meeting of the Council on September 9, 1717, Capt. Rich-

---

[14] *Colonial Records: First Series*, Vol. III., p. 29.

mond, Capt. Tower and Capt. Eyers waited upon the Board with the lists of the Palatines they had brought over from London, by which it appeared the first had carried one hundred and sixty-four, the second ninety-one and the last one hundred and eight.

There is no evidence however, that I am aware of, that anything further was immediately done towards carrying out the order passed in 1717. The minutes of the Council are silent on the subject for ten full years.

On September 14, 1727, again acting on the Governor's suggestion, a resolution was adopted by the Provincial Council holding shipmasters to a strict accountability and ordering an examination into the matter of bringing aliens into the Province. Here is the Resolution: " That the masters of vessels importing Germans and others from the continent of Europe, shall be examined whether they have leave granted to them by the Court of Great Britain for the importation of these foreigners, and that a List be taken of all these people, their several occupations, and the place from whence they came, and shall be further examined touching their intentions in coming hither; and that a writing be drawn up for them to sign, declaring their allegiance and subjection to the King of Great Britain, and fidelity to the Proprietary of this Province, and that they will demean themselves peaceably towards all his Majesty's subjects, and observe and conform to the Laws of England and the Government of Pennsylvania." [15] The arrival of a ship load of German immigrants on September 21, 1727, appears to have recalled to the Council the action it had decided upon ten years before. At a meeting held on September 21, 1727, the following appears on the minutes:

" A Paper being drawn up to be signed by those Pala-

---

[15] *Colonial Records: First Series*, Vol. III., p. 283.

tines, who should come into this Province with an Intention to settle therein, pursuant to the order of this Board, was this day presented, read & approved, & is in these Words :

"We Subscribers, Natives and late Inhabitants of the Palatinate upon the Rhine & Places adjacent, having transported ourselves and Families into this Province of Pennsylvania, a Colony subject to the Crown of Great Britain, in hopes and Expectation of finding a Retreat & peaceful Settlement therein, Do Solemnly promise & Engage, that We will be faithful & bear true Allegiance to his present MAJESTY KING GEORGE THE SECOND, and his Successors Kings of Great Britain, and will be faithfull to the Proprietor of this Province ; And that we will demean ourselves peaceably to all His said Majesties Subjects, and strictly observe & conform to the Laws of England and this Province, to the utmost of our Power and best of our understanding."

A signed list was then presented to the Board, on which were the names of one hundred and nine Palatines, who, with their families, numbered about four hundred persons, who had just arrived at the port of Philadelphia, on the ship *William and Sarah*, William Hill, Master, from Rotterdam, but last from Dover, England.   Captain Hill was asked whether he had a license from any Court in Great Britain to bring these people into the Province and what their intentions were in coming here.   He replied that he had no other authority than the ordinary ship clearance, and that he believed the immigrants designed to settle in the Province.   After this the persons who had come over on the *William and Sarah* were then called before the Board, and " did repeat & subscribe the foregoing Declaration."

As a matter of interest the names of this earliest importation of Germans under the new regulations are here
given. The list is the forerunner of hundreds more which
were placed on record during the following fifty years. It
has been doubted whether the lists preserved in the State
archives at Harrisburg are complete. At all events some
years are missing. The war with France put a stop to
nearly all this traffic, so that between 1756 and 1763 only
one or two arrivals of immigrant ships are recorded; in
1745 none at all.

The result of that action was that thereafter lists were
regularly made by the masters of ships bringing passengers
to this country, which lists are still preserved in the archives
of the State, at Harrisburg. Sometimes triplicate lists
were prepared. These were submitted to the Provincial
authorities for their satisfaction and guidance, and also became of service when contracts between these people and
those who hired or bought them were made.[16]

There are good reasons for believing that the ships lists
as we find them in Rupp, in Volume XVII. of the Second
Series of Pennsylvania Archives, and of course in the Colonial Records from which they were mainly compiled,
are in some cases defective, in that they do not in every
instance give the full list of those who came. To what
extent these omissions have been carried, it is impossible
to say from our present knowledge of the subject, but it is
possible that later investigations in Germany and Switzerland may bring fuller lists to light.[17]

---

[16] RUPP'S *Thirty Thousand Names,* p. 40.

[17] That indefatigable and successful searcher into the early ecclestiastical
and secular history of Provincial Pennsylvania, Professor W. J. Hinke, during
his researches in Europe, found, as we learn from a recent article contributed to
Notes and Queries, a pamphlet printed in Zurich, in 1735, called *The Limp-
ing Messenger from Carolina, or the Description of a journey from Zurich*

I. D. Rupp makes the following remarks concerning
these triple lists :

"The master's or captain's lists contain the names of
all male passengers above the age of sixteen, and some of
them, the names of all the passengers. If any had *died*,
or were *sick* on the arrival of the ship, they are marked
accordingly.

"Another list contains all the names of males above the
age of sixteen, who were made to repeat and subscribe the
Declaration of allegiance, with their own hands, if they
could write, if they could not the name was written by a
clerk, and the qualified person made his mark.

"The third list is an *autograph* duplicate of the second
one, signed in the same way, and is preserved in book
form." [18]

A LIST OF YE PALATINE PASSENGERS IMPORTED IN YE SHIP
WILLIAM AND SARAH, WILL'M HILL, MAST'R, FROM
ROTTERDAM, PHLID'A YE 18 SEPT'BRE 1727.

Hans Jerrick Swaess,   Hans Mich^le Siell,
Benedice Strome,   Jacob Josi,
Hans Jerrick Shoomaker,   Daniel Levan,
Hans Martain Shoomaker,   Andr^w Simmerman,
Hans Mich^le Pagman,   Hans Jerrick Wigler,
Johan Ilabaraker,   Johan Wester,
Hieromnius Milder,   Hans Adam Milder,
Henericus Bell,   Henrick Mayer,
Hans Seri Seigler,   Jacob Gons,

---

to Rotterdam, by Ludwig Weber, from Wallisellen, in which is given a list of
the Swiss emigrants to Pennsylvania on the ship *Mercury*. This list contains
a number of names not given in Rupp's list or that of Vol. XVII. of the Archives. Better still, it gives the name of the place from which each one of
the colonists went. These colonists left Zurich in October, 1734, and reached
Philadelphia May 29, 1735, having been more than six months on the way.

[18] RUPP'S *Thirty Thousand Names*, p. 40.

Sebastian Vink,
Jacob Swicker,
Hans Bernard Wolf,
Ann Floren,
Hans Jacob Ekinan,
Hendrick Wiltier,
Jacob Pause,
Hans Jerrick Wolf,
Hans Jerrick Bowman,
Hans Jerig Anspag,
Christ^r Milder,
Patrick Sprigler,
Joh Tob^s Serveas,
Johannes Eckman,
Christ^o Layhengyger,
Andrew Haltspan,
Hans Jerrick Schaub,
Christian Snyder,
Johannes Bartelme,
Johannes Dübendöffer,
Joseph Aelbraght,
Jacob Meyer,
Johannes Balt,
Christopher Walter,
Hans Adam Stall,
Hans Martin Wilder,
Hans Jerig Arldnold,
Hans Jerig Reder,
Hendrick Gonger,
Hans Jerig Roldebas,
Christopher Wittmer,
Clement Eirn,
Johannes Mich^{le} Peepell,
Philip Siegler,
Rudolph Wilkes,
Abraham Farn,

Hans Mart^n Levisbergn,
Jan. Hend^n Scaub,
Abraham Beni,
Frederick Hiligas,
Sebastian Creek,
Alex. Diebenderf,
Johan Willm May,
Casper Springler,
Michael Peitley,
Jno. Barne Levinstey,
Johannes Jlon,
Hans Mich^{le} Weider,
Leonard Seldonrick,
Willm Turgens,
Willm Tleer,
Anspel Anspag,
Adam Henrick,
Ulrich Sieere,
Junicus Meyer,
Hans Jor^g Glergelf,
Steven Frederick,
Philip Feruser,
Hans Filkcysinger,
Hans Jerrick Hoy,
And^w Saltsgerrer,
Jacob Wilder,
Johannis Stromf,
Philip Swyger,
Elias Meyer,
Martin Brill,
Peter Leyts,
Johanes Hen^{dk} Gyger,
Johannes Berret,
Jacob Swartz,
Hans Mich^l Phauts,
Bastiaen Smith,

Tobias Frye,	Albert Swope,
Jacob Mast,	Diederick Rolde,
Nicholas Adams,	Hans Adam Biender,
Johanes Leyb,	Hendrick Hartman,
Conrad Miller,	Philip Jacob Reylender,
Ulrich Hertsell,	Ernest Roede,
Hans Jerick Guyger,	Philip Roedeall,
Hans Jerig Viegle,	Hans Jerig Milder,
Hans Jerig Cramen,	Uldrick Staffon.

While this German immigration was considerable in some years prior to 1727, it was irregular and seemingly spasmodic. Apparently it was gathering strength and courage for the half century of irrepressible exodus which was to follow. In the fall of 1727, five ships laden with German immigrants reached the wharves of Philadelphia. It was no doubt these numerous arrivals that alarmed the

A PIONEER GERMAN HAMLET.

Provincial government anew and led to the imposition of the 40-shillings head tax on all aliens. From that time on the record of arrivals is almost continuous, and although there are several short breaks in it, we are enabled, nevertheless, to get a fairly accurate idea of its extent and also of the manner in which it was carried out.

TABLE SHOWING THE ARRIVAL OF GERMAN IMMIGRANTS DURING THE SPACE OF 44 YEARS, AND COVERING THE PERIOD OF THAT IMMIGRATION'S GREATEST ACTIVITY.

The following is the number of immigrant ships that reached the port of Philadelphia in the period between 1727 and 1775, both years inclusive, of which records have been preserved.

Year.	Number.	Year.	Number.	Year.	Number.
1727	5	1743	9	1759	none
1728	3	1744	5	1760	none
1729	2	1745	none	1761	1
1730	3	1746	2	1762	none
1731	4	1747	5	1763	4
1732	11	1748	8	1764	11
1733	7	1749	21	1765	5
1734	2	1750	14	1766	5
1735	3	1751	15	1767	7
1736	3	1752	19	1768	4
1737	7	1753	19	1769	4
1738	16	1754	17	1770	7
1739	8	1755	2	1771	9
1740	6	1756	1	1772	8
1741	9	1757	none	1773	15
1742	5	1758	none	1774	6
		1775			2

In all, 321 ships in 44 years: 43 in the first ten years, 67 in the second ten, 121 in the third decade, and 88 during the last eighteen years.

From the foregoing table it will be observed that the tide of immigration ebbed and flowed by years and periods. Sometimes these variations can be accounted for and then

again they appear inexplicable. It is reasonable to suppose the 40-shillings law was responsible to some extent
for this fluctuating immigration, as so onerous a head tax
as $10 would be likely to exercise a restraining effect on
the poorest class which was already compelled to endure
severe financial strains. It may be that some other cause,
the nature of which has not come down to us, was operative
in producing this result. At the same time it is well to remember there seems to have been a natural ebb and flow in
the numbers without any plausible reason for the same.

The 1,240 arrivals in 1727 were succeeded by 152 families numbering only 390 in 1728, and by only 243 in 1729.[19]
An improvement began in 1730, when the number increased
to 458, and they were succeeded by 631 in 1731. In 1732,
no fewer than 2,093 were landed; that was high-water
mark for a number of years, but in 1738 the number ran up
to 3,115. The numbers then proceed with considerable
regularity until 1745, when no ship with immigrants was
registered. Whether none arrived or whether the records
have been lost or mislaid I do not know; most likely the
latter, as we are in possession of no information that might
suggest a cause for this stoppage. Besides, there were no
other years without arrivals until 1757; during that and the
succeeding three years immigration ceased entirely. That
was due to the breaking out of hostilities between Great
Britain and France, which, as a matter of course, also involved the colonies of the two powers on this continent,
and which became known in America as the French and
Indian War; the Six Nations having united their fortunes
with France and her important colony of Canada. All

---

[19] During the year 1729, there were of English and Welsh passengers and
servants, 267, Scotch servants 43, Irish passengers and servants 1,155, Palatine
(alien, or 40 shilling) passengers 243; by way of Newcastle, chiefly passengers and servants from Ireland, 4,500.—HUGH'S *Historical Account*, p. 163.

manner of hostile French sea craft swept the Atlantic, depredating on English commerce, and however desirous Germans may have been to come to America, the danger of capture by the enemy's ships was a contingency that had to be considered.

After peace was concluded the tide once more began coming in a very steady stream until 1773, when it reached the highest point attained since 1754, and from which time it gradually dwindled until it no longer remained so prominent and distinctive a feature in the colonization of the State and Nation.

As throwing much light on the general question, as well as a matter of interest and curiosity, I here give the names of the ships, the dates of their arrival and the number of persons who came on them, during the period of a single year—that of 1738:

ARRIVALS IN A SINGLE YEAR.

Name of Ship.	Date of Arrival.	No. of Passengers.
Catharine	July 27	15
Winter Galley	Sept. 5	252
Glasgow	Sept. 9	349
Two Sisters	Sept. 9	110
Robert and Oliver	Sept. 11	320
Queen Elizabeth	Sept. 16	300
Thistle	Sept. 19	300
Nancy and Friendship	Sept. 20	187
Nancy	Sept. 20	150
Fox	Oct. 12	95
Davy	Oct. 25	180
Saint Andrew	Oct. 27	300
Bilender Thistle	Oct. 28	152
Elizabeth	Oct. 30	95
Charming Nancy	Nov. 9	200
Enterprise	Dec. 6	120

Very frequently two ships came into port on the same day. On September 3, 1739, and again on September 16, 1751, and September 27, 1752, three of these vessels sailed into port. The latter year is noted for its double arrivals, there having been two on the 22d of September, two on the 23d and three on the 27th. September 30, 1754, beat all records, no fewer than four immigrant ships having come into the port of Philadelphia on that day.

From 1737 to 1746, sixty-seven ships arrived bringing nearly fifteen thousand Germans, nearly all of whom sailed from Rotterdam. Of the first 100 ships that came with immigrants, four came in the month of May, one in June, one in July, fourteen in August, fifty in September, nineteen in October, five in November, four in December, and one each in January and February—the latter doubtless delayed by contrary winds or storms beyond their usual times. Among that 100 were seventy different ships. Some made a regular business of this kind of traffic and came a number of times. The *Samuel* has six voyages to her credit; the *Saint Andrew* four, the *Royal Judith* five and the *Friendship* five. Many names continue on the lists for many years. Some of these craft were called vessels, others ranked as ships, while there were still others known as " snows," " brigantines," " pinks," " brigs " and " billenders," names apparently applied to small craft, and which nomenclature, in part at least, is no longer current among ship-builders and sea-faring men.

The size of the ships on which these immigrants reached Pennsylvania, varied very considerably. A list of sixteen which I have found gives the smallest as 63 feet long over the gun deck, 20 feet 11 inches breadth of beam and 9 feet $7\frac{1}{2}$ inches as the depth of hold, with a tonnage of $108\frac{73}{94}$ tons; and the largest 99 feet 8 inches as length of deck,

Good Order Established
I N
Pennſilvania & New-Jerſey
I N
A M E R I C A,

Being a true Account of the Country ;
With its Produce and Commodities there made.

And the great Improvements that may be made by means of 𝔓ublick 𝔖to𝔯e-houſes for 𝔥emp, 𝔣lax and 𝔏innen-𝔠loth ; alſo, the Advantages of a 𝔓ublick-𝔖chool, the Profits of a 𝔓ublick-𝔅ank, and the Probability of its ariſing, if thoſe directions here laid down are followed. With the advantages of publick 𝔊𝔯anaries.

Likewiſe, ſeveral other things needful to be underſtood by thoſe that are or do intend to be concerned in planting in the ſaid Countries.

All which is laid down very plain, in this ſmall Treatiſe ; it being eaſie to be underſtood by any ordinary Capacity. To which the *Reader* is referred for his further ſatisfaction.

By *Thomas* *Budd*.

Printed in the Year 1685.

TITLE-PAGE OF BUDD'S *Tract*, PRINTED BY WILLIAM BRADFORD, PHILADELPHIA.

26 feet 5 inches as breadth of beam and a tonnage of $311\frac{16}{94}$ tons.   The average tonnage of the sixteen was 178 tons.

In some years the immigrants were nearly all from the Palatinate.   Then again Wurtembergers, Hannoverians, Saxons and Alsatians came, flocking by themselves, doubt- less because, coming from the same locality, they desired to settle together after their arrival.   At still other times the immigrants on a ship were composed of the subjects of half a dozen German rulers.

The principal port of embarkation was Rotterdam, and thence to Cowes, on the Isle of Wight.   Sometimes ships would load up in London, but generally with small num- bers.   Among the other points of departure were Rotter- dam and Leith; Rotterdam and Deal; Rotterdam and Plymouth, Rotterdam and Portsmouth; Hamburg and Cowes; Amsterdam and Cowes, and other places.   In 1770 three ships arrived from Lisbon, Portugal, with mostly Germans, but a few of other nationalities.   In October, 1774, the ships *Polly* and *Peggy*, arrived from Lisbon, bringing an entire cargo of Portuguese, Spaniards or French.

I quote the following from a prominent historian as pertinent to the question of numbers.

" In the summer of 1749 twenty-five sail of large ships arrived with *German* passengers alone; which brought about twelve thousand souls, some of the ships about six hundred each; and in several other years nearly the same number of these people arrived annually; and in some years near as many from *Ireland*.   By an exact account of all the ships and passengers annually which have arrived at Philadelphia, with Germans alone, nearly from the first settlement of the Province till about the year 1776, when their importation ceased, the number of the latter appears to be about thirty-nine thousand; and their internal increase has been very great. The Germans sought estates in this country, where industry and parsimony are the chief requisites to procure them." [20]

This statement is self-contradictory. In the first place, very few of the ships brought 600 passengers. That seems to have been about the extreme limit that came on any one vessel at a time. Only the very largest ships could carry that number. The smaller craft, and they were far more numerous than the large ones, carried less than half as many. Taking the records for a period of ten years, I find that the average carried by the nearly 70 ships that arrived during that period to have been about 300 each. Even that seems a large number when the average size of the ships—less than 200 tons—is considered. Then, again, if we take the number of recorded immigrant ships during the period mentioned by Proud, and allow them an average of only 200 passengers each, we get as a result nearly twice the total number of German immigrants as given by him. Besides, we are aware from many other sources that his is an underestimate as to totals, very much too low, in fact, as will be shown later on.

There was very little German immigration during the years immediately following the close of the Revolutionary War. The British Consul at Philadelphia puts the number of arrivals between 1783 and 1789 at 1,893 or only about 315 each year, on an average. In the latter named year, out of 2,176 arrivals only 114 were Germans.

But the action already taken did not wholly allay the fears of the Proprietary government. Those fears were supplemented by instructions from the British ministry, and two years after the Legislation already recorded, the impolitic

[20] PROUD'S *History of Pennsylvania*, Vol. II., pp. 273-274.

Act of the Assembly, laying a head tax upon all aliens who should come into the Province, was consummated.

Gordon intimates that "a regard to revenue may have assisted this determination, as many thousands of Germans were expected in the ensuing year. In justice to the Germans, it should be told, that this law was enacted in the face of a report of a committee of the House, containing satisfactory evidence of their good conduct." [21]

Here is the report alluded to in the foregoing paragraph : "The Palatines who had been imported directly into the Province, had purchased and honestly paid for their lands, had conducted themselves respectfully towards the government, paid their taxes readily, and were a sober and honest people in their religious and civil duties. Yet some who have come by the way of New York and elsewhere, had seated themselves on lands of the Proprietaries and others, and refused to yield obedience to the governments."

The latter allusion refers to the colony which came down the Susquehanna in 1729, under the leadership of John Conrad Weiser, the younger, and settled in the Tulpehocken region of Berks county. The persistence of the Germans in adhering to their mother tongue was perhaps the principal reason for this uneasiness; besides, they generally managed to settle near each other, so that communities composed almost exclusively of Germans grew up in many places.

As few acts of the Assembly at that early day have received more comment than the one laying a head tax on aliens, the law is here quoted. The word "Germans" is not found in the law, but as there were few other aliens besides these, at that time, the Germans were the persons against whom the statute was aimed.

---

[21] GORDON'S *History of Pennsylvania*, pp. 207–208.

An Act Laying a Duty on Foreigners and Irish
Servants Imported into this Province,
Passed May 10, 1729.

" Whereas an act of general assembly of this province
was made in the eighth year of the reign of the late King
George for preventing the importation of persons convicted
of heinous crimes, and, whereas, it appears necessary that
a further provision be made to discourage the great importation and coming in of numbers of foreigners and of lewd,
idle and ill-affected persons into this province, as well
from parts beyond the seas as from the neighboring colonies, by reason whereof not only the quiet and safety of
the peaceable people of this province is very much en-
dangered, but great numbers of the persons so imported
and coming into this government, either through age, im-
potency or idleness, have become a heavy burden and
charge upon the inhabitants of this province and is daily
increasing. For remedy whereof:
" Be it enacted by the Honorable Patrick Gordon, Esquire, Lieutenant Governor of the Province of Pennsylvania, &., by and with the advice and consent of the
freemen of the said Province in General Assembly met,
and by the authority of the same, That all persons being
aliens born out of the allegiance of the King of Great
Britain and being of the age of sixteen years or upwards
shall within the space of forty-eight hours after their being
imported or coming into this province by land or water,
go before some judge or justice of the peace of the said
province or before the mayor or recorder of the city of
Philadelphia for the time being and there take the oaths
appointed to be taken instead of the oath of allegiance and
supremacy, and shall also take the oath of adjuration, for

which each person shall pay to the person administering
the said oaths the sum of twelve pence and no more. And
if any such alien (being of the age aforesaid) shall refuse
or neglect to take the oaths aforesaid, it shall and may be
lawful to and for any judge, justice of the peace or other
magistrate of this government forthwith to cause such person or persons to be brought before them, (and) oblige
them to give security for their good behavior and appearance at the next court of general quarter-sessions of the
peace to be held for the city or country where such magistrate resides.

*   *   *   *   *   *   *   *

" Be it enacted by the authority aforesaid, That every
person being an alien born out of the allegiance of the
King of Great Britain and being imported or coming into
this province by land or water shall pay the duty of forty
shillings for the uses of this act hereinafter mentioned.

" And that all masters of vessels, merchants and others
who shall import or bring into any port or place within
this province any Irish servant or passenger upon redemption, or on condition of paying for his or her passage upon
or after their arrival in the plantations, shall pay for every
such Irish servant or passenger upon redemption as aforesaid the sum of twenty shillings." [22]

The foregoing includes only a portion of the first and
second sections of the Act, which runs to six sections in all.
The other sections allude to a number of other things, such
as the carrying out of the law, and the penalties imposed
for non-compliance. In section third occurs this clause,
which throws some light upon the methods employed by
ship-captains and importers to smuggle objectionable persons into the province without a compliance with the laws :

---

[22] *The Statutes at Large of Pennsylvania*, Vol. IV., pp. 135–140.

" And whereas it hath been a practice for masters of vessels, merchants and others trading into this province, with intent to avoid complying with the payment of the duties and giving the securities required in the cases of convicts by the aforesaid act of assembly, to land their servants in some of the adjacent governments, which servants and convicts have afterwards been secretly brought into this province."

I have found in Watson a case which was one of the many that caused the insertion of the last quoted paragraph in this Act. He copies the following paragraph from the *Pennsylvania Gazette:* " An errant cheat detected at Annapolis ! A vessel arrived there, bringing sixty-six indentures, signed by the Mayor of Dublin, and twenty-two *wigs*, of such a make as if they were intended for no other use than to set out the *convicts* when they should get on shore." [23] It was a clever ruse to get into the country a lot of convicts by means of fraudulent papers and other devices, and dispose of them as honest servants.

It will be observed that the foregoing Act also takes full cognizance of the importation of persons for sale, of redemptioners, the practice being already so general, not alone as to Germans, but also to Englishmen, Irishmen, Scotch and Welsh, a fact that is rarely alluded to by writers when discussing this subject. In another chapter this fact will be more fully examined and additional testimony offered, although this allusion to the practice in the Act of the Assembly puts the matter so plainly as to admit of no dispute.

Prior to 1741 all the Germans who came to Pennsylvania were called *Palatines* on the ship lists, irrespective of the place of their nativity. Subsequent to that time,

[23] WATSON'S *Annals of Philadelphia,* Vol. II., pp. 266–267.

however, the terms "*Foreigners,*" "inhabitants of the Palatinate and places adjacent" were applied to them. Still later, after 1754, the German principalities from which they came are not mentioned. [24]

---

[24] See note by Rupp in DR. RUSH'S *Manners and Customs of the German Inhabitants of Pennsylvania*, p. 6.

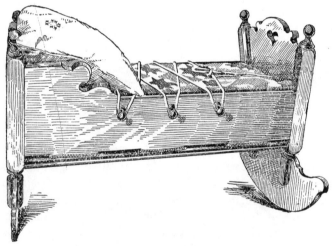

TYPICAL PENNSYLVANIA-GERMAN CRADLE,
With sacking bottom and top cords, showing how the infant was tied in.

CHAPTER V.

The Voyage Across the Ocean. — Discomforts and Privations Attending It. — Insufficient Room. — Deficient Supplies of Food and Drink. — Unsanitary Conditions and Excessive Mortality.

"Borne far away beyond the ocean's roar,
He found his Fatherland upon this shore ;
And every drop of ardent blood that ran
Through his great heart was true American."

"Lasst hoch die Heimath leben !
Nehmt all' ein Glas zur Hand !
Nicht Jeder hat ein Liebchen,
Doch Jeder ein Vaterland."

THE uncertainties attending the length of the voyages often entailed great hardships and misery upon the immigrants. The ships were crowded with passengers beyond their proper roomage, as Mittelberger and others relate. As I have shown elsewhere chests and other property which should have come with the voyagers, were left behind so that more human freight could be put on board.

(55)

These latter consequently often took up a part of the space that should have been given to provisions and water. When the voyages were prolonged—a very common occurrence—the food ran short in a corresponding degree, and not that only, but deteriorated to an extent that often rendered it uneatable, save in cases of dire necessity. Low fares were the rule and that of course also meant provisions of the cheapest kind, and as few of them as the captain of the vessel could keep his passengers alive on, and he was not always over-particular concerning the latter. As it was with the food so it was with the water supply. The allowance of the latter, never over-abundant, nearly always ran short, when the supply was of course curtailed to the passengers. Passing vessels were often stopped to secure fresh supplies both of water and food, and pastor Muhlenburg relates how passing showers were sometimes made to yield their contributions.

In this connection it deserves to be mentioned that in those days little or no regard was paid to sanitation on board ships. They were not constructed with such ends in view but to secure the largest amount of room for the least expenditure of money. In fact, these things were very poorly understood at that time. Therefore, with insufficient and often unwholesome food, short water supplies that were unfit to drink, and the crowded condition of the vessels into the bargain, we need feel no surprise at the dreadful mortality that so often occurred on board. We are well aware to-day that typhoid fever is very generally the result of the use of contaminated water, and that the demand for greater and purer water supplies is the unceasing cry from all large and small communities. Need we wonder that under the stress of all these unhappy concurrent conditions on shipboard, the mortality in many instances was frightful?

Under conditions of discouragement, robbery, wrong, deception and contumely that almost exceed the limits of human credulity, these poor but enthusiastic people continued to make their way to America. The story of their treatment and sufferings while on shipboard equals all the horrors we have been told of the " middle passage." On shore the land shark in the shape of the broker and merchant awaited their arrival to finish the work of spoliation if the ship captain had not already completed it. It was but little these helpless sons of toil had, but in their huge wooden chests were stored a few heirlooms, generations old sometimes; the few household treasures their scant earnings had enabled them to accumulate, and which, until now they had tried to keep together. These at once became the objects of English covetousness, and too often became the reward of English cupidity. We can scarcely realize the dismal tale, but it comes to us from so many sources, official and otherwise, that we can only read, pity and believe. Herein at least the world has grown better. If such things are still practiced, it is done secretly ; openly they have ceased to vex the earth with their detestable inhumanity.

Expatriation is usually a severe trial to the men of all nations, and perhaps to none so much so as to those of the Teutonic race. They are steady and constant by nature. Their affection even from days of childhood for their native soil is deep-rooted, while their love and reverence for home and fatherland is strong and abiding. Yet in this exodus to the New World all these deep-seated sentiments gave way under new feelings and impulses. They migrated to escape from the contracted and unfavorable conditions of their home environment, which were unbearable. That these people should venture their all in a quest for rest and comfort in a new and strange land, marks an era in the migrations of the human family. The German immigrants seem to have been regarded as legitimate game by nearly all the men who in any manner were brought into relations with them. We must, of course, believe that there was some honesty among the men who had control of this traffic for so many years, but truth compels us to say that such men were not the rule but its exceptions. They had no more interest in these incoming aliens than what they might make out of them, legitimately or otherwise. In this they were greatly aided by the fact that the Germans were unacquainted with the English language, and therefore prevented from defending their rights when they were assailed. Furthermore, honest themselves, they were prone to put trust and confidence in others. Here they committed a grievous mistake. They were dealing with men in whom all the ordinary instincts of humanity save that of cupidity appear to have been almost entirely absent. What show could the trustful German, fresh from the fields of the Fatherland, have against men who seemingly lived only to defraud?

A memorial letter written by a well-known Philadelphia clergyman in 1774 to the then Govenor, gives us an insight into the frauds perpetrated on these people.

THE MEMORIAL OF LEWIS WEISS, 1774.

" To the Honorable John Penn, Esqʳ, Govenor and Commander in Chief of the Province of Pennsylvania, &c.

" The Memorial of Lewis Weiss, most respectfully showeth,

" That altho' in the Bill now before your Honor, ' to prevent infectious Disease being brought into this Province,' great care and Tenderness is shewn for the unhappy sick

Miſſive van
CORNELIS BOM,
Geſchreven uit de Stadt
PHILADELPHIA.
In de Provintie van
PENNSYLVANIA,
Leggende op d'Ooſtzyde van de
Znyd Revier van Nieuw Nederland.

Verhalende de groote Voortgank
van de ſelve Provintie.

Waer by komt
De Getuygenis van
JACOB TELNER.
van Amſterdam.

Tot Rotterdam gedrukt , by Pieter van
Wijnbrugge, in de Leeuweſtraet. 168:

TITLE-PAGE OF CORNELIS BOM'S *Account.*

and of curing them if possible, yet there seems something very material that might be added by the Goodness and Humanity of the Legislative Body of this Province in order to enlarge the Benefit of an act that is partly intended to relieve the poor, the sick, and the Stranger, to wit, the Custody and preservation of their Property shipped on board of such sickly vessel.

" May it please your Honor to put a Benevolent Construction on this your Memoralist's humble application by him made (indeed not only on behalf of his Countrymen, the Germans, but) for all unfortunate Strangers taking refuge in your blessed Province. And for as much as he has these nineteen years of his Residence here lent his ear to their numerous Complaints ; he begs Leave to explain the Substance thereof in as concise a manner as he is able to contract in Words so extensive a Subject.

" Passengers having Goods of any value on board of the same Ship in which they transport themselves hardly ever take Bills of Lading for such Goods, the Merchants, Captains, or their Subordinates persuading them that it could do them no Good but rather involve them into Difficulties at their arrival.   If they leave any Goods in the Stores of the Freighter of such vessel they will now & then take a little Note ' that the Merchant has such Chests, Casks, Bales, &c., and under takes to send it by next Vessel free of Freight, &.,' to the person who deposited such Goods with him.   The Passenger puts the note in his Pocket Book, he has also the Invoice of his Goods, and his Money he has sowed up in his old Rags or in a Belt about his Waist.   But in the voyage he or his Wife or some of his Family, or all of them grow sick.   Then the plunder upon the sick or dead begin, and if the old ones recover or small Children survive the goods are gone, and the proofs that they had any are lost. The Captains never reported to any public officer how many passengers he took in at the Port from whence he sailed, or how many died on the voyage, never any manifest of the Goods belonging to passengers is produced. But in short hardly any vessel with Palatine Passengers has arrived in the Port of Philadelphia but there has been Clamours and Complaints heard of Stealing & pilfering the Goods of the Sick & of the dead. And if your Honour will be pleased to inquire of the Register General, whether within the space of twenty-five years or since the passing of the Act 23. Geo. 2, intitled 'An Act for the prohibiting of German & other Passengers in too great Numbers in any one Vessel,' any considerable Number of Inventories of Goods & Effects of Persons who died in their Passage hither or soon after have been exhibited into that Office, you will find that the practice is otherwise than the Law.

" Upon the whole your Memorialist humbly apprehends that if sick Passengers shall by Virtue of the Bill now before your Honour be landed & nursed at the Province Island and their Chests and other Goods go up to Philadelphia, it will require a particular Provision of what shall be done for the preservation of their Goods on board.

" L. Weiss.

" Philad^a, Jan. 19. 1774."

In some instances these German immigrants have recorded in writings which are still accessible the story of their sufferings and their wrongs. We have a case of this in the record of the voyage of the ship *Love and Unity*, than which no vessel was perhaps ever more unaptly named. This ship under the command of Captain Lobb, sailed from Rotterdam for Philadelphia in May, 1731, with more than one hundred and fifty Palatines. Instead of going to Philadelphia, these people, or rather the survivors, were landed on the island of Martha's Vineyard, off the southern coast of Massachusetts. Of their number, only thirty-four reached Philadelphia in May, 1732.[25]

In a letter written by Johannes Gohr, Jacob Diffebach, Jonas Daner, Jacob Kuntz and Samuel Schwachhamer, dated February, 1732, to the Rev. Michael Weiss, a German Reformed minister in Philadelphia, they say among other things : " Captain Lobb, a wicked murderer of souls, thought to starve us, not having provided provisions enough, according to agreement; and thus got possession of our goods; for during the voyage of the last eight weeks, five persons were only allowed one pint of coarse meal per day, and a quart of water to each person. We were twenty-four weeks coming from Rotterdam to Martha's Vineyard. There were at first more than one hundred and fifty persons—more than one hundred perished. * * * To keep from starving, we had to eat rats and mice. We paid from eight pence to two shillings for a mouse; four pence for a quart of water. * * * In one night several persons miserably perished and were thrown naked overboard; no sand was allowed to be used to sink the bodies but they floated. We paid for a loaf of Indian corn eight shillings. Our misery was so great that we often begged the captain to put us on land that we might buy provisions. He put us off from day to day for eight weeks, until at last it pleased Almighty God, to send us a sloop, which brought us to Home's Hole, Martha's Vineyard. * * * Had he detained four days longer every one of us would have famished; for none had it in his power to hand another a drop of water. * * * All our chests were broken

---

[25] *Philadelphia Gazette*, May 18, 1732.

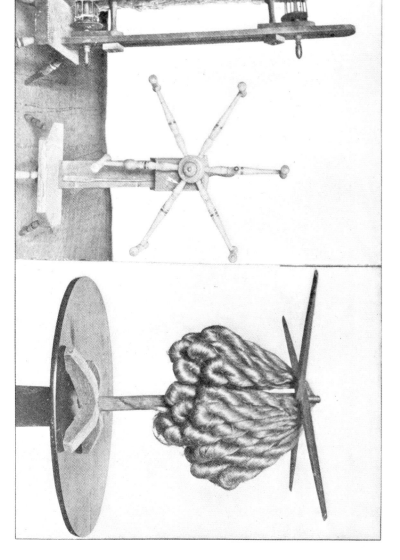

DOMESTIC INDUSTRIES.

TOW AND FLAX REELS. HANKS OF SPUN FLAX.

open. * * * The captain constrained us to *pay the whole freight of the dead and living*, as if he had landed us at Philadelphia, and we agreed in writing to do so, not understanding what we signed; but we are not able to comply, for if we are to pay for the *dead*, we should have taken the *goods of the dead;* but in discharging the vessel, we found that most of *their chests* were broken open and plundered.

"The captain however, has determined, that we shall pay him in three weeks; we, therefore, desire you to instantly assist us as much as is in your power. For if we have to pay, the wicked captain will make us all beggars. * * * We would have sent two or three men with this letter, but none of us is yet able to stir, for we are weak and feeble; but as soon as there shall be two or three of us able to travel they will follow." [26]

The whole history of American colonization may confidently be challenged to present so pathetic and sorrowful a tale. The voyage of the "Mayflower" has been told and retold in song and story. It is the entire stock in trade of certain writers. If I remember it aright its one hundred and two Puritans were all landed after a voyage of sixty-five days duration. Not a death from any cause, certainly none from starvation. Yet that voyage is extolled as the one beyond all others where the courage, fortitude and endurance of colonists were tried to their utmost. If the student of American colonization wishes to learn where humanity's sorest trial on this continent occurred, he must turn to the German immigration to Pennsylvania in the eighteenth century.

In this instance the deception and rascality perpetrated

[26] *Gentleman's Magazine*, Vol. II., April, 1732, p. 727.

on these poor people became the subject of official investigation.[27]

The sequel to this tale of oppression and suffering is not the least interesting part of the story. It appears that several of these wretched German immigrants had charged Captain Lobb with killing several of their countrymen by his brutal treatment. Such an accusation could hardly

---

[27] The particulars of this case, contributed to the *Pennsylvania Magazine of History and Biography*, Vol. XXI., pp. 124-125, by Mr. ANDREW M. DAVIS, as taken from the "Journal of the House of Massachusetts," are as follows : " *December 29, 1731.*

"A Petition sign'd *Philip Bongarden*, in the Name and behalf of sundry poor distressed Palatines, now at Martha's Vineyard, within this Province (Massachusetts), setting forth, That they were lately brought into said *Martha's Vineyard* from *Rotterdam*, in the Ship *Loving Unity*, Jacob Lobb Commander, with whom they entered into a written Agreement at Rotterdam aforesaid (a Copy of which said Agreement was therewith exhibited, translated into *English*). That the said Captain had in a most barberous manner dealt with the Petitioners in their voyage : praying that the Court would Order that the said Capt. *Lobb* may be obliged to answer for the Injuries, Wrongs and Abuses by him done and offered as herein mentioned ; as also, that he may be obliged to comply with his Contract, for the transporting of the Petitiones and their Goods to *Philadelphia*, and that they may meet with such other Relief as shall be agreeable to Justice. (Brought down this Afternoon by Ebenezer Burrel Esq ;) Pass'd in Council, *viz.* In Council, *December* 29, 1731. Read and *Voted*, That His Excellency be desired to issue out a *Special Warrant* for citing the before mentioned *Jacob* Lobb to appear before the Governour and Council to answer to the Complaint ; and that in the meantime the Goods and Effects of the Palatines, brought on the ship *Loving Unity* be secured at *Martha's Vineyard*, and the said Ship stopped in one of the Harbours there, till the Order of the Governour and Council thereupon ; and that any two of his Majesty's Justices of the Peace in *Dukes County*, be directed to take care that two or three of the principal Persons of the Palatines be sent up to attend the Governour and Council, to support this Complaint ; and that they likewise examine some of the Seamen on Oath, upon this Affair and send up their Examinations to the Secretary.— Sent down for concurrence.—Read.

"*Ordered*, That the Treasurer of this Province, be and hereby is directed to supply the Select-Men of *Edgartown* with the Sum of *Two Hundred Pounds*, to be disposed of, according to their best Discretion, for the Relief and Comfort of the *Palatines*, lately brought into *Martha's Vineyard;* The Treasurer to account therefore, in his next Accompt of Disbursements

Sent up for Concurrence.

" December 30. The Order of Council on the *Palatines* Petition entered Yes-

be passed over in silence, so he haled his accusers into the Massachusetts courts, and after a prolonged trial, the captain was not only acquitted of the charge but the witnesses against him were saddled with the costs of the trial and sent to jail until they were paid. The *Philadelphische Zeitung* of 1732 has an account of the proceedings.[28]

terday, Read again, and after a Debate, the House passed a Non-Concurrence thereon, and

" *Ordered*, That *William Sherley* Esq ; be desired to be of Council to Mr. Philip Bongarden, and assist him in seeking Relief for the *Palatines* (in whose behalf he appears) in the legal and customary Way in such cases.

Sent up for Concurrence.

"December 31. *Thomas Palmer* Esq ; brought down from the Honorable Board, the Order of the 29th Instant for an Allowance to the *Palatines* pass'd in Council viz. In Council Dec. 31, 1731. Read and Concurred; with the Amendment.

"Sent down for Concurrence. Read and Concurred."

[28]Nachdem auf anstifftung und eingebung verschiedener Persohnen, welche den Kapitain des Schiffs "Liebe und Einigkeit," Jacob Lobb, mit grosser Barbarey gegen gewisse Pfältzer in seinem Schiffe auf ihrer Passage von Holland zu Martha's Vineyard, beleget haben, die Ehrsame Richter des Köeniglichen Obergerichts gut gefunden haben denselben zu verpflichten dass er vor dem Obergerichte von Rechts-sachen, &c welches den vierdten Dienstag im Mertz letzthin zu Barnstable vor die County von Barnstable gehalten worden, erscheinen, und dasjeinge so von des Königs wegen gegen ihn eingebracht werden möchte, beantworten solle ; da er dann diesem folge erscheinen, und wegen Zweyer unter Schiedenen Beschuldigungen des mords von der grossen jury dieser County gegen ihn gefunden, examinirt worden und nach einem 6 stunden lang gewähretem Wortwechsel die Kline Jury in, urtheil geschwint einbrachten als unschuldig von der erstem anklage, und wenig minuten hernach ein gleiches wegen der andern beschuldigung. N. B. Es wurde bey der examinirung observiret, dass das elend so diesen Passagieren begegnet, nicht von einer gewinnsüchtigen begierde des Capitains, oder vorsetzlichen Intention die Reise zu verlangern hergekommen, sondern die länge derselben müste, wie aus dem Tag-register des Capitains, und der Eydlichen aussage aller Matrosen erhellerte, dem contraierem Winde und der Wind-stille zugeschrieben werden : Und konten die Gezeugen von des Königs seiten den Capitain mit keiner einzigen ausübung einer Härtigkeit während der reise belegen. Weswegen der Capitain sich zu rechtfertigen gutgefunden, seinen verletzten caracter öffentlich zu defendiren ; insonderheit in ansehung der falschen und schändlichen advertissementen, welche sind publiciret worden denselben zu beflecken und die gemüther des volcks mit vorurtheilen gegen ihn einzunehmen ehe er examinirt worden und sich selbst rechtmässig befreyen konte. Weiters ist er nun darauf aus, diejenigen gerichtlich zu ver-

The foregoing action on the part of Massachusetts had its counterpart in Pennsylvania in January, 1796. A ship arrived in Philadelphia in the fall of 1795 with a large number of French immigrants, many of whom were women and children. On January 13th of the first named year, the Legislature passed an Act appropriating $1,500 for their relief, and two hundred and twenty persons were thus aided.[29]

In addition to this Martha's Vineyard episode, there is still another New England Palatine story, less fully authenticated, but of the truth of the main details there seems to be no question. As the story goes, a number of Palatine immigrants were either shipwrecked or landed under very destitute circumstances on Block Island towards the middle of the eighteenth century. No record of the oc-

---

folgen, welche ihn so boshaftig verleumdet und einen Process verursachet haben, der nach untersuchung gantz ohne grund gefunden worden.

See article on the first German newspaper published in America. *Proceedings of the Pennsylvania-German Society*, Vol. X., pp. 41–46.

[29] "To THOMAS MIFFLIN : Governor of the Commonwealth of Pennsylvania.

"The Commissioners appointed by the act of the Legislature, dated the 13th of January, 1796, to afford relief to certain distressed French Emigrants ; Report that they have endeavoured to fulfil the benevolent views of the Legislature, by personally distributing the sum of fifteen hundred Dollars, granted for that purpose, in money, wood, clothing and other necessaries to about two hundred and twenty necessitous French People, as by the annexed Schedule ; many of whom were old, and some of them lame, blind, sick, or otherwise unable to support themselves.

"It was a very seasonable relief to them during the last winter, and spring, for which many of them have expressed their gratitude, on leaving the Continent to return to their own country. Others remain, endeavouring to habituate themselves to our language, customs and modes of life ; of whom a number will, we hope in future be able to gain an honest livelihood, with but little assistance ; yet some worthy Individuals will probably continue entirely dependent upon the aid of charity.

"Signed in Philadelphia, the 5th day of November, 1796.

"SAMUEL P. GRIFFITHS,
"ROB. RALSTON,
"GODFREY HAGA,
"JOSEPH PANSOM,
"JOSEPH LOWNES."

curence has been preserved so far as is known; tradition only has dealt with it, and that says many of these people were landed there and that some of them perished.　Some of the survivors got away from the island.　A woman who remained is reported to have married a negro.

The name of the vessel is said to have been the *Palatine*, but perhaps that is a mere supposition, the result of confounding it with the country whence these unfortunates came.　The fancy of the poet has been called in to lend attractiveness to the tale, and Whittier tells a weird story about the ship *Palatine* in his "Tent on the Beach."　Listen to his melodious verse:

> "And old men mending their nets of twine,
> 　Talk together of dream and sign,
> 　Talk of the lost ship Palatine.
> 　　*　*　*　*　*　*
> "The ship that a hundred years before,
> 　Freighted deep with its goodly store,
> 　In the gales of the equinox went ashore.
> 　　*　*　*　*　*　*
> "Into the teeth of death she sped:
> 　(May God forgive the hands that fed
> 　The false lights over the rocky head!)
> 　　*　*　*　*　*　*
> "And then, with ghastly shimmer and shine
> 　Over the rocks and the seething brine,
> 　They burned the wreck of the Palatine.
> 　　*　*　*　*　*　*
> "And still on many a moonless night,
> 　From Kingston head and from Montauk light,
> 　The spectre kindles and burns in sight.
> 　　*　*　*　*　*　*
> "And the wise Sound skippers, though skies be fine,
> 　Reef their sails when they see the sign
> 　Of the blazing wreck of the Palatine."

It has been conjectured that this ship was one which, although destined for Pennsylvania, was nevertheless diverted from her course by the captain, as was frequently done for improper purposes, and that the disaster, whatever its character, was the result of ignorance of the coast on his part.

A "DUTCH OVEN."

This was placed upon the hearth and live coals and ashes heaped over it.

CHAPTER VI.

Pennsylvania the Favorite Home of German Immigrants.— What Occurred in Massachusetts.— The Germans Especially Adapted to the Requirements of Penn's Province.— Bishop Berkeley's Prevision.

"It is a peculiarly noble work rescuing from oblivion those who deserve immortality, and extending their renown at the same time that we advance our own."

"Those who take no pride in the achievements of their ancestors, near or remote, are not likely to accomplish much that will be remembered with pride by their descendants."

FROM the time of the arrival of the first regular German colony at Germantown down until 1776, and later, Pennsylvania was the most favored of all the countries in America, by the German immigrants. There were two all-sufficient reasons for this. First was the liberal government of Penn's Province, and second the illiberal spirit which greeted them everywhere else. To this may be added still another, the character of the

(69)

soil, so well adapted to the needs of an agricultural people such as a majority of these colonists were. Then, too, as the earliest settlers found plenty and contentment under liberal laws, they were not slow in keeping their friends and relatives in the old home beyond the sea informed of all that had happened to them. These favorable accounts—for in nearly every case they were favorable—turned the incoming tide in the same direction. Naturally, these people desired to go where their friends and kindred were, or if neither of these had preceded them, then where their fellow countrymen were, where the German language was spoken and where the manners and customs of the Fatherland met them on every hand.

Came they with modest wealth or came they steeped in poverty as so many were, they could at least expect a welcome, nor was it often that this was not accorded in the fullest possible measure. There have been preserved in many families, and they are still told among their descendants, pleasant tales of welcome to new arrivals by those who were already on the spot and comfortably fixed. The nearest neighbors to the new squatter may have lived five or ten miles away, but they quickly gathered about the new comer and aided him in the construction of his humble log dwelling, and in putting out such grain and vegetables as the season would allow. Often a cow and other domestic animals were bestowed by a well-to-do neighbor, and in this way the early hardships and needs were relieved until the settler was in a measure prepared to take care of himself and family. Could these charitable and neighborly deeds be looked for from men of alien races and tongues? No, but the German heart beat true, and never made a nobler record than that which was recorded to its credit in the wilds of Pennsylvania nigh two hundred years

Vier kleine
Doch ungemeine
Und sehr nützliche

Tractätlein

De omnium Sanctorum Vitis
I. De omnium Pontificum Statutis
II. De Conciliorum Decisionibus
V. De Episcopis & Patriarchis Constan-
tinopolitanis.

Das ist:
1. Von Aller Heiligen Lebens-Ubung
2. Von Aller Päpste Gesetz-Einführung
3. Von der Concilien Stritt-Sopirung.
4. Von denen Bischöffen und Patriarchen
zu Constantinopel.

Zum Grunde
Der künfftighin noch ferner darauf
zu bauen Vorhabender Warheit
præmittiret,
Durch

FRANCISCUM DANIELEM

PASTORIUN. J. U. L.

Aus der
In Pensylvania neulichst von mir in
Grund angelegten / und nun mit gutem
Succes aufgehenden Stadt:

GERMANOPOLI

Anno Christi M. DC. XC.

TITLE-PAGE OF PASTORIUS' *Four Useful Tracts.*

ago.   It was, therefore, not mere chance that directed this, the most remarkable migration of the last century.   It followed along lines that we can easily understand to-day, and wherever else credit may be due, it is undeniable that the first impulse came from William Penn himself, and that as a law giver, a commonwealth builder and as a MAN, he clearly stands before us as the grandest character that ever landed upon the shores of the New World.

A single life measures but a span in the life of a nation, therefore it was not given to William Penn to witness the splendor of his success in commonwealth building.   He died long before his scheme of German immigration reached even the promise of its later development.   But yet it was granted to him to enjoy something of the satisfaction and pride that comes to the man of great plans and ideas, when even the limited present projects its brightness into the coming years, filling the future with its radiance. Well could he exclaim, with true modesty, and with honest exultation :   " I must without vanity, say, I have led the greatest colony into America that ever any man did upon a private credit, and the most prosperous beginnings that ever were in it, are to be found among us."[30]   With the eye of faith he

" — Dipt into the future far as human eye could see ; Saw the vision of the world, and all the wonder that would be."

William Penn in Pennsylvania and the Governors of New York and other nearby States were not the only persons who made efforts to secure these immigrants.   During the first half of the eighteenth century some of the large landed proprietors in the New England colonies were intent on the same game.   They sent agents across the Atlantic,

---

[30] Penn to Lord Halifax, in WATSON'S *Annals of Pennsylvania*, p. 19.

who fairly flooded the Palatinate and other German provinces with hand-bills and other documents to encourage immigration into that region. Nor were their efforts unsuccessful. A number of small colonies were persuaded to come over, and they were settled along the bleak seacoast. But the unkindly climate, added to the sterility of the soil, and in some cases also fraudulent titles to their lands, soon had the effect of driving them away, they finding more congenial homes in the Middle and Southern Colonies.

It cannot be gainsaid that the Germans were preëminently such settlers as the Province of Pennsylvania needed. From the earliest times they lived in the forests and cultivated the soil. One of the greatest of the Latin historians has told us that none of the German nations lived in cities, " or even allow contiguous settlements. They dwelt scattered and separate, as a spring, a meadow or a grove might chance to invite them. Their villages are laid out in rows of adjoining buildings, but every one surrounds his house with a vacant space, either by way of security against fire, or through ignorance of the art of building. For indeed they are unacquainted with the use of mortar and tiles and for every purpose employ rude misshapen timber fashioned with no regard to pleasing the eye."[31] Cæsar speaks to the same purpose, and says, "they think it the greatest honor to a nation to have as wide an extent of vacant land around their dominions as possible."[32]

An eminent German historian has said that the overplus population of Germany has ever emigrated; in ancient times for the purpose of conquering foreign powers; in modern times for that of serving under them. In the days of German heroism, her conquering hordes spread towards

[31] TACITUS, *Germania*, C. 16.
[32] CÆSAR, *Bell. Gall.*, IV., 3.

the west and south. During the Middle Ages her mail-
clad warriors took an easterly direction and overran the
Slavonian countries.   In modern times, her political and
religous refugees have emigrated in scarcely less considerable numbers to countries far more distant, but in the
humble garb of artificers and beggars, the Parias of the
world. Her ancient warriors gained undying fame and
long maintained the influence and the rule of Germany in
foreign lands.   Her modern emigrants have quitted their
native country unnoted, and as early as the second generation intermixed with the people among whom they settled.
Hundreds of thousands of Germans have in this manner
aided in aggrandizing the British colonies, while Germany
has derived no benefit from the emigration of her sons.
The industry and honesty for which the German workmen
are remarkable caused some Englishmen to enter into a
speculation to procure their services as white slaves. The
greatest encouragement was accordingly given by them to
emigration from Germany.[33]

Early in the eighteenth century one of the most distinguished of the sons of Ireland came to the New World. He
had all the culture of the schools. There were few departments of learning that were unfamiliar to him. Best of all,
his heart was full of love for the human race, for he caught
his inspiration in the same school that gave the world men
like Locke and Penn and Hampden. He came here full of
high hopes and the most exalted ambition. Unfortunately,
his schemes for the uplifting of the American people, from
the Red Man in his forest home to the refined dweller
in the cities, were not realized, and George Berkeley returned to Europe, eventually to receive a bishopric he did
not covet. But the heart of the gentle prelate turned with

---

[33] MENZEL'S *History of Germany*, Chap. CCLXXIV.

ARRANGED AND PHOTO. BY J. F. SACHSE.

SPECIMENS IN DANNER COLLECTION.

PENNSYLVANIA-GERMAN ENTERPRISE.

GLASSWARE MADE BY BARON STIEGEL (1768-1774), MANHEIM, PA.

an unquenchable and ever-living love to the green fields, the prosperous villages, and to the happy men who dwelt in America. Through the mists of the future he thought he saw what was destined to transpire in that land of his affection in the years that were still to come, and when the spirit of prophecy came upon him, he wrote words that have come down to us, their music reverberating through the corridors of time.

> " In happy climes, the seat of innocence,
>   Where nature guides, and virtue rules ;
>   Where men shall not impose for truth and sense
>   The pedantry of courts and schools :—·

> " There shall be sung another golden age,—
>   The rise of empire and of arts,—
>   The good and great inspiring epic rage—
>   The wisest heads and noblest hearts.

> " Not such as Europe breeds in her decay ;
>   Such as she bred when fresh and young,
>   When heavenly flame did animate her clay,
>   By future poets shall be sung.

> " Westward the cause of empire takes its way.
>   The first four acts already past,
>   A fifth shall close the drama with the day.
>   Time's noblest offspring is the last."

Is it too much to say to-day that the hopes of William Penn and the prophetic visions of the poet-Bishop have already had their realization? Is not Pennsylvania at this very hour the grandest colony ever founded in the New World. Which surpasses her? Which equals her? Does she not stand peerless, an empire Republic, largely the result of this German immigration?

CHAPTER VII.

A Glance at the Quarrels between the Proprietary Governors and the Legislatures.— It was not the Political "Golden Age" to which we sometimes Refer with so much Pride and Pleasure.

> "In Deutsche Eichenforste,
> Auf Berge, hoch und grün
> Zu frischen Au'n der Donau
> Zog mich das Heimweh hin."

> "Wie wird es in den fremden Waldern
> Euch nach der Heimathberge grün,
> Nach Deutschlands gelben Weizenfeldern,
> Nach seinen Rebenhügeln ziehn."

A GREAT deal is said and read in these latter days of the golden age of our provincial times. The present generation is told to refer to that idyllic period as a time and when the golden rule was the reigning law among men, to contrast it with the spirit of legislative strife, contention and corruption which we are told hold sway to-day. The myth has done duty for many a year and those who are content to take things at second hand, accept and believe it. But that golden colonial period derives its fine reputation from the glamor the passing generations of men have thrown upon it. Let the student carefully study the Colonial Records and the First Series of Pennsylvania Archives, and he will have his mind promptly disabused of these pleasing ideas. The trouble began even before the death of Penn and it was continued between nearly all the succeeding Governors and the Assemblies until the Proprietary rights were extinguished by the Revolution. No, quarrels between the legislative and executive departments of our fair Province of Pennsylvania were a constantly recurring affair, and often were anything but beneficial to the inhabitants.

This fact is recalled now to exemplify a case where it resulted in the neglect to do a very necessary thing, which both the Governor and the Assembly seemed anxious to do, but which through their obstinacy and recriminations, was long delayed. The need of a hospital or lazaretto for the reception of immigrants and others who came to Philadelphia on pest-infected vessels, was recognized long before action was taken to establish one. Not only did the German residents of Philadelphia urge it, but English subjects also. In 1738 the influence brought to bear on Governor Thomas was so strong that at a Council meeting held on January 2d of the above mentioned year, he made an address, in which among other things he highly complimented the German immigrants and declared the progress and prosperity of the Province was largely due to their industry and thrift. He further said: "The condition, indeed, of such as arrived here lately has given a very just alarm; but had you been provided with a Pest House or

Hospital, in a proper Situation, the Evils which have been apprehended might, under God, have been entirely prevented. The Law to Prevent Sickly Vessels from coming into this Government, has been strictly put in Execution by me. A Physician has been appointed to visit those Vessels, and the Masters obliged to land such of the Passengers as were sick, at a distance from the City, and to convey them at their own Expence, to Houses in the Country convenient for their Reception. More could not have been done without inhumanly exposing great Numbers to perish on board the Ships that brought them. This accident, I cannot doubt, will induce you to make a Provision against the like for the future." [34]

Owing, however, to the causes just alluded to, the Assembly ignored the Governor's suggestion about providing a hospital for sick immigrants, and the records make no further mention of the matter until the 26th of January, 1741, when the Governor laid before the Council the following address or message which he said he had sent to the General Assembly, viz:

" Gentlemen :

" Several of the most substantial Germans now Inhabitants of this Province, have joined in a petition to me, setting forth in Substance, That for want of a Convenient House for the reception of such of their Countrymen as, on their Arrival here, laboured under Diseases Contracted in a long Voyage, they were obliged to continue on board the Ships which brought them, where they could not get either Attendance or Conveniences suitable to their Condition, from whence many have lost their Lives ; And praying that I would recommend to the Assembly the Erecting

---

[34] *Colonial Records*, Vol. IV., p. 315.

of a proper Building at the public Expence, not only to accommodate such as shall arrive hereafter under the same Circumstances, but to prevent the future Importation of Diseases into this City, which has more than once felt the fatal Effects of them.

"The numbers of People which I observed came into this Province from Ireland & Germany, pointed out to me the necessity of an Hospital or Pest House, soon after my arrival here; (August, 1738.) and in 1738 I recommended it to the Assembly of that year, who seemed so far from disapproving it, that they gave me hopes of building one so soon as the Circumstances of the Province should admit. I very heartily wish for the sake of such ffamilys, Inhabitants of this City, as suffered in the late Mortality by the Loss of some who were their Chief Support, and will therefore feel it for Years to come, and on account of the Irish & German Strangers, that it had indeed been done as soon as the Circumstances of the Province did admit of it. But as it can profit nothing to bewail Evils past, I hope you will now make the proper Use of them by doing all in your Power to Prevent the like for the time to come.

"I am not insensible that some look with jealous Eyes upon the yearly concourse of Germans to this Province, but the Parliament of Great Britain see it in a different Light, and have therefore given great Encouragement by a late Act to all such foreign Protestants as shall settle in his Majesty's Dominions; And indeed every Man who well Considers this Matter must allow that every industrious Laborer from Europe, is a real addition to the wealth of this Province, and that the Labor of every foreigner in particular is almost so much clear Gain to our Mother Country.

"I hope I need not take up more of your or my own Time to convince you that what is now again recommended is both for the interest of the Province and the Health of this City. Evils felt are the most convincing Arguments. I shall only add, that as Christians and as Men, we are obliged to make a Charitable Provision for the sick Stranger, and not by Confining him to a Ship, inhumanly expose him to fresh Miserys when he hopes that his Sufferings are soon to be mitigated. Nothing but the building an Hospital or Pest House in a proper situation can, in my Opinion, be a suitable Charity or an Effectual security for the future, more especially as the Country people are grown so apprehensive of the Disease that they will not be persuaded to admit the infected into their Houses."

To the foregoing message, every word of which was true, the Assembly returned the following answer:

"A Message to the Governor from the House of Representatives.

"May it please the Governor:

"As great numbers of People from Ireland & Germany are yearly imported into this Province, some of whom have been affected with Malignant & Dangerous Distempers, it is Evident to Us that a convenient House to accommodate such as shall hereafter arrive under the like Circumstances, may be of great Use to them, and a means to prevent the spreading of infectious Distempers among Us, the Effects of which the City of Philadelphia has lately felt, altho' we think a due Execution of the Laws might in part have prevented them. How this failure happened, at whose Door it ought to lye, and the Means of preventing it for the future, we shall take another Occasion to Consider, and therefore we wave further Notice of it here.

"When the Governor was pleased to recommend the Building an Hospital or Pest-house to the Assembly in the Year 1738, it was thought too great an undertaking for the Circumstances we were then in; and if it be Considered that the Province hath since been at great and unusual Expences, we think it may justly be said that the State of the Public Treasure neither at present nor at any time since the year 1738 hath been in a much better Condition for such an Undertaking than it was at that time. Nevertheless, as it will not only be Charitable to Strangers who may hereafter come among us in the distressed Circumstances before mentioned, but also of benefit to the inhabitants of this Province, we are therefore determined to take this Matter into Consideration, and to direct a plan to be proposed and an Estimate made of the Money which would be requisite for the Building and yearly maintenance of such an Hospital, to be laid before Us at our next Sitting. In the mean Time, as it is a Matter of Considerable Importance, we may have the Opportunity of Knowing more generally the Minds of our Constituents, and it will give such of them as shall think it fit an Opportunity of applying to us touching the necessity of such a Building, and the Manner of doing it which may render it most useful & least burthensome to the Province; And on the whole we may the better be enabled to judge of the part it will become Us to act in the Affair.

"Who they are that look with jealous Eyes on the Germans the Governor has not been pleased to inform Us, nor do we know; Nothing of the kind can justly be attributed to Us, or any preceeding Assembly to our knowledge; On the Contrary, the Legislature of this Province, before the late Provision made in the Parliament of Great Britian, have generally, on application made to them, admitted the Germans to partake of the Privileges enjoyed by the King's natural born Subjects here, and as we look upon the protestant part of them in general to be Laborius, Industrious people, we shall cheerfully perform what may reasonably be expected from Us for the benefit of those already among Us, and such who may hereafter be imported.

" Signed by Order of the House.

" John Kinsey,
" Speaker."

It will readily be seen that the foregoing reply is so much petty quibbling, intended to excuse the non-performance of a duty, for neglect of which there really was no excuse. But Governor Thomas was a good politician, had as good a command of the English language as the members of the Legislature, and above all had the right side of the question. He promptly sent that body a rejoinder on the following day, January 8th, in the following words :

" Gentlemen :

" I am not a little pleased to find by your Message of Yesterday, that you agree to the necessity of building a Pest House for the reception of Sick strangers, and to prevent the Spreading of infectious Diseases they may happen to have Contracted in their Voyage hither, and I cannot allow myself to doubt of your taking a speedy & proper Means for the Completion of so charitable a Work.

" Whilst the German petitioners complain that many have lost their Lives by being confined to the ships, you express your Dissatisfaction that the Laws have not been Executed ; that is, I suppose, that sick passengers were not confined to the Ships. A former Assembly however, com-

Kurtze
Beschreibung
Des H. R. Reichs Stadt
Windsheim/

Samt

Dero vielfältigen Unglücks-Fällen/
und wahrhafftigen Ursachen ihrer so grossen Decadenz und Erbarmungs-wür-
digen Zustandes/

Aus

Alten, glaubwürdigen Documentis und
Briefflichen Urkunden (der itzo lebenden lieben
Burgerschafft/ und Dero Nachkommen / zu guter
Nachricht) also zusammen getragen / und in
den Druck gegeben

durch

Melchiorem Adamum Paftorium,
ältern Burgemeistern und Ober-Rich-
tern in besagter Stadt.

Gedruckt zu Nürnberg
bey Christian Sigmund Froberg.
Im Jahr Christi 1692.

TITLE-PAGE OF MELCHIOR ADAM PASTORIUS' TRACT ON *Windsheim*
and Pennsylvania.

posed of many of the same Members with the present, after the very same Measures taken as to me, were pleased to tell me in their address ' That they had a grateful sense of my Care in putting in Execution the Law for preventing Sickly vessels from coming into this Governmenᵗ.' But all I say or do now must be wrong. The Resolutions of the last Assembly on this Matter sufficiently explain to me what is meant by ' taking another occasion to consider at whose Door the late sickness in Philadelphia ought to lie.' I shall be glad to see your attempt to justify what was insinuated & assumed in those Resolves; Accusations & Complaints are no new things to me, but thanks to my Integrity they have been so far from doing me a prejudice that they have shown me to his Majesty & his Ministers in a Light more advantageous than I could otherwise have expected; ffor this favor tho' not designed as such, Gentlemen, I thank you.

" If I do not strictly adhere to form in imputing to you what was done by the two preceeding Assembly's I hope you will excuse me, for as you are nine in ten of you the same Members, I do not know how to separate your actions from your Persons.

" I cannot but differ with you (which I am sorry is too often the Case) in the State of the Public Treasury since 1738, for the Public accounts in my Opinion Show that the Province has at no point of Time since been unable to Erect the proposed Building; you have, I confess, been at some unusual Expence, but I cannot call it great as you do, since £1,500 out of the £2,500 said to be Expended has been stopt out of my support. I know of no other call Upon the Province since for an Unusual Expence. If you have generously and out of Compassion for the Sufferings of your Subjects in Britain remitted

£3,000 to your Agent for their Relief, I conclude you were well able to Spare it, And that otherwise you would not have done it.

" Either the Memory of some of your Body who were members in 1738, must have failed them very much; or their Sentiments of the Importation of foreigners are, for very Substantial Reasons, much alter'd; ffor, not to dwell upon a small Instance of the assembly's Displeasure to me at that Time for saying a little too much of the Industry of the Germans, I refer you to the Minutes for the Assembly's address to the Proprietor in 1738, to convince you that what I said of their having been looked upon with Jealous Eyes by some, was not altogether without foundation. What follows may be found in that address :

" And this House will, in a proper Time, readily join with the Governor in any Act that may be judged necessary, as well for protecting the property of the Proprietors and others from such unjust Intrusions for the future and for the preservation of the peace of the Government, as for Guarding against the Dangers which may arise from the great & frequent Importation of fforeigners." [35]

It is not necessary to follow this quarrel between the Governor and the Assembly any further. Suffice it to say that eight days later the Assembly replied to the last quoted communication of the Governor in a screed nearly thrice as long, in which an attempt is made to traverse the latter's very effective and convincing homethrusts.

It appears that a Dr. Grœme had for many years, more than twenty, by appointment of an earlier Governor and the consent of the Provincial Council, visited unhealthy vessels. About this time he presented a bill reading as

---

[35] From the Minutes of the Provincial Council, in *Colonial Records*, Vol. IV., pp. 570–571.

follows: " To going on Board Visiting & reporting to
his Honour, the Governor, the State and Condition as to
Sickness & Health of six Palatine vessels, and one with
Negroes from South Carolina, at a Pistole each, £9. 16s."
Of course the Assembly found fault: there was no explanation of the service rendered; the names of the ships
were not given, there was no evidence they were infected;
so the House would not approve the bill. It turned up
again in the following year accompanied by another bill
for £8. 8s., but without the desired explanations. Finally
he was allowed £10 in payment of both. After that he
refused to serve any longer, and Dr. Lachany and some
other doctors, no doubt moved by professional etiquette,
also refused to act in this capacity, and the result was another war of words between the Governor and his unman-
ageable Assembly. The latter body drew up and passed
a series of resolutions, the first one of which read as follows : " That for the Governor & Council to draw in
Question, arrange & Censure the proceedings of the
Representatives of the ffreemen of this Province in Assembly met, after the Adjournment of such Assembly, is
assuming to themselves a power the Law hath not intrusted
them with, is illegal, unwarrantable, a high breach of their
Privileges, and of Dangerous Example." [36] With the discharge of this Parthian shot we shall leave these belig-
erents, who kept up their quarrels for a long time after
with all their original impetuosity.

The outcome of this quarrel was, however, that in 1742,
Fisher's Island was purchased for the sum of £1,700 by a
Committee who were to hold the estate in trust. This
island contained three hundred and forty-two acres, and
was situated near the junction of the Schuylkill with the

---

[36] *Colonial Records*, Vol. IV., p. 523.

HEAD DRESS AND UTENSILS.

(A) QUILTED HOOD, BEAVER HAT, LEGHORN BONNET AND TORTOISE-SHELL COMBS.
(B) SEINE FLOAT, BREAD TRAY, FRUIT BASKET, SPARK CATCHER AND WARMING PAN.

Delaware, on the southwest side of the Schuylkill, near its mouth. The name Fisher's Island was taken from the man who owned it. The named was changed to Province Island, and later to State Island. There were some buildings on it at the time and these were utilized as hospitals. Fines were imposed upon any one harboring a person who had been ordered to the Island. In January, 1750, the Assembly appropriated £1,000 to erect a pest house.[37]

Sometimes when the passengers on an arriving ship were afflicted with a severe disorder, they were not permitted to land, but were compelled to remain on board the close quarters of the infected vessel, a practice which it may be supposed did not contribute much to their speedy restoration to health.[38]

Under date of October 27, 1738, Lloyd Zachary and Th. Bond, physicians, presented a certificate to the colonial council to the following effect: " We have carefully examined the state of health of the marines and passengers on board of the ship St. Andrew, Captain Steadman, from Rotterdam, and found a great number laboring under a malignant, eruptive fever, and are of the opinion, they cannot, for some time, be landed in town without the danger of infecting the inhabitants."

Again: "The foreigners, in number 49, imported in the ship Francis and Elizabeth, Captain Beach, being

---

[37] WATSON'S *Annals of Philadelphia,* Vol. III., p. 333.
"The crowded condition of emigrant ships both from Germany and Ireland had frequently received the attention of the Legislature. The landing of the sick was forbidden, but for a long time no adequate provision was made for their care. But in 1741 an island of 342 acres, subsequently called Province Island, lying at the confluence of the Schuylkill with the Delaware, was purchased and a lazaretto established, where such were landed. * * * Strange to say, no provision was made for their support. The expense was chargeable to the importers and ship captains, who had their recourse against the effects of the immigrants."—GORDON'S *History of Pennsylvania,* pp. 237-238.

[38] *Colonial Records,* Vol. IV., p. 306.

sickly, were not permitted to be landed.   Likewise the
foreigners, in number 53, imported in the ship Rachel,
Captain Armstrong, were so sickly that it was thought
dangerous to suffer them to land altogether; whereupon
the sick were ordered to be separated from the well, and
such as recovered, with the well were to be qualified occasionally." [39]

[39] *Colonial Records*, Vol. V., p. 410.

SKIMMER AND MUSSTOPF.

CHAPTER VIII.

EARLY DEMAND OF THE GERMANS FOR NATURALIZATION.
— REQUEST DENIED, BUT GRANTED LATER.— HOW THEY
SPREAD OVER ALL THE LAND AND BECAME THE SHIELD
AND BULWARK OF THE QUAKERS BY GUARDING THE FRON-
TIERS AGAINST THE INDIANS.

"From Delaware's and Schuylkill's gleam,
    Away where Susquehanna twines,
And out o'er Allegheny's stream
    In places distant fell their lines."

By river and by fountain,
    Where'er they touched this strand ;
In wood and vale and mountain,
    They found a fatherland.

ROYAL ARMS OF HOLLAND,
A. D. 1694.

AS has already been stated the great and persistent influx of Germans alarmed the Provincial Assembly, which at that early period was composed almost exclusively of British born subjects. Several efforts to secure naturalization met with much coldness. Their industry and abstention from politics were well known, but failed to remove the existing jealousy. As early as 1721, Palatines, who had long been residents in the Province, applied for the privileges of naturalization, but their claims were quietly ignored until 1724, when permission was granted to bring in a bill, conditionally however, that each applicant should obtain from a justice of the peace a certificate of the value of their property and the nature of their religious faith.

A bill carrying the foregoing provisions was passed and laid before the Governor in 1725, but was returned by him without his approval, on the ground that in a country where English law and liberty prevailed, a scrutiny into the private conversation and faith of the citizens, and especially into the value of their estates was a measure at once unjust in its character and establishing a dangerous precedent. The House yielded to the Governor's reasoning and the bill was withdrawn. But the Palatines became more urgent for the privileges of citizenship as they saw a disposition on the part of the authorities to defer their request, doubtless apprehending that sinister motives controlled the action of the Assembly.

In 1729 the question was once more brought up and the following bill was introduced. It was passed on October 14, 1729, and received the assent of Governor Gordon:

Whereas, By encouragement given by the Honorable William Penn, Esq., late Proprietary and Governor of the province of Pennsylvania, and by permission of his Majesty, King George the First, of blessed memory, and his predecessors, Kings and Queens of England, &c., divers Protestants, who were subjects to the Emperor of Germany, a Prince in amity with the Crown of Great Britain, transported themselves and estates into the Province of Pennsylvania, between the years one thousand seven hundred and eighteen; and since they came hither have contributed very much to the enlargement of the British Empire, and to the raising and improving sundry commodities fit for the markets of Europe, and have always behaved themselves religiously and peaceably, and have paid a due regard to the laws and Government of this province; And whereas, many of said persons, to wit, Martin Meylin, Hans Graaf and others, all of Lancaster county, in the said province, in demonstration of their affection and zeal for his present Majesty's person and Government, qualified themselves by taking the qualification, and subscribing the declaration directed to be taken and subscribed by the several acts of parliament, made for the security of his Majesty's person and Government, and for preventing the dangers which may happen by Popish Recusants, &c., and thereupon have humbly signified to the Governor and Representatives of the freemen of this province, in General Assembly, that they have purchased and do hold lands of the proprietary, and others, his Majesty's subjects within this province, and have likewise represented their great desire of being made partakers of those privileges which the natural born subjects of Great Britain do enjoy within this province; and it being just and reasonable, that those persons who have *bona fide* purchased lands, and who have given such testimony of their affection and obedience to the Crown of Great Britain should as well be secured in the enjoyment of their estates, as encouraged in their laudable affection and zeal for the English constitution:

Be it enacted by the Hon. Patrick Gordon, Esq., Lieutenant Governor of the province of Pennsylvania, &c., by and with the advice and consent of the freemen of the said province, in General Assembly met, and by the authority of the same, that (here follow the names of one hundred and five heads of German families) all of Lancaster county, be, and shall be to all intents and purposes deemed, taken and esteemed, His Majesty's natural born subjects of this province of Pennsylvania, as if they, and each of them had been born within the said province; and shall and may, and every one of them shall and may, within this province, take, receive, enjoy, and be entitled to all rights, privileges and advantages of natural born subjects, as fully, to all intents and constructions and purposes, whatsoever, as any of His Majesty's natural born subjects of this province, can, do, or ought to enjoy, by virtue of their being His Majesty's natural born subjects of His Majesty's said province of Pennsylvania." [40]

From this time forward long lists of persons, mostly Germans, however, were presented to the Assembly, asking that the petitioners be granted the privileges of naturalization and citizenship. As we are nowhere informed that these hard-working, industrious citizens anywhere turned in and kicked the Quaker law makers out of their places of honor and profit, it may be taken for granted they did all they promised in their oaths of naturalization. When the troublesome times of the Revolution came along none were stauncher in their support of the Independence of the Colonies.

From the following endorsement which appears on the copy of an act passed by the General Assembly, sitting from October 14, 1738, until its adjournment on May 1, 1739, naturalizing a large number of Germans, I infer there must have been a charge for naturalization and that considerable revenue was derived from this source: [41]

---

[40] *Statutes at Large of Pennsylvania*, Vol. IV., pp. 147–150.

[41] J. I. MOMBERT'S *History of Lancaster County*, pp. 424–426.

PHILADEL'Y, the 18th of September.
Then received of Abraham Witmer the sum of one pound and two shillings (and one pound before) which is in full for his Naturalization. I say received by me.

Christian Grassold,
Collector.

It was customary to take the immigrants upon disembarkation to the Court House in Philadelphia to be qualified, but this practice was varied. Sometimes this ceremony occurred at the office of the Mayor, and again at the office of some attorney, no doubt authorized for that purpose.[42]

The names of the incoming Palatines were published in the *Colonial Records* from September 21, 1727, until August 30, 1736, when the practice was discontinued.

WHERE SOME OF THEM WENT.

It is interesting to follow these people after reaching Pennsylvania. The little colony of 33 persons who planted

CONESTOGA TEAM AND WAGON.

themselves at Germantown under the headship of Francis Daniel Pastorius, in 1683, was slowly augmented during the following two decades. But by 1702, as Judge Penny-

---

[42]See note in RUPP's *Thirty Thousand Names*, p. 47.

packer tells us, they began to penetrate into the regions beyond their own limited domain.   The acquisition of land seems ever to have been a prominent characteristic with the Germans, and it may be said to continue to this very hour. Even then the spirit of speculation was rife among them. Their early cleared farms had become valuable.   There were always those who, having money, preferred to buy farms from which the heavy timber had been cleared and on which good buildings were erected.   The prices for wild lands were so reasonable that men were tempted to sell their early holdings and, with the aid of their sturdy sons and daughters, to enter upon and conquer new lands in the interior.

Then, too, the inflowing tide became so strong that there were no longer lands near the older settlements to be taken up, and they were perforce compelled to move far into the backwoods.   Lancaster County, Berks County, Lebanon County, York and Dauphin, Schuylkill, Lehigh and Northampton all heard the tread of the invading hosts.

One characteristic of these German immigrants deserves especial mention.   While many of them were handicrafts-men, by far the greater number were bauern — farmers — and to this calling they at once betook themselves.   Indeed, the first thing upon their arrival in Philadelphia was to find out the nearest route to the unsettled lands of the Proprietary, and thither they betook themselves at the earliest possible moment.   The backwoods had no terrors for them.   As a race of tillers of the soil, they were well aware that the character of the timber was an indication of the nature of the ground on which it stood.   They were not afraid to work.   The felling of the trees and the clearing of the land neither intimidated nor deterred them from locating where these impediments to farming were greatest. The fatness of the land they knew was greatest where trees were largest and stood thickest. The mightiest forests fell at the resounding blows of the woodman's axe, even as the arch enemy of mankind shrunk at the potent thrust of Ithurial's spear. Their presence was manifested in every fertile valley. Wherever a cool spring burst from the earth, on every green hillside and in the depths of the forest, their modest homes appeared. The traditional policy of the Proprietary Government also pushed them to the frontiers — the places of danger. Let the truth be told, even as history is to-day writing it. It is the boast of the historian that so mild and generous was the dealing of the Quaker with the aborigines that "not a drop of Quaker blood was ever shed by an Indian."[43] Shall I tell why? It was because the belt of Quaker settlement was enclosed in a circumference described by a radius of fifty miles from Penn's city on the Delaware. Beyond that point came the sturdy Germans, the Reformed, the Lutherans, the Dunkers, the Mennonites and the Moravians, whose settlements effectually prevented the savages from spilling Quaker blood. Instead, the tomahawk and scalping knife found sheath in the bodies of the sturdy children of the Palatinate. Let the sacrificed lives of more than three hundred men, women and children from the Rhine country, who fell along the Blue Mountains between 1754 and 1763, give the true answer to the Quaker boast.[44]

There were many entire settlements throughout eastern Pennsylvania as early as 1750 where no language but the German was heard. They went to the north, the south, and to the west. Soon they reached the Appalachian chain of mountains, climbed its wooded sides and de-

[43] BANCROFT'S *United States*, Vol. II., p. 383.
[44] RUPP'S *Thirty Thousand Names*, p. 17.

bouched into the wild regions beyond until the Ohio was in sight. But on, still on, went that resistless army of Commonwealth-builders. To-day they are spread over the fairest and most fertile lands of the great West. Ohio, Indiana, Illinois, Iowa, Kansas, Nebraska and other states, the entire continent in fact, count among the best of their citizens the men who went out of Pennsylvania with Luther's bible in their hands and the language of Schiller and Goethe upon their lips. Wherever they went their fervent but unobtrusive piety went with them. As early as 1750 there were already forty well-established German Reformed and thirty Lutheran congregations in Pennsylvania.[45] Of the minor church organizations, or rather of those who had no such organizations, "the sect people," like the Mennonites, the Dunkers, Schwenkfelders and many more, we cannot speak. In the aggregate they were very numerous and in their quiet way brought credit on their country and on their lineage, wherever they located themselves; and all that was said of them at that early period attaches to them to-day.

---

[45] OSWALD SEIDENSTICKER'S *Bilder aus der Deutsch-pennsylvanischen Geschichte*, Vol. II., p. 254.

CHAPTER IX.

The German Population of Pennsylvania as Estimated by various Writers at various Epochs. — Often Mere Guesses. — Better Means of Reaching close Results now. — Some Sources of Increase not Generally Considered.

> "Ay, call it holy ground,
>   The soil where first they trod ;
> They left unstained what there they found
>   Freedom to worship God."
>
> O mighty oaks centennial,
>   On field and fell that stand ;
> Keep watch and ward perennial
>   Above that faithful band.

HOW many Germans came to Pennsylvania during the eighteenth century? That query will probably occur to many readers, because it is one of the most interesting of all the questions connected with this subject. In the absence of direct and indisputable evidence every effort to solve the problem must of necessity be in the nature of an approximation, or if you will, only a guess. A score of writers have tried their hands at the problem, and their guesses are as various as the writers themselves. In fact, these estimates are hopelessly discordant and some of them are here given that the reader may understand the situation and exercise his own judgment in the matter from the evidence that has been laid before him in the course of this narration.

Sypher, for example, says " in 1727, nearly 50,000 persons, mostly Germans, had found a new home in Pennsylvania," [46] which I venture to think exaggerates the number at that time so far as the Germans are concerned. Dr. Charles J. Stillé has estimated the population of the State in 1740, at 100,000, and he adds, " of the inhabitants of the Province one-fourth or one-fifth were Quakers, about one-half Germans and the rest emigrants from the North of Ireland." [47] Governor Thomas, who ought to be good authority, expressed the opinion that in 1747 the population numbered 120,000 of which three-fifths or 72,000 were Germans. I find an estimate in the *Colonial Records,* on what authority is not stated, which gives the population at 220,000 in 1747 of which it is said 100,000 were Germans. In 1763, a Committee of which Benjamin Franklin was chairman, reported to Parliament that 30,000 laborers, servants and redemptioners had come into the Province within twenty years and yet " the price of labor had not diminished." [48] This is an interesting fact and is conclusive evidence that nothing was so much needed in the growing Province in those early days as men who knew how to work and were willing to do so. In 1776 Dr. Franklin's estimate was 160,000 colonists of whom one-third or 53,000 were Germans, one-third Quakers and the

[46] SYPHER'S *History of Pennsylvania,* p. 73.

[47] STILLÉ'S *Life and Times of John Dickinson,* pp. 46-47.

[48] GORDON'S *History of Pennsylvania,* p. 273.

DOMESTIC UTENSILS.

1 WROUGHT IRON CANDLE STICK.
2 FAT LAMP ON EARTHENWARE STAND.
3 WALL SCONCE.
4 FAT LAMP ON PORTABLE BASE.
5 LARD LAMP.

6 CAN FOR WARMING LARD.
7 WOODEN LANTERN.
8 TIN CANDLE STICK.
9 FISH OIL LAMP.
10 BUNCH OF SULPHUR STICKS.

rest of other nationalities. Michael Schlatter, the eminent missionary and organizer in the Reformed Church, in 1751 gave 190,000 as the total population of Pennsylvania, of whom one-third or 63,000 were Germans. Proud, the historian, who ought to be a very competent authority, estimated the entire population of Pennsylvania in 1770 at 250,000, with the Germans as one-third of that number or 83,000. Menzel, in his history of Germany, informs us that from 1770 to 1791, twenty-four immigrant ships arrived annually at Philadelphia, without reckoning those that landed in other harbors.[49] This is a wholesale exaggeration of the actual facts. This statement indicates the arrival of more than 500 ships during the 21 years mentioned. We know that is more than the total recorded number from 1727 to 1791. From 1771 until 1775 there were only 47 arrivals. There were hardly any German arrivals during the Revolutionary War, and comparatively few from 1783 until 1790. We know there were only 114 in the year 1789. It is easy for historians to fall into error when they draw on their fancy for their facts. According to Ebeling, the German inhabitants of Pennsylvania numbered 144,660 in the year 1790.[50] Seidensticker gives the inhabitants of the Province in 1752 at 190,000, of which he says about 90,000 were Germans. The Lutherans in 1731 are supposed to have numbered about 17,000 and the German Reformed 15,000.[51] In 1742 the number of Germans was given at 100,000 by Hirsching.[52] Rev. J. B. Rieger estimated the number of Germans in the Province in 1733 at 15,000. In the notes to the *Hallische Nach-*

---

[49] MENZEL'S *History of Germany*, Vol. III., Chap. CCLXXIV.

[50] EBELING, *Beschreibung der Erde, Abtheilung, Pennsylvanien.*

[51] OSWALD SEIDENSTICKER, *Geschichte der Deutschen Gesellschaft von Pennsylvanien*, S. 18.

[52] HIRSCHING, *Histor. Literar. Handbuch VII.*, 230.

richten, we find this: "If we estimate the Germans of Pennsylvania, at the middle of the eighteenth century, at from 70,000 to 80,000, we shall not be far out of the way." [53]

Franz Löher, in his *Geschichte und Zustände der Deutschen in Amerika,* has some interesting remarks on this subject. [54]

Amid this multiplicity of estimates the writer of to-day is reluctant to enter the field with some of his own. The observant men who lived here between 1725 and 1775, should certainly have been more capable of forming an accurate estimate than those who came a century or more after them. But it is evident that many made mere guesses, without actual knowledge, and their views are, therefore, without special value. The tendency in almost every case was to exaggerate. But to-day we know with tolerable accuracy the number of ships that reached Philadelphia, and have the ship lists. We know, too,

---

[53] *Hallische Nachrichten,* Vol. I., p. 463.

[54] Löher says: "There was hardly a single year between 1720 and 1727 that a large number of ships bearing German immigrants did not arrive in Philadelphia, and even greater numbers came between 1730 and 1742 (*Hallische Nachrichten,* 665–668). Already in 1742, the number of Germans in Pennsylvania was estimated at 100,000 (HIRSCHING'S *History of Literature*). Eight years later (1750) it was thought the number was well nigh 230,000. Still other estimates give the number in 1732 at 30,000, and in 1763 at 280,000 (*Grahame History of Pennsylvania,* Vol. II., p. 514. *Holmes',* Vol. I., 554; II., 142). Philadelphia had in 1749 six English and four German Churches. * * * From 1740 on, thousands of Germans landed in Philadelphia every fall. In 1749 alone 25 ships reached that port with 7,049; others say 12,000 (*Hallische Nachrichten,* 369. *Grahame,* Vol. II., p. 201). During the following three years, 1750, 51, 52, also came 6,000 (*Hall. Nachrichten,* 369. *Grahame,* II., 201). It is said that in 1759 alone, 22,000 came from Baden, the Palatinate and Wirtenberg (*Mittelberger,* p. 25). In the terrible famine years of 1771 and 1772 came the greatest number, but, in the succeeding four years, from 20 to 24 ships reached Philadelphia with German immigrants (*Halle Nachrichten,* 125, 735, 682). In 1771 and 1772, 484 persons left Canton Basel for America (*Mittelberger,* p. 26)."

An Hiftorical and Geographical Account

OF THE

PROVINCE and COUNTRY

O F

PENSILVANIA;

AND OF

Weft-New-Jerfey

IN

AMERICA.

The Richnefs of the Soil, the Sweetnefs of the Situation
the Wholefomnefs of the Air, the Navigable Rivers, and
others, the prodigious Encreafe of Corn, the flourifhing
Condition of the City of *Philadelphia*, with the ftately
Buildings, and other Improvements there. The ftrange
Creatures, as *Birds, Beafts, Fifhes,* and *Fowls,* with the
feveral forts of *Minerals, Purging-Waters,* and *Stones,*
lately difcovered. The *Natives, Aborogmes,* their *Language, Religion, Laws,* and *Cuftoms*; The firft Planters,
the *Dutch, Sweeds,* and *Englifh,* with the number of
its Inhabitants; As alfo a Touch upon *George Keith's*
New Religion, in his fecond Change fince he left the
QUAKERS.

With a Map of both Countries.

By GABRIEL THOMAS,
who refided there about Fifteen Years.

London, Printed for, and Sold by *A. Baldwin,* at
the *Oxon Arms* in *Warwich-Lane,* 1698.

TITLE-PAGE OF ORIGINAL EDITION OF GABRIEL THOMAS' *Account.*

that many were here when the registry law went into operation and who go to swell the whole number; that in addition, others came from New York prior to 1700.

In the year 1738 sixteen immigrant ships reached port, bringing from 15 to 349 each, or a total of 3,115. The average per ship was about 200. It is reasonable to suppose that was also a fair average for previous and succeeding years. Between 1727 and 1750, the latter year and that of 1745 when there were no arrivals not included, there were 134 arrivals of ships of all sizes. Allowing these an average of 200 each, we get as a result 26,800 souls, or an average of about 1,220 annually. As has elsewhere been stated the number of arrivals in 1732 was 2,093, and in 1738, 3,257. In 1728, 1729 and 1730 the arrivals were 390, 243 and 458 respectively, which, of course, counter-balance such big years as 1732 and 1738.

We are in the dark as to the ship arrivals between 1714 and 1727, but the accounts are agreed the number was considerable. I am inclined to accept the Rev. Rieger's estimate of 15,000 in 1727, instead of in 1733, where he places it. That number added to estimated arrivals between 1727 and 1749, both years included, gives us in round numbers about 42,000 in 1750, to which must be added the natural increase which was, perhaps, 5,000 more, or a total German population of 47,000 souls in the Province in 1750. Between 1750 and 1775, both years inclusive (but not counting 1757, '58, '59 and '60, during which there were no arrivals) we have a total of 196 ships in 21 years, which reckoned at the average of 200 to each vessel gives us 39,000 arrivals or rather less than an average of 1,900 yearly. This added to our previous estimate for 1750 gives us with the natural increase fully 90,000 Germans in the Province when the Revolutionary war broke out. Indeed, I am inclined to believe the number was nearer 100,000 than 90,000, for these early Germans were noted for their large families. There is, however, considerable unanimity in one particular among most of the authorities, and that is that the Germans at any and every period between 1730 and 1790 constituted about one-third of the total population. This statement is unquestionably correct as we approach the years nearest the Revolutionary period. The English Quakers and the Welsh had not been coming over in any considerable number, and the same may, perhaps, be said of the Scotch-Irish. The Germans formed the bulk of the immigrants and necessarily increased their numerical ratio to the total population of the Province which, according to the first census in 1790, was 434,373. Accepting the ratio of one-third being Germans, we get 144,791 as the German population at that period.

There is still another large increase in the German population of Pennsylvania prior to 1790 which writers do not reckon with, but which must not be left out of our estimates. It is those German soldiers who remained in the State at the close of the Revolutionary War. The number of these men who were sent to America and fought under the banner of George III., was, according to the best authorities, 29,867.[55] Of that number, 17,313 returned to Europe in the autumn of 1783. The number that did not return was 12,554. These have been accounted for as follows:

Killed and died of wounds	1,200
Died of illness and accident	6,354
Deserted	5,000
Total	12,554

[55] KAPP'S *Soldatenhandel*, 2d edition, p. 209; SCHLOZER'S *Stats-Anzeigen*, VI., pp. 521-522.

Here we have five thousand men, most of whom remained scattered among their countrymen throughout Pennsylvania. The few hundred who perhaps settled in other states were more than made up by those German soldiers who, by agreement with the several German States, enlisted in the English regiments, some of which had recruiting stations at various places along the Rhine, and who were not counted in the financial adjustment of accounts between Great Britain and the German Princes, nor compelled to return to Europe.[56]

It is well known that during the first quarter of the nineteenth century the German immigration to this State was well sustained so that probably the Germans and their descendants have pretty nearly kept up the percentage of population accorded them by general consent so long as one hundred and fifty years ago.

The opinion seems to prevail very generally that in 1700 all the Germans in Pennsylvania were those who were gathered at the Germantown settlement, along the Wissahickon and immediately around Philadelphia. Rupp expressly states that there were only about 200 families of Germans in the Province in 1700. I do not coincide with that view. The colonists which Sweden had begun to send to the Delaware as early as 1638, were not composed of Swedes and Finns only; special privileges were offered to Germans and these, too, came along.

An examination of the *Colonial History of New York* and O'Callagan's *Documentary History of New York*, shows that a number of settlements had been planted on the Delaware by the City of Amsterdam. Colonies of Mennonites are mentioned as having settled in New York prior to 1657. In a report on the *State of*

---

[56] See LOWELL'S *Hessians*, pp. 21–300.

Religion in New York, dated August 5, 1657, addressed to the Classis of Amsterdam, I find this : " At Gravesend, on Long Island, there are Mennonists * * * yea they for the most part reject infant baptism, the Sabbath, the office of preacher and the teachers of God's word, saying that through these have come all sorts of contention into the world. Whenever they meet together one or the other reads something for them."[57] I also find that Governor Fletcher, of New York, wrote in 1693 that " more families are daily removing for Pennsylvania and Connecticut to be eased from taxes and detachments."[58] The Rev. John Miller writes in 1696 that "the burdens of the Province (N. Y.) have made two or three hundred families forsake it and remove to Pennsylvania, and Maryland chiefly."[59]

Here we are told of the migration of as many German families from New York to Pennsylvania prior to 1693, as are credited to all Pennsylvania in the year 1700. I regret that time has not allowed me to examine more fully the documents here mentioned. There are a great number of references in them to Mennonites in New York, and as these disappeared from that colony at an early date, there seems to be abundant reason for believing that they nearly all found their way into Pennsylvania, swelling the German population to no inconsiderable extent. We undoubtedly have here a factor which must be reckoned with in any summary we may make of the early population of Pennsylvania.

I am therefore not ready to accept the generally believed statement that the colony of Crefelders who settled at Germantown in 1683 were the only Germans around Philadelphia at that time. The evidence is scattering but none the

---

[57] *Documentary History of New York*, Vol. III., p. 69.

[58] *Colonial History of New York*, Vol. IV., p. 55.

[59] *Ibid.*, Vol. IV., p. 183.

less direct. Watson tells us that one Warner had settled at William Grove, two miles beyond the city limits as early as 1658. Also that Jurian Hartsfelder took up 350 acres of land in March, 1676, nearly six years before Penn's arrival.[60] Pennypacker says he was " a stray Dutchman or German, who had been a deputy Sheriff under Andross in 1676."[61] Rupp tells us that one Heinrich Frey had reached Philadelphia two years before Penn's arrival, and a certain Plattenbach somewhat later.[62] There was a large general immigration in 1682, about 30 ships having arrived with settlers.[63] We can no more divest ourselves of the belief that there were many Germans among these than we can that there were many Germans among the Swedes and Finns who first came fifty years earlier, because we know Gustavus Adolphus asked the Protestant German princes to allow their subjects to join his own subjects in forming the Swedish settlements on the Delaware. Johannes Printz, who succeeded Peter Minnewit as Governor, was a German, a Holsteiner, and he brought with him fifty-four German families, mostly from Pomerania.[64] It is a very logical supposition that these were only a portion of the Germans who planted themselves along the Delaware at various times between 1638 and 1682. When therefore Rupp tells us that there were only about 200 German families in Pennsylvania in 1700, I cannot accept his statement, because I cannot escape the conclusion from all the evidence accessible, that those figures should be increased several hundred per cent. Neither do I doubt that in the fullness of time an abundance of confirmatory evidence of this view will be forthcoming.

---

[60] WATSON'S *Annals of Philadelphia*, Vol. I., p. 11.

[61] PENNYPACKER'S *Settlement of Germantown*, p. 19.

[62] RUPP'S *History of Berks and Lebanon Counties*, p. 90.

[63] PROUD'S *History of Pennsylvania*, Vol. I., p. 220.

[64] LOUIS P. HENNINGHAUSEN, Esq., *The First German Immigrants to North America*, p. 20.

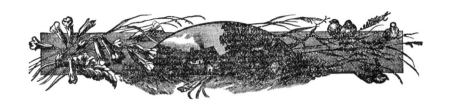

CHAPTER X.

Their Detractors and their Friends. — What Both Parties have said. — The Great Philosopher Mistaken. — How the Passing Years have Brought along their Vindication.

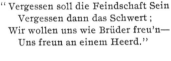

" Vergessen soll die Feindschaft Sein
Vergessen dann das Schwert ;
Wir wollen uns wie Brüder freu'n—
Uns freun an einem Heerd."

IT will hardly be questioned, I suppose, that Benjamin Franklin was the greatest American of the Revolutionary era. He certainly was from a political point of view. Coming into the Province in 1723 and dying in the State in 1790, his residence here covers almost three-quarters of a century. He literally grew up with the Province, saw it in almost every phase of its career, from its earliest struggles until the strong Commonwealth was established, let us hope for all time. The proprietary period was by no means an ideal one. The student of that early time is confronted on almost every

(107)

page of our history by the quarrels and disputes between the Governors of the Province and the Provincial Assemblies. The former in standing up for the rights of the Penn heirs, and the latter jealous of the rights and interests of the people, presented a condition of turbulence hardly equalled in any of the American colonies.

Franklin was on the spot when the great German immigration set in. He saw it all and could hardly help understanding it. He could not avoid coming in contact with these people. He did, in fact, come into very close and profitable relations with them. For years he owned and conducted the best equipped printing establishment in the Province, if not in the entire country. This brought him into very close business relations with the Germans, for there were many men of high culture among them, who wrote learned books which Franklin printed for them at his establishment. Had he understood the Germans better he might have appreciated this more. At all events he seems to have misunderstood them, and through that misunderstanding to have done them a great wrong. It may not have been willful, but it was, nevertheless, inexcusable.

Other men prominent in affairs, Secretary Logan and some of the early Governors, have had their fling at the German colonists, but they also in time paid ample testimony to their excellent qualities. But from none of them came so severe a blow as from Dr. Franklin. Under date of May 9, 1753, he wrote a letter to his friend Peter Collinson, in which he speaks thus unkindly of these people, the very bone and sinew of the great State that was to be :

" I am perfectly of your mind, that measures of great temper are necessary touching the Germans, and I am not without apprehensions, that, through their indiscretion, or ours, or both, great disorders may one day arise among us.

BENJAMIN FRANKLIN.

Those who came hither are generally the most stupid of their own nation, and as ignorance is often attended with great credulity, when knavery would mislead it, and with suspicion when honesty would set it right; and, few of the English understand the German language, and so cannot address them either from the press or pulpit, it is almost impossible to remove any prejudices they may entertain. Their clergy have very little influence on the people, who seem to take pleasure in abusing and discharging the minister on every trivial occasion. Not being used to liberty, they know not how to make modest use of it. * * * They are under no restraint from ecclesiastical government; they behave, however, submissively enough at present to the civil government, which I wish they may continue to do, for I remember when they modestly declined intermeddling with our elections; but now they come in droves and carry all before them, except in one or two counties.

" Few of their children in the country know English. They import many books from Germany, and of the six printing houses in the Province, two are entirely German, two half German, half English, and but two are entirely English. They have one German newspaper, and one-half German Advertisements intended to be general, are now printed in Dutch (German) and English. The signs in our streets (Philadelphia) have inscriptions in both languages, and some places only in German. They begin, of late, to make all their bonds and other legal instruments in their own language, which (though I think it ought not to be), are allowed in our courts, where the German business so increases, that there is continued need of interpreters, and I suppose in a few years, they will also be necessary in the Assembly, to tell one-half of our legislators, what the other half says. In short, unless the stream of importation could be turned from this to other colonies, as you very judiciously propose, they will soon outnumber us, that all the advantages we will have, will in my opinion, be not able to preserve our language, and even our government will become precarious." [65]

The wisest mortals are sometimes short-sighted and Dr. Franklin must be allowed a place in that category. His letter is unsound throughout. First he calls them stupid and ignorant; later he admits they import many books. If so ignorant and stupid what did they want with so many books? If so steeped in mental darkness, how is it that there were more German newspapers printed in the Province at that very hour than in English? The generally shrewd philosopher, patriot and statesman involved himself in contradictions such as not even the "stupid" Germans would have done. I may even go further and say, that at the time Dr. Franklin's letter was written there were many Germans in Pennsylvania incomparably superior to him in the learning of the schools. He does not appear to have thought of that. Perhaps he did not know it—could not comprehend it.

Well-nigh one hundred and fifty years have come and gone since his unjust tirade against the German colonists. Not one of the fears that seemed to have possessed his soul has been realized. It is true the Quaker no longer governs the land. He went to the rear as the Germans came to the front and assumed control of the Government. They became the dominant race, and they are so to-day. They did no violence to the laws; they upheld them and enforced them. They have made the State the grandest of all the forty-five. Dr. Franklin lived to see how idle his predictions were, and even he recanted.

---

[65] SPARK'S *Works of Franklin*, Vol. VII., pp. 71-73.

CONTINUATIO
Der
Beschreibung der Landschafft
PENSYLVANIÆ
An denen End-Gräntzen
AMERICÆ.
Uber vorige des Herrn Pastorii
Relationes.
In sich haltend:
Die Situation, und Fruchtbarkeit des
Erdbodens. Die Schiffreiche und andere
Flüsse. Die Anzahl derer bißhero gebauten Städte.
Die seltsame Creaturen an Thieren / Vögeln und Fischen.
Die Mineralien und Edelgesteine Deren eingebohrnen wil-
den Völcker Sprachen / Religion und Gebräuche. Und
die ersten Christlichen Pflantzer und Anbauer
dieses Landes.
Beschrieben von
GABRIEL THOMAS
15. Jährigen Inwohner dieses
Landes.
Welchem Tractätlein noch beygefüget sind:
Des Hn. DANIEL FALCKNERS
Burgers und Pilgrims in Pensylvania 193.
Beantwortungen uff vorgelegte Fragen von
guten Freunden.

Franckfurt und Leipzig /
Zu finden bey Andreas Otto/ Buchhändlern.

There were a number of others whose views coincided with those of Franklin, at least in some particulars. On the other hand there were those who spoke and wrote as decidedly in their behalf. Among these was the historian Macaulay, who calls them "Honest, laborious men, who had once been thriving burghers of Mannheim and Heidelberg, or who had cultivated the vine on the banks of the Neckar and Rhine. Their ingenuity and their diligence could not fail to enrich any land which should afford them an asylum."

Against the jaundiced views of Dr. Franklin I set those of a man of our own times, one who from his public position and his superior opportunities for forming correct views of the early German immigrants is eminently entitled to be heard on this question. I mean Dr. James P. Wickersham, for nearly fifteen years Superintendent of Public Instruction in Pennsylvania. Of Quaker descent, he was nevertheless broad-minded and liberal, and did not strive to close his eyes to the good qualities of the early Germans, with whose descendants he became so intimately connected and acquainted. He says: "Pennsylvania as a land of promise became known in Holland, Germany and Switzerland. * * * But it was not long until numbers of the oppressed inhabitants of nearly all parts of Germany and Switzerland, and especially of districts along the Rhine, began to seek homes, with wives, children and all they possessed, in the wilds of Pennsylvania. Among them were members of a dozen different religious denominations, large and small. They all came with the common object of bettering their condition in life, and securing homes in a country where they could enjoy unmolested the right to worship God as their consciences dictated. In Pennsylvania, if nowhere else, they knew they would secure civil and religious liberty. Some of them were very poor, even coming without sufficient money to pay the expenses of their passage, but others were well to do, bought land, built houses, and soon by patient industry had about them the comforts to which they had been accustomed. The German immigrants were mostly farmers, but among them there was a smaller proportion of different kinds of mechanics. They brought few books with them, but nearly every individual possessed a Bible and a Prayer or Hymn-book, and many had in addition a Catechism or a Confession of Faith. These were the treasures that could not be left behind, and they are still preserved as heirlooms in hundreds of old German families.

" When they came in bodies, they were usually accompanied by a clergyman or a schoolmaster, or both. They were not highly educated as a class, but among them were some good scholars, and few could be found who were not able to read. The impression has prevailed that they were grossly ignorant; it is unjust; those who make the charge either do not take the pains to understand, or wish to misrepresent them. Their average intelligence compared favorably with that of contemporary American colonists of other nationalities. If they did not keep pace with others in subsequent years, their backwardness is easily accounted for by their living for the most part on farms, frequently many miles separated, and extending over large sections of country; their division into many religious denominations, among which there was little unity; their inability, scattered and broken as they were, to support ministers and schoolmasters, or even to secure the advantages of an organized community; their use of a language which in a measure isolated them from the neighboring settlers, and shut them out from the social, political and business currents that gave life to the communities around them; their unacquaintance with the proper forms of local self-government, and the habit brought with them, in all public concerns, of deferring to some outside or higher authority; and above all, perhaps, their quiet, confiding disposition, quite in contrast with the ways of some of the more aggressive, self-asserting classes of people with whom they were brought in competition. * * *

"Although invited to settle in Pennsylvania, the Germans, arriving in such large numbers and spreading over the country so rapidly, seem to have created a fear on the part of other settlers and of the provincial authorities that they would form an unruly element in society, and eventually work the overthrow of the government, or assume possession of it, as their countrymen had done long before in England. Laws restraining their immigration were passed, and the alarm disturbed even such well-balanced minds as those of Logan and Franklin. It is almost needless to add now that such a fear was groundless and arose wholly out of the political and sectarian prejudices of the day. On the contrary, it is only just to say that to all that has gone to build up Pennsylvania, to enlarge her wealth, to develop her resources, to increase her prosperity, to educate her people, to give her good government from the first, the German element of the population has contributed its full share. Better citizens cannot be found in any nation on the face of the globe." [66]

No truer tribute was ever paid the German immigrants than this one, before the Assembly on January 2, 1738, by Lieutenant-Governor George Thomas when urging the es-

---

[66] JAMES PYLE WICKERSHAM, LL.D., *A History of Education in Pennsylvania*, pp. 122-124.

tablishment of a hospital for sick arrivals : " This Province has been for some years the Asylum of the distressed Protestants of the Palatinate, and other parts of Germany, and I believe it may with truth be said that the present flourishing condition of it is in a great measure owing to the industry of these People; and should any discouragement divert them from coming hither, it may well be apprehended that the value of your Lands will fall, and your Advances to wealth be much slower; for it is not altogether the goodness of the Soil, but the Number and Industry of the People that make a flourishing Colony." [67]

[67] *Colonial Records*, Vol. IV., p. 315.

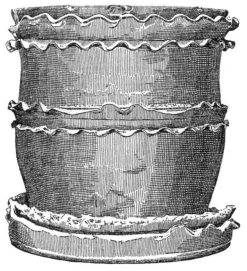

SPECIMEN OF EARLY PENNSYLVANIA POTTERY.

CHAPTER XI.

THE GERMANS AS FARMERS.— ANSWER TO A RECENT HIS-
TORIAN WHO ASSERTS THEY, A RACE OF FARMERS, DID
NOT TAKE THE SAME ENJOYMENT IN AGRICULTURAL PUR-
SUITS AS THE SCOTCH-IRISH AND SOME OTHERS!!

> "Oft did the harvest to their sickle yield,
>   Their furrow oft the stubborn glebe has broke ;
> How jocund did they drive their teams afield !
>   How bow'd the woods beneath their sturdy stroke ! "

> "Und der Vater mit frohem Blick,
>   Von des Hauses weitschauendem Giebel
> Überzählet sein blühend Glück,
>   Siehet der Pfosten ragende Bäume,
>   Und der Scheunen gefüllte Räume,
> Und die Speicher, vom Segen gebogen
> Und des Kornes bewegte Wogen."

THIS chapter is supplemen-
tary. It had no place
in the original plan of the
writer. It has been called
forth by a brief sentence found in a recently published history of Pennsylvania, and is the last written chapter of this
book—written long after the rest. While not germane to
the general title, it yet deserves a place here inasmuch as

(116)

it strikes at one of the innumerable errors and misrepresentations concerning the early German population of Pennsylvania which crowd the pages of some recent writers. These errors, I am persuaded, are more the result of ignorance than of design, but they are errors nevertheless, and should be killed at their birth. That is the only plan known to me to keep down the abundant crop of ignorance which springs up as often as writers draw on their imagination for their facts. It is rarely, however, that anything so gross as the blunder to which I shall refer appears in print, as genuine history.

I was much surprised to find in a recently issued history of Pennsylvania, the following surprising statement : " The Germans perhaps were less given to the enjoyment of agriculture than the Scotch-Irish and other settlers, yet in their own way they enjoyed existence, etc." [68] By no conceivable possibility is such a statement likely to be accepted by any one who has actual knowledge of the German immigration into this or any other country in America. It shows such a superficial acquaintance with the subject discussed as to carry its own condemnation with it. Yet, lest future writers of our history be lured into making similar statements, I shall take it upon myself to adduce such proof in contradiction of the statement quoted, as will, I believe, set the question at rest effectually and permanently.

I think it will be conceded, as a general proposition, that men in all civilized countries follow those pursuits to which they are best adapted and most inclined, whether for profit or enjoyment. It is true that when Roman civilization first came into contact with the Germanic tribes, the latter were more given to war and the chase than to agriculture.

---

[68] ALBERT BOLLES, Ph.D., LL.D., *Pennsylvania, Province and State*, Vol. II., p. 161.

But even then they grew corn and lived largely upon the products of the field. In time they became agriculturists and for hundreds of years parts of Germany have been among the best cultivated portions of Europe, even as they are to-day. In the seventeenth century, the Palatinate and the Rhine provinces generally were the garden of Europe. They hold the same rank at this very hour. Other pursuits were followed, it is true, but outside the cities the prevailing pursuit was agriculture. The German immigration to Pennsylvania was very largely from the Palatinate, not only in its early stages, but subsequently.

Lying before me are lists of those who reached London during the great German Exodus in 1709, on their way to America. One of these gives the pursuits of the 2,928 adult males; of that entire number 1,838 were farmers, while the remaining 1,073 were classified under 24 other distinct mechanical and other professions. Another list containing 1,593 had 1,083 farmers and 510 men trained to 26 other pursuits; more than 67 per cent. of the entire number were farmers.

I think it is entirely within bounds to say that 75 per cent. of the German colonists in Pennsylvania were agriculturists. The first thing they did was to take up land, generally in the legally prescribed way, but sometimes irregularly. Nine-tenths of them went into the country, that is beyond the immediate bounds of Philadelphia, and most of them took to farming. In fact there was nothing else for them to get at for many years. Even most of those who had mechanical trades were compelled to take to farming because there was not much of a demand for bakers, glass-blowers, millers, engravers, and some other classes of handicraftsmen.

Look at the counties settled principally by these people

—Lancaster, Berks, Lebanon, York, Lehigh and Northampton. They comprise to-day the great agricultural region of the Commonwealth, and the men who are doing the farming on their fertile acres are the lineal descendants three, four or five generations removed from the first farmer immigrants. It was in every instance the agriculturists that pushed and were pushed to the outskirts of civilization. Did they go there for the profit and enjoyment they had in farming or for the fun of the thing, as we are asked to infer? What is more, they were the best and most successful farmers Pennsylvania had during the eighteenth century, just as they are the best and most successful farmers in United States to-day, and yet we are deliberately and the gravely informed they did not enjoy agriculture as much as the Scotch-Irish and other settlers! What is the record? Where are all the Scotch-Irish farmers to-day? Why are they not on the ancestral acres as the Germans are? Cumberland county was settled mainly by Scotch-Irish. In Northampton county there were many Irish and Scotch-Irish. Three-fourths of all the land in both these agricultural counties are to-day tilled by Pennsylvania-Germans. There are several townships in Lancaster county once largely occupied by Scotch-Irish of the best class. One can ride through them an entire day now without finding one farm tilled by an Ulster Irishman. Nine-tenths of the farmers in eastern Pennsylvania to-day are descendants of the men who, we are gravely informed, did not find the same enjoyment in agriculture as the Scotch-Irish, Welsh, English and others. If such an array of facts, susceptible of verification by any one who cares to make the test, is not deemed sufficient, I will produce further evidence from contemporary sources to fortify the position here taken.

The most eminent medical man in Pennsylvania, if not in the United States during the last century, was Dr. Benjamin Rush. In the course of a very busy life he found time to write and publish a little volume dealing with the Germans of this State and especially with the German farmers.[69] I will be pardoned if I quote numerous passages from this book, written by one who had a thorough personal knowledge of all he tells us.

"The principal part of them were farmers. * * * I shall begin this account of the German inhabitants of Pennsylvania by describing the manners of the German farmers. The Germans, taken as a body, especially as farmers, are not only industrious and frugal, but skillful cultivators of the earth. I shall enumerate a few particulars in which they differ from most of the other farmers of Pennsylvania. In settling a tract of land, they always provide large and suitable accommodation for their horses and cattle, before they lay out much money in building a house for themselves. * * * The first dwelling house upon this farm is small and built of logs. It generally lasts the lifetime of the first settler of a tract of land; and hence, they have a saying, that 'a son should always begin his improvements where his father left off,' that is by building a large and convenient stone house.

"They always prefer good land, or that land on which there is a large quantity of meadow land. From an attention to the cultivation of grass, they often double the value of an old farm in a few years, and grow rich on farms, on which their predecessors of whom they purchased them had nearly starved. They prefer purchasing farms with improvements to settling on a new tract of land.

---

[69] BENJAMIN RUSH, M.D., *An Account of the Manners of the German Inhabitants of Pennsylvania.* Written in 1789.

PENNSYLVANIA-GERMAN FARM LIFE.

RAKING THE BAKE-OVEN.

" In clearing new land, they do not girdle or belt the trees simply, and leave them to perish in the ground, as is the custom of their English or Irish neighbors; but they generally cut them down and burn them. In destroying underwood and bushes, they generally grub them out of the ground, by which means a field is as fit for cultivation the second year after it is cleared as it is in twenty years afterwards. The advantages of this mode of clearing, consists in the immediate product of the field, and in the greater facility with which it is ploughed, harrowed and reaped. The expense of repairing a plow, which is often broken, is greater than the extraordinary expense of grubbing the same field completely, in clearing.

" They feed their horses and cows well, of which they keep only a small number, in such a manner that the former perform twice the labor of those horses, and the latter yield twice the quantity of milk of those cows, that are less plentifully fed. There is great economy in this practice, especially in a country where so much of the labor of the farmer is necessary to support his domestic animals. A German horse is known in every part of the State; indeed, the horse seems 'to feel with his lord, the pleasure and the pride' of his extraordinary size or fat.

" The fences of a German farm are generally high and well built, so that his fields seldom suffer from the inroads of his own or his neighbors' horses, cattle, hogs or sheep.

" The German farmers are great economists in their wood. Hence they burn it only in stoves, in which they consume but a fourth or fifth of what is commonly burnt in ordinary open fireplaces; besides their horses are saved by means of this economy, from that immense labor of hauling wood in the middle of winter, which frequently unfits the horses of their (Scotch) neighbors for the toils of the ensuing spring. Their houses are, moreover, rendered so comfortable, at all times, by large close stoves, that twice the business is done by every branch of the family, in knitting, spinning and mending of farming utensils, that is done in houses where every member in the family crowds near a common fireplace, or shivers at a distance from it, with hands and fingers that move, by reason of the cold, with only half their usual quickness. They discover economy in the preservation and increase of their wood, in several other ways. They sometimes defend it, by high fences, from their cattle; by which means the young forest

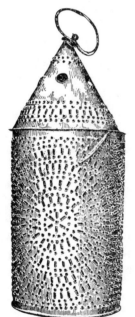

PRIMITIVE LANTERN.

trees are suffered to grow, to replace those that are cut down for the necessary use of the farm.

" They keep their horses and cattle as warm as possible, in winter, by which means they save a great deal of their hay and grain, for these animals when cold, eat much more than when in a more comfortable situation.

" The German farmers live frugally in their families, with respect to diet, furniture, and apparel. They sell their most profitable grain, which is wheat, and eat that which is less profitable, that is rye, or Indian corn. The profit to a farmer, from this single article of economy, is equal, in the course of a life-time, to the price of a farm for one of his children.

" The German farmers have large or profitable gardens near their houses. These contain little else but useful vegetables. Pennsylvania is indebted to the Germans for the principal part of her knowledge in horticulture. There was a time when turnips and cabbage were the principal vegetables that were used in diet by the citizens of Philadelphia. This will not surprise those persons who know that the first settlers in Pennsylvania left England while horticulture was in its infancy in that country. Since the settlement of a number of German gardens in the neighborhood of Philadelphia, the tables of all classes of citizens have been covered with a variety of vegetables in every season of the year, and to the use of these vegetables in diet may be ascribed the general exemption of the citizens of Philadelphia from diseases of the skin.

" The Germans seldom hire men to work upon their farms. The feebleness of that authority which masters possess over their hired servants is such that their wages are seldom procured from their labor, except in harvest when they work in the presence of their masters.[70] The wives and daughters of the German farmers frequently forsake for a while their dairy and spinning wheel, and join their husbands and brothers in the labor of cutting down, collecting and bringing home the fruits of the fields and orchards. The work of the gardens is generally done by the women of the family.

" A large strong wagon, the ship of inland commerce, covered with linen cloth, is an essential part of the furniture of a German farm. In this wagon, drawn by four

---

[70] I avail myself at this place of the liberty to state that one of the main reasons why the Scotch-Irish were not so successful as farmers as the Germans, was because their lands were mainly cultivated by negroes as indentured servants. They did not care for farm work, and the consequence was the farms did not care for them, and in the end they sold their improved lands to the Germans who under a better system had been successful in accumulating the money to pay for them. They then went into politics and trade, where they succeeded better.

or five horses of a peculiar breed they convey to market, over the roughest roads from 2,000 to 3,000 pounds weight of the produce of their farms. In the months of September and October, it is no uncommon thing, on the Lancaster and Reading roads, to meet in one day fifty or one hundred of these wagons, on their way to Philadelphia, most of which belong to German farmers.[71]

"The favorable influence of agriculture, as conducted by the Germans, in extending human happiness, is manifested by the joy they express upon the birth of a child. No dread of poverty, nor distrust of Providence, from an increasing family, depresses the spirit of these industrious and frugal people. Upon the birth of a son, they exult in the gift of a plowman or a waggoner; and upon the birth of a daughter, they rejoice in the addition of another spinster or milk-maid to the family.

" The Germans set a great value upon patrimonial property. This useful principle in human nature prevents much folly and vice in young people. It moreover leads to lasting and extensive advantages, in the improvement of a farm; for what inducements can be stronger in a parent to plant an orchard, to preserve forest trees or to build a commodious house than the idea that they will all be possessed by a succession of generations who shall inherit his blood and name.

" From the history that has been given of the German agriculture, it will hardly be necessary to add that a German farm may be distinguished from the farms of the

---

[71] These were the famous Conestoga wagons and the equally famous Conestoga horses, whose fame is as enduring as that of the Commonwealth itself.

"Die entfernsten, besonders deutschen Landleute, kommen mit grossen, mit mancherlei Proviant beladenen bedeckten Wagen auf denen sie zugleich ihren eigenen Mundvorrath und Futter für ihre Pferde mitbringen, und darauf übernachten." SCHOEPF's *Reise durch Pennsylvanien*, 1783, p. 165.

other citizens of the State, by the superior size of their barns, the plain but compact form of their houses, the height of their inclosures, the extent of their orchards, the fertility of their fields, the luxuriance of their meadows, and a general appearance of plenty and neatness in everything that belongs to them."

I think the eminent professor of the University of Pennsylvania, of 1789, writing with a thorough knowledge of the German agriculture of his time, may be fairly set against the professor in the same great school, writing in the year 1900, whose statement concerning them is so at variance with the facts, so incorrect and misleading, that the inference is irresistible that he wrote without a due examination of the question.

But we need not rely on Dr. Rush alone for evidence that the Germans were the best farmers in the State, that they were given to enjoyment in agricultural pursuits and that their descendants are to this day keeping up the reputation of their ancestors on the ancestral acres. The evidence is so manifold and so conclusive that I almost feel like making an apology for introducing it.

Watson, the annalist, says the best lands in Lancaster county, and deemed, in general, the finest farms in the State, are those possessed by the German families." [72]

Another writer says this :

" The Germans wisely chose some of the best land in the State, where they soon made themselves comfortable, and next grew quietly rich. * * * The German population of Pennsylvania, naturally increasing, and augmented by continual accessions from the Fatherland, has since spread over a large portion of the State, still inheriting the

---

[72] WATSON'S *Annals of Philadelphia*, Vol. II., p. 148.

economy and prudent foresight of their ancestors, and generally establishing themselves on the most fertile soils." [73]

Bancroft, in speaking of the German immigrants to this country, says : " The Germans, especially of the borders of the Rhine, thronged to America in such numbers, that in course of a century, preserving *their line of rural life*, they appropriated much of the very best land from the Mohawk to the valley of Virginia." [74]

EARLY SETTLERS AND THEIR VISITORS.

Rupp bears this testimony : " The Germans were principally farmers. They depended more upon themselves than upon others. They wielded the mattock, the axe and the maul, and by the power of brawny arms, rooted up the grubs, removed the saplings, felled the majestic oaks,

[73] CHARLES B. TREGO, *A Geography of Pennsylvania*, p. 89.
[74] BANCROFT'S *United States*, Vol. X., pp. 83-84.

laid low the towering hickory; prostrated, where they grew, the walnut, poplar, chestnut—cleaved such as suited for the purpose, into rails for fences—persevered untiringly until the forest was changed into arable fields." [75]

"The Germans," says Proud, "seem more adapted to agriculture and improvements of a wilderness; and the Irish for trade. The Germans soon get estates in this country, where industry and economy are the chief requisites to procure them." [76]

In the fall of 1856, the Philadelphia *Ledger*, in reply to some stupid strictures in a New York journal, said : "No one familiar with the German farmers of Pennsylvania, need be told that this (the article referred to) is a stupid and ignorant libel. Its author has either never travelled through our State, or has maliciously misrepresented what he saw. So far from our German farmers being on a level with the serfs of a hundred and fifty years ago, they are vastly in advance of contemporary German or French farmers, or even of English farmers of similar means. On this point we need go no further for authority than to Mr. Munch, who though hostile in politics to our German farmers in general, was forced, during his tour through Pennsylvania, to admit their sterling worth. Mr. Munch is an experienced and practical agriculturist, so that his judgment on such a question is worth that of a score of visionary, ill-informed, prejudiced, disappointed demagogues. After eulogizing the picturesque natural features of the landscape of our German counties, praising the excellent taste which has preserved the woods on the hillsides, and extolling the appearance of the farms, this gentleman adds significantly that he found the population of

---

[75] RUPP'S *Thirty Thousand Names*, p. 11.
[76] PROUD'S *History of Pennsylvania*, Vol. II., p. 274.

' a genial, solid and respectable stamp, enviably circumstanced in comparison with the European farmer, and very far his superior in intelligence and morals.' * * * In many particulars, the German farmers surpass even the people of New England, who, of late, have put in a claim, it would seem to be the *ne plus ultra* in all things. The German farmers understand, or if they do not understand, they observe the laws of health, better than even the rural population of Massachusetts; and the result is that they are really the finest race of men, physically, to be found within the borders of the United States. * * * To be plain, if some of our crochetty, one-ideaed, dyspeptic, thin, cadaverous, New England brethren would emigrate to our German counties; follow, for a generation or two, the open-air life of our German farmers; and last of all marry into our vigorous, anti-hypochondriacal German families, they would soon cease to die by such scores of consumption, to complain that there were no longer any healthy women left, and to amuse sensible people with such silly vagaries of Pantheism, or a thousand and one intellectual vagaries which are born of their abnormal physical condition." [77]

Still another quotation will be allowed me : " Latterly much has been heard of an ' endless chain,' used in a financial sense. There is an endless chain of another kind in existence among the substantial Germans in the German counties of this State. While many of New England's sons have sold or abandoned their ancient acres and sought new homes in other States, the lands of these first Palatine emigrants still remain in the possession of their descendants, held by ancient indentures, supplemented by

---

[77] Quoted by RUPP in his RUSH'S *Manners and Customs of the Pennsylvania Germans.*

an endless chain of fresh titles from father to son, reaching backward to the original patents from Penn."[78]

One of our most eminent historians remarks :

"A still larger number of these German exiles found refuge in Pennsylvania, to which colony also many were carried as indentured servants. * * * It was this immigration which first introduced into America compact bodies of German settlers, and along with them the dogmas and worship of the German Lutheran and German Reformed churches. Constantly supplied with new recruits, and occupying contiguous tracts of territory, the immigrants preserved and have transmitted to our day, especially in Pennsylvania, the German language and German manners. Their industry was remarkable; they took care to settle on fertile lands, and they soon became distinguished as the best farmers in America."[79]

A traveller who passed through the Shenandoah Valley during the French and Indian War writes as follows : "The low grounds upon the banks of the Shenandoah River are very rich and fertile. They are chiefly settled by Germans (and Pennsylvania-Germans at that, who went there prior to 1748), who gain a sufficient livelihood by raising stock for the troops, and sending butter down into the lower parts of the country. I could not but reflect with pleasure on the situation of these people, and I think, if there is such a thing as happiness in this life, they enjoy it. Far from the bustle of the world, they live in the most delightful climate and richest soil imaginable. They are

---

[78] F. R. DIFFENDERFFER, *The Palatine and Quaker as Commonwealth Builders*, pp. 29-30.

The writer has himself, in the fifth generation ploughed and planted, hoed and harvested upon the original tract patented to his great-great-grandsire, by the Penn heirs, in 1734.

[79] HILDRETH'S *History of the United States*, First Series, Vol. II., p. 264.

everywhere surrounded with beautiful prospects and sylvan scenes; lofty mountains and transparent streams, falls of water, rich valleys and majestic woods, the whole interspersed with an infinite variety of flowering shrubs constitute the landscapes surrounding them. They are subject to few diseases, are generally robust and live in perfect liberty. They know no wants, and are acquainted with but few vices. Their inexperience of the elegancies of life precludes any regret that they have not the means of enjoying them; but they possess what many princes would give

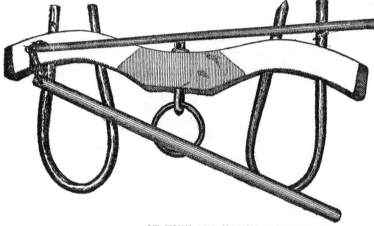

OX YOKE AND THRESHING FLAIL.

half their dominions for—health, contentment, and tranquility of mind." [80]

Dr. Oswald Seidensticker, while living, an honored professor in the University of Pennsylvania, and who has, perhaps, given the German immigration into Pennsylvania as much careful and intelligent study as any one else, has this to say of them as farmers: "Often as the Germans

---

[80] HOWE'S *Historical Collections of Virginia*, p. 468.

have been spoken of contemptuously in certain matters, that was not valid when urged against them as farmers. The very sight of their farms is sufficient to tell that they are well and carefully managed, providing blessed and happy homes. Their knowledge of properly preparing the soil, of growing fine cattle, and of erecting proper buildings, and their manner of life led the eminent Dr. Rush to study their character and habits and in his book to encourage others to imitate their example." [81]

Still another and a recent author writes thus : " In all they did, they were moved thereto by one great, irresistible desire, and that was the love of home. * * * Now that they had found this " home," they were content to abide on it and to make of it a very garden spot and horn of plenty for the Province. * * * Because the Germans were truly in earnest did they persevere until they have spread abroad over the entire land, supplementing their less stable brethren of other nationalities. Before even the break of day, during the heat of the noontide sun they toiled on, and until its rays had disappeared beneath the western horizon, when darkness made work impossible, and then they sought their needed rest in slumber, but not before each little family had gathered about its altar to sing their hymns of praise and invoke the same Divine blessing upon their future undertaking which had been showered upon their past.

" Other settlers have likewise toiled and struggled, but it may well be asked what other settlers can show an equal result to these Palatine immigrants within the same length of time. Hardly had a decade of time elapsed, when, on all sides, were to be seen flourishing farms, with fields

[81] OSWALD SEIDENSTICKER, *Bilder aus der Deutsch-pennsylvanischen Geschichte*, Vol. II., p. 255.

of waving grain, orchards laden with fruit, and pastures filled with well-conditioned domestic animals. The temporary log house has given place to a two-story stone structure, a most durable, commodious and comfortable home; in place of the shedding, hurriedly erected, now stands the great red barn, upon its stone base, and with its overhanging frame superstructure bursting with plenty; and everywhere are scattered the many little adjuncts of prosperity and comfort. How well the fathers then built is evidenced by the existence of scores of these buildings, still homelike and inviting as of old." [82]

A recent writer, in discussing some changes that have taken place, how German virility and race-tenacity have resulted in the elimination of some peoples and the substitution of themselves, humorously but truly remarks: " Penn attempted to engraft on his English stock other scions, trusting to the virility of his masterful race to preserve the English type, but the strong German sap has outworn them all in Lancaster county. The descendants of the early English who own acres of land here to-day are becoming rare. The children of the Scotch-Irish by a kind of natural selection have quit farming and taken to politics and business, and their ancient acres are covered with the big red barns that betoken another kindred. The Welshman has been lost in the shuffle, and the Quaker is marrying the Dutch girl in self defense. So reads the record at the close of the nineteenth century. It has taken almost two hundred years to get there. But ' by their fruits ye shall know them.' " [83]

---

[82] Rev. M. H. Richards, D.D., *Proceedings and Addresses of the Pennsylvania-German Society*, Vol. IX., pp. 413-414.

[83] E. K. Martin, Esq., *Proceedings and Addresses of the Pennsylvania-German Society*, Vol. VIII., p. 13.

THE OLDEST HOUSE IN LANCASTER COUNTY.

THE CHRISTIAN HERR, BUILT 1719.

Although the foregoing evidence abundantly disproves the absurd statement that the German colonists found less enjoyment in agriculture than other nationalities, the panel of witnesses is by no means exhausted and the testimony could be expanded into a volume. Most of it is from contemporaneous sources and deals with the question as it stood one hundred or one hundred and fifty years ago. Let us turn from that long-gone time and look at the situation as we find it at this very hour.

I invite the reader to accompany me for a brief interval to Lancaster county, as typical a Pennsylvania region to-day as it was one hundred and fifty years ago. Its earliest settlers were Germans and Swiss Huguenots. They were agriculturists. They bought lands, settled on them, farmed them, and their descendants in the fourth and fifth generations are engaged in the same enjoyable pursuit to-day. Other men also came into the county: Quakers, Scotch-Irish and Welsh, but to-day nineteen twentieths of the more than 10,000 farms in the county are owned and cultivated by the descendants of the early German settlers. The townships of East and West Donegal, Conoy, Mt. Joy and portions of West Hempfield were settled almost exclusively by the Scotch-Irish. To-day there is not a single farm in

---

[84] The country architecture of Germany as is well known, runs more to durability than ornamentation. The German immigrants brought their old-world building ideas with them. The result is there are to-day many substantial stone structures, dwelling houses and barns standing all over the earliest settled portions of the State, whose well-laid walls have bid defiance to the storms of a century and a half, and even more, and are to-day in such a state of preservation as to promise another century or two of life. So far as is known with certainty, the structure shown on the opposite page is the oldest house still standing, erected in Lancaster county. The legend 17 C. H.–H. R. 19, carved on a sandstone forming part of the wall, tells the story of its building. It was erected in 1719, by the Rev. Christian Herr, a minister of the Mennonite church, who came into the country from the Palatinate, in 1709. The house stands several miles south of Lancaster city.

any of those districts owned and farmed by a Scotch-Irishman! In this instance at least, it was "the other fellow" and not the German farmer that did not find enjoyment in his vocation. In the townships of Fulton and Little Britain the settlers were almost exclusively Scotch-Irish; these have maintained themselves more stubbornly on the ancestral acres, but in recent years an invasion of German farmers has been steadily encroaching on their ancient domain, and the fate that has befallen the Donegals seems to be awaiting them also.

Let the man—or men, if there be more than one—who does not believe the German pioneers had pleasure, enjoyment and content on their broad acres, go into that same county of Lancaster and look the landscape over. He will find a territory of unsurpassed fertility—another evidence of the sound agricultural judgment of these people—yielding as abundantly to-day as when it was virgin, two centuries ago. It has enriched every generation of those who have owned it. There have, of course, been some failures, but the record on the whole, stands unchallenged. Pride of ownership went hand in hand with agricultural skill. The land was treated even as their cattle were, carefully and plentifully. The result is there are no deserted farms and ruined farmhouses, as may be seen all over New England. Even at the present depreciated prices for real estate, the farms still sell at $200 and more per acre. Look at the great barns in which their crops are stored and their cattle housed! Large as they are they are generally inadequate to contain the farm prod-

EARLY PENNSYLVANIA
PRINTING PRESS.

ucts, and a dozen grain and hay ricks are built elsewhere on the farm until the grain can be threshed. Nor is the barn the only building besides the dwelling house, on the farm; sheds, stables, and other outhouses are scattered around until the farmer's home resembles a hamlet in itself. All the modern farm machinery, and that too of the best possible type, is there; cunning devices of many kinds that rob labor of half its terrors.

The farmer's house is generally a model of a farmhouse. There are some that have all the best modern accessories— steam heat, gas, electric bells, cemented cellars, and similar improvements. Within, there is not only comfort but luxury—fine furniture, pictures, costly carpets, imported crockery, generally an organ and often a piano. There are books, magazines and newspapers, and much else. The son, and often the sons, have their individual teams, and they use them too. No farmer's outfit in these days is complete without a fine vehicle or two. It may safely be said that there is no spot encompassed by the four seas that hem in this North American continent, nay, none beneath the blue canopy that overspreads the entire earth, where the agriculturist is better educated, more intelligent in his calling, better fed and clothed and enjoys so many of the luxuries of life as the Lancaster county families in the year of grace, 1900. Go and look at him where he is; sit at his table and see the fullness thereof, and you will then be able to give a fitting answer to the calumny, born of ignorance, that says the German colonists in Pennsylvania did not, and inferentially do not, find that enjoyment in agricultural pursuits as the races whose farms they have bought and now own and cultivate.

One paragraph more will be pardoned : the theme is an attractive one and I leave it with reluctance. To understand fully what these Germans have done for themselves and for the county of Lancaster a few figures may be introduced. Being official, and on record they will be accepted. Lancaster county is not one of the large counties of the State or Nation, but it is the richest so far as its agricultural wealth and products are concerned of all the three thousand or more within all the States and Territories. For a quarter of a century it has stood at the head of them all in the money value of its agricultural products. The census of 1890 gives them at $7,657,790. Her nearest competitor does not come within a million and a half dollars of equalling it. The assessors' lists for 1899 give the value of her real estate, at the usual low estimate, at $86,796,064 and of her horses and cattle at $1,958,802. Her citizens report $20,802,634 at interest: the real amount is three times that sum. To give even a more condensed idea of what these farmers, who took such little enjoyment in their chosen pursuit, have done to make their county rich, it may be stated that there are at the present moment on this little area of 973 square miles, 26 National Banks, with an aggregate capital of $3,750,000, and deposits aggregating $7,000,000; also 3 Trust companies, with large assets, and 7 Building and Loan Associations, controlling large sums of money.

It is aggravating that it should be necessary at this late day to be compelled to enter into a discussion of this subject. But we cannot forget that all the opprobrium and misrepresentation that has been cast upon the Germans of Pennsylvania has long been borne without a protest. The chief offenders during the present century are men who have had no intimate acquaintance with the characteristics of the men whom they falsely deride and abuse. New England has contributed even more than her quota to the number of these defamers. Their scurrilous falsehoods have so long gone unchallenged that some have accepted them as truths and reiterated them with all their original fervency. The day for that has gone. The faults and shortcomings of the German pioneers and their descendants were many and obvious. I do not seek to extenuate them in the slightest degree, but I do assert—and the authorities to prove it are legion—that with all their shortcomings, they were the peers of any race of men that set its feet upon the Western Hemisphere, and that in every qualification that goes to the making of the highest class of citizenship, they stand at the very forefront to-day.

They brought with them none of the vindictive bigotry that burnt witches and swung Quakers from the scaffold. They at once made their own the doctrines of the broadminded Penn, that religious and political tolerance were among the natural and inalienable rights of men. The subjects of kings and princes in Europe, they left kingcraft behind them and proclaimed the evangel of freedom in their new home. Let it not be forgotten through all the years, that these people, whom a few historians and a host of inconsequent minor scribblers have denounced and derided as indifferent boors, were nevertheless the first men on the continent of America to denounce the wrong of human slavery and petition for its abolition; yea, a century before the sensitive soul of New England even took thought of the subject, while it was still selling Indians and Quakers into West Indian slavery and only forty years after the great celebrity of Massachusetts, Governor Winthrop, disposed of slaves in his will.

The age of the defamer has not gone by, and most probably never will. Like the liar and the thief he will maintain his footing among men even unto the end. The men who have assailed the good name of the German immigrants to Pennsylvania are, however, in a fair way to die out. The truth confronts their falsehoods at every stage and the latter are borne down in the contest. Even now their numbers are growing fewer and their idle gossip no longer receives credence as history. The Commonwealth of Pennsylvania, the greatest and grandest of all the members in the Brotherhood of States, confronts them and confutes their idle tattle, born of misapprehension and ignorance, and here I may safely leave them.

ARMS OF GREAT BRITAIN.

The Redemptioners.

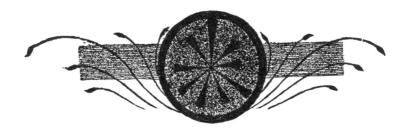

CHAPTER I.

WHO AND WHAT THEY WERE.— A CONDITION BORN OF NE-
CESSITY BEYOND THE SEA AND TRANSFERRED TO AMERICA.
— THE SEVERAL KINDS OF BOND SERVANTS.— A STRIKING
FEATURE IN THE HISTORY OF PENNSYLVANIA.

"Haz gala, Sancho, de la humilidad de tu linage, y no te desprecies de decir
que vienes de labradores ; por que viendo que no te corres, ninguno se pondrá
a correrte."

"Und wenn wir dankbar auch ermessen,
Was uns das neue Heim beschied,
So können wir doch nie Vergessen
Der alten Heimath, Wort und Lied."

THE history of the Germanic immigration to the Province of
Pennsylvania naturally divides itself
into two well-defined parts or chapters. Of one of these, dealing with
the arrival and dispersion of these
people, I have endeavored to write
with that fullness and exactitude
which the importance of the subject deserves, in the earlier part of
this work. The other, which remains to be taken up, will deal
with that portion of these people
whose means were scant even at
the outset of their journey, and wholly inadequate to

(141)

bear the strain of a long and tedious sea voyage. Who arrived virtually penniless and dependent; who had not been able to pay for their passage across the ocean, and who, upon their arrival, were compelled to barter or sell their personal services for a stated period of time, at a stipulated price, and under prescribed legal regulations, to such of their fellowmen as stood in need of their labor, and who were willing to discharge the debts they had been compelled to incur through their desire to reach this promised land, this modern Eden, a new Canaan in a new world.

The inflowing tide of German immigrants to the Province of Pennsylvania, through the port of Philadelphia, is not secondary in importance to the coming of William Penn himself and the establishment of his Government on the banks of the Delaware. Considered in its historic bearings, it is not only one of the most noteworthy events associated with the colonization of America, but is besides invested with a more special interest, all its own, of which I shall attempt to give the more important details.

The first Germans to come to America, as colonists in Pennsylvania, were, as a rule, well to do. Nearly all of them in the beginning of that mighty exodus had sufficient means to pay all the charges incurred in going down the Rhine to the sea, and enough besides to meet the expenses for carrying them across the ocean, and yet have some left when they arrived to pay for part or all of the lands they took up.[85] The large tracts taken up by the colony at Germantown and at Conestoga are all-sufficient evidences of this. And this continued to be the rule until about 1717,[86]

---

[85] FRANZ LÖHER, *Geschichte und Zuständen der Deutschen in America*, p. 80.

[86] Also RUPP.

and perhaps later, when the great exodus from the Palatinate set in. Then the real race to reach the New World began. The poorer classes had not been unobservant of what was going on. If America was a place where the rich could become richer still, surely it must be a place where the poor also might better themselves. At all events, nothing could be lost by going, because they had the merest pittance to begin with. Besides, all the accounts were favorable. Those already in Pennsylvania sent back glowing descriptions of the ease with which land could be acquired, the productiveness of the soil, the abundance of food, the freedom from taxation and the equality of all men before the law to their natural rights and their religious creeds.

Such arguments were irresistible to men whose fathers and themselves had felt all the pangs that poverty, persecution and wrong can bring upon the citizen. The desire to flee from the land of oppression to the land of promise became paramount, and to attain their wish, no hardship was too great, no sacrifice too costly. Unable to raise the sum necessary to bring them here, they sold their few meager belongings, and with the proceeds were enabled to reach a seaport. Once there, they found plenty of men ready to send them across the Atlantic. The terms were hard. They knew they would be, but long before they reached the western Patmos, the "Insel Pennsylvanien" as it was frequently written in those days, they often realized what kind of a trap it was into which they had fallen. What they suffered on the voyage, how they were maltreated, and how many of them died, forms perhaps the most pathetic picture in the history of American colonization, not excepting that drawn by Las Casas three hundred and fifty years ago, nor the later one limned in Longfellow's Evangeline.

The evidence concerning the manner in which this immigration was aroused, fostered and carried on, is cumulative rather than diverse, and there is a close resemblance in the many narratives I have examined. It is true, the same series of facts presented themselves to every investigator and the result is a somewhat tedious sameness in the various accounts. Once the facts were put on record they became public property and the latest writer simply followed those who had preceded him. So graphic, however, are some of these accounts that I have deemed it a matter of interest to give several of them, those of Mittelberger, Pastor Muhlenberg and Christoph Saur at some length. Their testimony, coming from both sides of the ocean, and from men personally familiar with all the circumstances they describe, has never been challenged and has accordingly become part and parcel of the history of German immigration into America.

The persons without means, who availed themselves of the facilities offered them by shipmasters to come to this country, were called " Redemptioners " by their contemporaries, and down even to our own times. It deserves to be stated, however, that this term does not appear in the indentures entered into between themselves and those by whom their obligations were discharged and to whom they sold their personal services for a term of years. Neither is the term to be found in any of the legislative acts of the period. Such persons, whatever their nationality—many came from British lands—were called indentured or bond servants, and those terms were invariably applied to them. As such they were known in all the Acts of the Assembly of the Province of Pennsylvania and those of the three lower counties, New Castle, Kent and Sussex. It was the common term prevailing in the mother country and natur-

DOMESTIC UTENSILS.

1 COPPER KETTLE
2 JAPANNED TINWARE.
3 EARTHENWARE PIE DISH.
4 JAPANNED COFFEE POT.

DANNER COLLECTION.

SHAVING OUTFIT. A.D. 1733.

1 SHAVING GLASS
2 BASIN TO CATCH LATHER.
3 RAZOR AND STROP.
4 SHAVING MUG.
5 POWDER AND PUFF BOX.
6 BASIN AND STAND.

ally followed them to this. It is found in Penn's *Conditions and Concessions* issued while he was still in England, in 1681, and was reiterated many times subsequently.

But while we must distinguish between the men who had money to transport themselves and their families to Pennsylvania, and those who came under conditions to sell their services until their obligations were repaid, we must not lose sight of a broad distinction between some of these indentured immigrants. They may very appropriately be divided into two classes. The first was composed of persons who were honest men and good citizens; men who came here of their own volition, who had undergone many trials at home, some because of their religion and most of them because of the hard conditions of life they were compelled to face from youth to old age. Political changes were of frequent occurrence and each one was generally accompanied by fresh exactions on the part of the new ruler. After the demands of the tax gatherer had been met, about the only things that were left were visions of fresh exactions and possible starvation. Such people were excusable for contracting terms of temporary servitude in a distant land to encountering an unending repetition of their former intolerable state. Their action was at least voluntary.

But the other class was a widely different one. They did not come to America because of any special desire on their part to do so. On the contrary they would doubtless have preferred to remain in the land of their birth had they had a voice or a choice in the matter. They were criminals and felons, the scum of the population, which the mother country dumped upon her new Province in order to rid herself of the most objectionable portion of her criminal classes. The very jails were emptied of their in-

mates and the latter sent to her colonies, North and South.
This action was naturally resented by the honest and industrious colonists of Pennsylvania, and as early as 1722
the Provincial Assembly attempted to prevent the coming
of these people by imposing a tax upon every criminal
landed in the Province, and in addition made the shipowner responsible for the future good conduct of his passengers. But nothing could keep them out and the early
criminal record of Pennsylvania is no doubt largely made
up from this class of her population. It is probably owing
to the dual classes of these indentured servants or redemptioners, that much of the obloquy, which some persons,
ignorant of the circumstances, have visited upon this class
of our colonists, is owing. Ignorance has been the prolific
mother of many of the silly and untruthful accusations
that have from time to time been trumped up against the
German colonists of Pennsylvania.

They differed wholly from the Germans who came to
better their condition and frequently against the protests
of the potentates under whose
rule they were living. They
were, indeed, the very flower
of the German peasantry, and
Europe boasted of no better
citizens. They were men of
robust frame, hardy constitution, inured to toil and
accustomed to earn their living with their hands—Men
who trod the soil of the New
World as if it was their right-
ful inheritance, and able to help themselves. They fought
the battle of civilization in the depths and solitudes of the

A PIONEER'S CABIN.

wilderness. There they established the equality of man in place of hereditary privileges. They were born commonwealth-builders, and their handiwork in Pennsylvania is one of the marvels of modern colonization.

Under conditions of discouragement, deceit and contumely, of wrong and robbery that almost exceed the limits of human belief, these poor people continued to come over to the land of promise. The story of their treatment on shipboard equals all the horrors of the " middle passage " during the African slave traffic, while here, land sharks in the shape of the commission merchant and money broker, stood ready upon their arrival to complete the work of spoliation and plunder. It was little that many of these forlorn sons of toil had. In their wooden chests heirlooms that were sometimes generations old were gathered, and the few remaining household treasures they had been able to save out of the wreck of their fortunes, small though the latter were. These at once attracted the cupidity of the thieves who lay in waiting for their prey. Thousands of them found themselves possessed only of their lives and their strong arms when they stepped on the Philadelphia wharfs, wherewith to begin anew the battle of life, the struggle for existence. But handicapped as they were, they faced adverse fate with stout hearts and fulfilled their contracts with their purchasers and masters as faithfully as if their efforts were directed to keep alive their own hearth-fires or to support their wives and children.

To all the foregoing, separately and collectively, must be added the sufferings and numerous deaths from smallpox, dysentery, poor nutrition, and worst of all the fatal ship-fever, resulting from the contaminated water and other causes. The literature of that time, the few news-

papers, the letters of those who made the voyage and were
not only witnesses but actual sufferers, and the books
and pamphlets that were written and printed, bear ample
testimony to the horrible scenes and sufferings that only
too often came upon the overcrowded immigrant ships. It
is not a pleasant duty to enter into some of the details that
have come down to us. The pen assumes the disagree-
able task only because the truth and the requirements of
history demand it. It is only another, although perhaps
the most sorrowful, of all the episodes that attended the
colonization of Pennsylvania. It may perhaps be truth-
fully said that in the first instance the practice had its
origin in laudable and benevolent motives. Those who
lent it their assistance in the beginning, at that time hardly
conceived the extent the hegira was to assume or the depth
of the misery it was to entail. Fraud and deception had
their origin in opportunity ; some men are quick to spring
from good to evil when it pays, and the occasion offers
itself. So I apprehend it was in this case.

I have tried to collect and arrange the evidence still ob-
tainable and present it in these pages as best I could.
Every writer of our local or general history has dealt with
the question in a summary way, rather than otherwise.
The story is broken into many fragments, and these are
scattered through hundreds of volumes, without anything
approaching completeness or regularity of detail in any.
In the fullness of time, no doubt, some one with love and
leisure for the work will address himself to the task and
write the story of the REDEMPTIONERS with the philosophic
spirit and the amplitude it deserves. Meanwhile the following chapters are offered as a substitute until something
better comes along.

CHAPTER II.

Bond Servants a Universal Custom of the Times.—
Brought from Great Britain and Taken to All the
Middle Colonies.—Synopsis of the Colonial Legis-
lation on Indentured Servants.

> " Such were to take these lands by toil
>   To till these generous breadths and fair,
>   Turning this Pennsylvania soil
>   To fruitful gardens everywhere."

> "Kommt zu uns frei von Groll und Trug
>   Und est das Freundschafts mohl,
>   Wir haben hier der Hütten g'nug
>   Und Länder ohne Zahl."

THERE was not a little rivalry among the various English colonies planted along the Atlantic seaboard of America, in their race for wealth, progress and commercial supremacy. Into that competition, Pennsylvania, although the youngest of all the English settlements, entered with as much ambition and ardor as the people to the north and south of her. Penn was a Quaker, and a man of sincere

(149)

convictions and unquestioned piety, but we cannot shut our eyes to the fact that he united a very liberal share of worldly shrewdness with his colonization schemes. In fact, the competition in material progress and advancement in the seventeenth and eighteenth centuries was quite as sharp between what are to-day called the Thirteen Colonies as it is to-day. The older settlements had the advantage of age and experience, and this naturally compelled the newer ones to redouble their efforts to overtake them in the race for advancement and to surpass them if possible.

In some particulars they endeavored to work out their destinies along similar lines. They copied from each other when they thought such imitations would prove advantageous—not blindly, but always with an eye to the main chance. When Lord Baltimore found that his older neighbor Virginia was increasing her population and her wealth by the extensive importation of male and female servants from the mother country under indentures that meant years of servitude, and under conditions not wholly dissimilar to her negro slave traffic, he at once availed himself of the Virginia idea, and ship-loads of these people came from Ireland, Scotland and even England herself.

It can hardly be questioned that the authorities in Pennsylvania took the same view of the case, and early in the history of the Province introduced, or at least connived at the system. At all events the fact remains that Penn's government had hardly got under way, before indentured servants became a feature in the civil life of the community. Here, as elsewhere, labor was scarce, and here, perhaps more than anywhere else, extra labor was required to cut down the forests, clear the land and keep abreast of the march of civilization that was moving forward on all sides of the new settlement.

All this is to be inferred from the number of these sold and purchased servants that were brought into Pennsylvania, and from the legislation that was enacted in consequence. That legislation grew out of the necessities of the traffic in these people and consequently reflects its successive stages. It must be borne in mind, however, that while it had even in its earlier stages all the characteristics that marked it during its most flourishing period, from 1730 to 1770, it had not the same name. The men and women who were sent over here from Ireland and Scotland, or who came voluntarily under contracts to render personal service for their passage money, board and any other expenses that might be incurred, were always called " servants " or " indentured servants " by the laws of the Province. The word " redemptioner " belongs to a later period and was of more recent coinage, and this fact must not be lost sight of, although in reality there was no material difference recognized either by statutory enactments or by custom, between the two. The word " redemptioner " does not occur in the Pennsylvania Statutes at Large.

" We may with propriety," says Gordon, " notice here another class of the people who were not freemen. Many valuable individuals were imported into the province as servants, who in consideration of the payment of their passages and other stipulations, contracted to serve for a definite period. This class was a favorite of the law. Provision was made by the laws agreed on in England for recording the names, times and wages of servants; masters were allowed to take up lands for their use, and the servants themselves, after the expiration of their service, were permitted to become land-holders on easy terms; they were provided with sufficient clothing and implements of labor; they could not be sold out of the Province without their consent, and, in case of marriage, husband and wife could not be parted. On the other hand, due care was taken to preserve the rights of the master. Many of the German and Irish settlers were of this class, from whom have sprung some of the most reputable and wealthy inhabitants of the Province." [87]

In speaking of servants about the year 1740, Watson says : " The other kind were those who were free after a time. Many came from England, Germany and other countries who could not pay their passage, who were sold on their arrival for so many years, at about three to four pounds Pennsylvania currency per annum, as would pay their passage : generally fourteen pounds for four years' service would cover their passage money. Those who were too old to serve would sell their children in the same way. *Some would sell themselves to get a knowledge of the country before starting in the world.* The purchaser could resell them for the unexpired time. The purchaser also had to give them a suit of clothes at the expiration of the time." [88]

I propose to offer a brief résumé of the various legislative enactments bearing on this class of immigrants to show the status held by them, and also the precautions that were from time to time taken by the law-making power for their protection.

While the condition of this large class was in innumerable cases to be commiserated, the fact nevertheless remains that the Legislature threw over them the ægis of its protection, and in so far as it could, tried to deal fairly with them. Their rights were as scrupulously guarded as

[87] GORDON'S *History of Pennsylvania,* pp. 555–556.
[88] WATSON'S *Annals of Philadelphia,* Vol. III., p. 469.

GABRIEL THOMAS' MAP OF PENNSYLVANIA, 1698.

those of their masters.   It deserves also to be remembered that no fault was found with the system of buying these servants and holding them to their service until their obligations were discharged.   That was a recognized custom of the period, already in existence both north and south of Pennsylvania, and universally acquiesced in.   Nobody thought it wrong.   People entered into these obligations of their own free will.   There was no compulsion.   The great wrongs grew out of the practices under which it was carried on.   As these developed and were brought to the attention of the Legislature, numerous laws were passed to better guard the rights of the deceived and defrauded immigrants.   But the laws could not reach the infamous Newlander beyond the sea, and he took good care to keep the broad Atlantic between himself and his outraged victims.

The Provincial Government did not do all perhaps it should or even might have done looking to the protection of these people.   It is important that we keep before us a clear idea of the spirit of those days.   It was very different from what we find to-day.   Public sentiment leaned towards severity rather than towards charity.   The laws dealt more severely with crime, and were often pushed to the verge of inhumanity.   Take for example, the laws against creditors.   In 1705 the first insolvent law in the Province was passed, and it has justly been said that it " was formulated in sterner justice than is consistent with human frailty."   When the property of a debtor was insufficient to discharge his debts, the law compelled him to make good the deficiency by personal servitude in case his creditors demanded it, and there were always those who did.   Single men not more than fifty-three years old could be sold for a period of not more than seven years,

but married men under forty-six could be held for a period
not exceeding five years. A milder law was enacted to
supersede the above one in 1730, but so many creditors
abused its provisions, that satisfaction by servitude was
engrafted upon it in a supplemental clause.[89]
There were, too, often quarrels and bickerings between
the Governors and the members of the Assembly. The
one tried to thwart the wishes and will of the other. When,
for example, the Legislature in 1755 drew up a bill on
this very subject of the better protection of German immigrants, especially to prevent the breaking open of their
chests and the theft of their goods, Governor Thomas cut
out this very matter and returned the rest with his approval. There seems to have been a reason for his action,
and the Assembly in a sharp reply told him, in so many
words, that some of his own political household were
regularly engaged in these robberies, and that was no
doubt why he refused to do this act of simple justice. No
doubt they knew what they were talking about.

Many of the English and Welsh settlers who came to
Pennsylvania within twenty years after it was founded
brought indentured servants with them. To hold such
people was evidently an old English custom, and at the
very outset of his proprietary career, provision was made
by Penn for the welfare of these people on regaining their
freedom. No sooner had Penn obtained the royal charter
to his province than he issued a long and tedious document for the enlightenment of "those of our own and
other nations that are inclined to transport themselves or
families beyond the seas." On July 11, 1682, while still
in England he issued a series of "conditions or concessions," running to twenty separate paragraphs or articles,

---

[89] GORDON'S *History of Pennsylvania*, pp. 218–219.

for the government of the relations between himself and his province and those who should purchase lands from him and settle here. The seventh of these conditions reads as follows : " That for every Fifty acres that shall be allotted to a servants, at the end of his service, his Quitrent shall be two shillings per annum, and the master or owner of the servant, when he shall take up the other Fifty acres, his Quit-rent shall be Four shillings by the year, or if the master of the servant (by reason in the Indentures he is so obliged to do) allot to the Servant Fifty acres in his own division, the said master shall have on demand allotted him from the Governor, the One hundred acres, at the chief rent of six shillings per annum." [90]

" The more wealthy of the Scotch emigrants (to New Jersey) were noted for the accompaniment of a numerous retinue of servants and dependents, and, in some instances they incurred the expense of transporting whole families of poor laborers whom they established on their lands for a term of years, and endowed with a competent stock, receiving in return one half of the agricultural produce." [91]

From the first, large numbers of these servants came to Pennsylvania. Claypole says, writing on Oct. 1, 1682, " above fifty servants belonging to the Society are going away in a great ship for Pennsylvania." [92]

The foregoing establishes the existence of this species of servitude before the founding of Pennsylvania. It also shows that in order to give these people a fair start in life the terms on which they could secure lands from the Proprietary were more favorable than those accorded to their masters themselves.

---

[90] HAZZARD'S *Annals*, pp. 505-513.
[91] GRAHAME'S *United States*, Vol. II., p. 295.
[92] HAZZARD'S *Annals of Pennsylvania from 1609 to 1682*, p. 593.

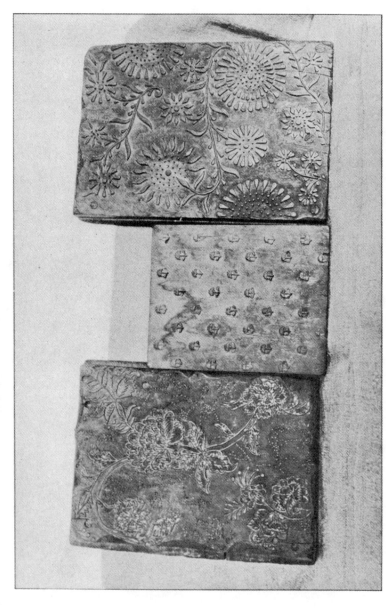

J F SACHSE, PHOTO.

PENNSYLVANIA-GERMAN ENTERPRISE.

CARVED BLOCKS MADE AT EPHRATA CLOISTER FOR PRINTING DRESS GOODS.

I find the word " servant," evidently used in the sense already indicated, in many acts of the General Assembly. It occurs in a law prohibiting work on the " First day of the week, called the Lord's Day," passed Nov. 27, 1700.[93] Also in another law passed on the same day and year,[94] and in still another passed at the same time with reference to " servants " assaulting their masters or mistresses.[95]   A fourth law enacted on the same day of the aforementioned year provides that " if any ' servant' or servants shall procure themselves to be married without consent of his or her master or mistress, (he or she) shall for such, their offense, each of them serve their respective masters or mistresses, one whole year after the time of their service (by indenture, law, or custom) is expired ; and if any person being free shall marry with a servant as aforesaid, he or she so marrying shall pay to the master or mistress of the servant, if for a man twelve pounds ; if a woman, six pounds or one year's service ; and the servant so being married shall abide with his or her master or mistress according to indenture or custom, and one year after as aforesaid." [96]   In still another law passed on the same day and same year, designed for raising county revenues, it is provided, " that no person that has been a bond servant by indenture or otherwise in this government, shall be rated the above four shillings per head until he has been free from his servitude the space of one year." [97]

An excellent law concerning servants was passed by the General Assembly, met at Newcastle, in the Lower Counties, in May, 1700.   It appears to be the model after which

---

[93] *Statutes at Large of Pennsylvania*, Vol. II., p. 4.
[94] *Ibid.*, Vol. II., p. 6.
[95] *Ibid.*, Vol. II., p. 13.
[96] *Ibid.*, Vol. II., p. 22.
[97] *Ibid.*, Vol. II., p. 35.

later legislation was largely formulated, and is therefore
quoted :

" AN ACT FOR THE BETTER REGULATION OF SERVANTS IN THE PROVINCE AND TERRITORIES.

" For the just Encouragements of Servants in the Discharge of their Duty, and the Prevention of their Desert-
ing their masters or Owners Services, Be It Enacted by
the Proprietary and Governor, by and with the Advice and
Consent of the Freemen of this Province and Territories,
in General Assembly met, and by the authority of the
same, that no Servant, bound to serve his or her Time in
this Province or Counties annexed, shall be sold or disposed of to any person residing in any other Province or
Government, without the Consent of the said Servant and
two Justices of the Peace of the said County wherein he
lives or is sold, under the Penalty of *Ten Pounds*, to be
forfeited by the Seller.

"AND BE IT FURTHER ENACTED, That no Servant shall
be assigned over to another person by any in this Province
or Territories, but in the presence of one Justice of the
Peace of the County, under the Penalty of *Ten Pounds;*
which Penalty, with all others in the Act expressed, shall
be levied by Distress and Sale of Goods of the Party
Offending.

" AND BE IT ENACTED, by the authority aforesaid, that
every Servant that shall faithfully serve four years, or
more, shall, at the expiration of their Servitude have a Discharge, and shall be duly Cloathed with two compleat suits
of Apparel, whereof one shall be new, and shall also be
furnished with one new Ax, one Grubbing-hoe, and one
Weeding-hoe ; at the Charge of their Master or Mistress.

"And for the Prevention of Servants quitting their Masters service, Be It Enacted by the authority aforesaid, that if any Servant shall absent him or herself from the Service of their Master or Owner for the space of one Day or more, without Leave first obtained for the same, every such Servant shall for every such Days absence be obliged to serve five days after the Expiration of his or her Time, and shall further make such Satisfaction to his or her Master or Owner, for the Damages and charges sustained by such Absence, as the respective County Court shall see meet, who shall order as well the Time to be served, as other Recompence for Damages sustained.

"And whoever shall Apprehend or take up any runaway Servant and shall bring him or her to the Sheriff of the County, such Person shall for every such Servant, if taken up within ten miles of the Servants Abode, receive *Ten Shillings* Reward of the said Sheriff ; who is hereby required to pay the same, and forthwith to send notice to the Master or Owner, of whom he shall receive Ten Shillings, Prison fees upon Delivery of the said Servant, together with all other Disbursements and reasonable Charges for and upon the same.

"And to prevent the clandestine employment of other Mens Servants, Be It Enacted, by the authority aforesaid, That whosoever shall conceal any Servant of this Province or Territories or entertain him or her twenty-four hours, without his or her Master's or Owners Knowledge and Consent, and shall not within the said time give an Account thereof to some Justice of the Peace of the County, every such Person shall forfeit *Twenty Shillings* for every Day's Concealment. And in case the said Justice of the Peace shall not, within twenty-four Hours after complaint made to him, issue his Warrant, directly to the next Constable, for apprehending and seizing the said Servant, and commit him or her to the Custody of the Sheriff of the County, such Justice shall for every such Offence forfeit FIVE POUNDS. And the Sheriff shall by the first Opportunity after he has received the said Servant, send notice thereof to his or her Master or Owner: and the said

PEASANTS AND COSTUMES OF THE PALATINATE.

Sheriff neglecting or omitting in any case to give Notice to the Master or Owner of the Servant being in his Custody as aforesaid, shall forfeit *Five Shillings* for every Day's neglect after an Opportunity has offered; to be proved against him before the County Court, and to be there adjudged.

"AND for the more effectual Discouragement of Servants embezzling their Masters' or Owners goods, BE IT ENACTED, by the Authority aforesaid, that whosoever shall clandestinely deal or traffick with any Servant white or black, for any Kind of goods or Merchandises, without Leave or Order from his or her Master or Owner, plainly signified or appearing, shall forfeit treble the value of such goods to the Owner; and the Servant, if a white, shall make Satisfaction to his or her Master or Owner by Servitude, after the expiration of his or her Time, to double the Value of the said Goods; and if the Servant be a black, he or she shall be severely whipt in the most Publick Place of the Township where the Offence was comitted." [98]

An act for the better regulation of servants in the Province and Territories, and for the just encouragement of servants in the discharge of their duties, also passed on November 27, 1700, throws so much light on this "servant" question that I give an abridgment of it. It provides that no servant bound to serve a certain time, shall be sold or disposed of to anyone residing in any other province or government, without his consent and that of two justices of the peace of the county where the servant resides, under a ten-pound penalty by the seller. No servant is to be sold or assigned to another person in the Province unless in the presence of a justice, under a ten-pound penalty.

---

[98] *Charters and Acts of the Assembly of the Province of Pennsylvania.* Printed by PETER MILLER & COMPANY, Phil. M.D.C.C.L.XII., Vol. I., pp. 5 and 6 of Section II.

See also GALLOWAY'S *Laws of Pennsylvania*, C. 49, p. 7.

Sec. III. of this law is so important that I quote it entire. "And be it enacted by the authority aforesaid, That every Servant that shall faithfully serve four years or more, shall, at the expiration of their servitude, have a discharge, and shall be duly clothed with two complete suits of apparel, whereof one shall be new; and shall also be furnished with one new axe, one grubbing hoe and one weeding hoe at the charge of their master or mistress." Other sections provide that servants who absent themselves from their service for one day without permission, shall for every such day, serve five days longer at the expiration of their time, and besides make satisfaction for all damage the master may have sustained by such absence. Persons apprehending runaway servants and taking them to the sheriff shall receive ten shillings for the same or twenty shillings when the runaway is taken more than ten miles from his master's abode. Persons concealing servants without the master's knowledge, or entertaining them twenty-four hours and who shall not notify either the master or a justice of the peace, shall be fined twenty shillings for every day's concealment. The final clause in the act provided that whosoever should clandestinely deal or traffic with any servant for any kind of goods or merchandize, without leave or order from the master, shall forfeit treble the value of the goods to the master; and the servant, if white, shall make reparation to his or her master or owner, by servitude after the expiration of his or her time, to double the value of the said goods.[99]

On October 18, 1701, the law of November 27, 1700, regulating the marriages of servants as already quoted, was reënacted.

It seems that sometimes "bought servants" left their

---

[99] *Statutes at Large of Pennsylvania*, Vol. II., pp. 54–56.

masters, greatly to the damage of the latter, and enlisted in the Queen's service over in New Jersey. In consequence of this hardship, an act was passed by the Assembly on August 10, 1711, providing that " any master who shall prove that a servant belonging to him has enlisted in the Queen's service since a certain date without the approval of his master or mistress, shall receive for every month's unexpired service of such servant, the sum of ten shillings, and the full sum which the unexpired time of servitude shall at that rate amount to, the entire sum not to exceed twenty pounds however. The master or mistress shall deliver up the covenant or indenture of such servant and assign thereon their right to such servant's services."

In an act regulating fees to be charged by public officials, passed on May 28, 1715, a shilling is allowed " for writing the assignment of a servant and signing it." [100] On August 24, 1717, an act for levying taxes passed the Assembly and among its other provisions was one requiring the constables in the several districts of the Province to carefully register the number of bound servants that are held. [101] A similar law was reënacted on February 22, 1717–1718, but servants not out of their servitude six months are exempted. [102] A licensing act passed on the 26th day of August, 1721, prohibits the sale of rum, brandy and other spirits to be drunk by servants and others in companies near the place of sale ; nor shall such servants be trusted or entertained, if warned by the master or mistress of the same ; and any one arresting a servant for a debt contracted in this way, such actions shall abate, and the servant or his master or mistress may plead the act in bar. [103]

---

[100] *Statutes at Large of Pennsylvania*, Vol. III., p. 100.
[101] *Ibid.*, pp. 250–251.
[102] *Ibid.*, p. 181.
[103] *Ibid.*, p. 129.

Under an act passed May 5, 1722, a duty was imposed on persons convicted of heinous crimes who should be imported into the Province.   The law recites that many persons trading here had, for purposes of gain, imported and sold as servants for a term of years, persons convicted of crimes, who soon ran away, leaving their masters' service, to the great loss of persons thus buying them.   The law inflicted a penalty of five pounds on any shipmaster who should bring such a convict into the Province to be paid before the servant was landed and be in addition held bound in the sum of fifty pounds for the good behavior of such convicted person, for the period of one year.   Examinations were to be made of suspected persons by justices of the peace, and if any were brought and disposed of without complying with the law, twenty pounds fine was to be levied on the offender.   All servants under the age of twelve years were exempted from the provisions of the law.[104]

This brings the legislation of the Province down to the period when the German immigration began to assume large proportions, and the importation and selling of the same appears to have taken its rise.   During all that period the word " Servant " was used ; that of " Redemptioner " never, nor at any time thereafter in legal enactments, so far as I am aware.

Under the law, all contracts between redemptioners and their purchasers were required to be registered by officials designated for that purpose.   It would be of much interest if these complete records were still in existence, but as they have not been discovered thus far, this is hardly to be hoped for now.   The Historical Society of Pennsylvania has two volumes of such records.   The title of the books is *German Redemptioners, from 1785 to 1804.*   That

---

[104] *Statutes at Large of Pennsylvania*, Vol. III., pp. 264-268.

period included three volumes, but the second one is missing. The books are in manuscript, folio in size, and the first one contains 409 pages. The third volume is smaller, only 130 pages, and the date runs from 1817 to 1831. Perhaps we have in this latter date the period when the traffic in these indentured people ceased. The smallness of the volume shows how few were recorded during the long period from 1817 to 1831. The books have a written index.

As a sample of the general character of this registry, the following entry from Volume I., page 57, is given:

" Maria Magdalina Shaffer assigned by John Fromberg, to serve Peter Muhlenberg, Esq. of Montgomery county State of Pennsylvania, the remainder of her indentures, recorded page 14. consideration £6."

" Maria Magdalena Shaffer bound herself to John Fromberg, of the city of Philadelphia, merchant, to serve him three years and six monchs : to have customary freedom suits."

All the other records follow the same general style.

The conditions under which British bond servants were brought to this country may be seen by the following indenture copied from the volume noted above. In this case, however, the document was in shape of a printed form, with names and dates filled in. It was the only one found in the book.

" This Indenture Made the 13th Day of May, in the year of our Lord, 1784, Alex.ʳ Beard of Broughshane, in the Co. of Antrim, Tayler, by consent of his father on the one Part, and John Dickey of Callybarthey in the said county, Gentleman, of the other Part, Witnesseth that the said Alexander Beard, doth hereby covenant, promise and

THE LONDON COFFEE HOUSE.[105]

grant to and with the said John Dickey his Executors, Administrators and Assigns, from the Day of the Date hereof, until the first and next arrival at Philadelphia, in America, and after for and during the Term of Three years to serve in such Service and Employment as the said John Dickey or his assigns shall there employ him according to the Custom of the Country in the like kind. In consideration whereof the said John Dickey doth hereby covenant and grant to and with the said Alexander Beard to pay for his Passage and to find and allow him Meat, Drink, Apparel and Lodging with other Necessaries, dur-

---

[105] The London Coffee House was the most celebrated establishment of its kind ever opened in Philadelphia. The original building was erected in 1702 by Charles Reed. It was first used as a "Coffee House" in 1754 by William Bradford, the famous provincial printer. Bradford's petition for a license reads as follows : "Having been advised to keep a Coffee House for the benefit of merchants and traders, and as some people may at times be desirous to be furnished with other liquors besides coffee, your petitioner apprehends it is necessary to have the Govenor's license."

The house (still standing) is at the southwest corner of Front and Market streets. It became the resort of everybody of consequence in the city and of all the prominent people who visited Philadelphia. It was the focus of all the news that was going on. The Governor, and merchants of every degree, went there at stated times to drink their coffee, learn the news and gossip. There was a covered shed connected with it, vendues of all kinds were regularly held, and often auctions of negro slaves, men, women and children were held there. Some of the more memorable events in the history of the city occurred on the spot. The Stamp Act papers, which were seized wherever they could be found, were burned there. The ship captain who first brought news of the repeal of the Stamp Act, was wined and dined there. In 1774, the effigies of Governor Hutchinson, of Massachusetts, and of Alexander Wederburn were burnt because of their insults to Dr. Franklin. The Declaration of Independence was read there by John Nixon, after which the Royal Arms were torn down from the Court House, carried there and burned. There General Thompson had a personal altercation with Justice McKean, leading to a challenge by the former, which was declined by the latter, because to accept it would be to violate the laws he was sworn to maintain. Even the Common Council proceedings are frequently dated at the "Coffee House." It is alluded to by all writers of the period as the place of general meeting when any event of importance, foreign or domestic, was to the fore. (WATSON'S *Annals of Philadelphia*, Vol. I., p. 203 ; III., p. 203.)

ing the said Term and at the End of the said Term to pay
unto him the usual Allowance, according to the Custom of
the country in the like kind.   In Witness whereof the Parties above Mentioned to these indentures have interchangeably put their Hands and Seals, the Day and Year first
above written.

" Signed, Sealed and Delivered
    " in the presence of

" PETER DILLON,	ALEX.ᴿ BEARD,
" JOHN WIER,	JOHN DICKEY."

Just when this business came to a close I have not been
able definitely to ascertain.[106]   That it died out gradually is
hardly to be doubted.   A more enlightened sentiment
among the American people, and the still more important
fact that the migrating " fever " had about run its course
among the poorer classes, for a time, were no doubt the
most important factors towards bringing this about.

So far as I have been able to learn, no Redemptioners
were brought into Lancaster county after 1811.   In that
year Mr. Abram Peters, a prominent farmer of the county,
while hauling wheat to the mills on the Brandywine, near
Wilmington, stopped at Chester to buy a small German
girl, his wife needing the services of such a person.   He
secured an orphan girl named " Kitty," at the price of $25.
The mother had died at sea, leaving Kitty and her sister
to be disposed of as Redemptioners.   The master of the
ship desired to sell the sisters to one person, that they
might not be separated, and offered the two for $40.   Mr.
Peters, having no use for two, declined to take them both,
but he promised to find a purchaser for the other sister at

---

[106] From a document quoted elsewhere, it would seem the traffic reached its
close about the year 1831.

$15, if possible. On his way home he met a Quaker gentleman and his wife. The latter wished to buy Kitty. Peters declined to part with her but told them of the other sister still at Chester. The old Quaker at once went to that place and bought her. The two purchasers had exchanged addresses and promised to keep the two sisters in correspondence with each other. Both girls found kind mistresses and good homes, corresponded and visited each other regularly. Kitty finally married a wealthy German, a baker named Kolb, of Philadelphia.[107]

---

[107] I am indebted to S. M. Sener, Esq., for the facts of the above narrative.

EARLY PENNSYLVANIA POTTERY.   EARTHEN PIE-PLATE.

CHAPTER III.

Origin and Meaning of the Term "Redemptioner."— Narrative of Gottlieb Mittelberger, who after Residing in Pennsylvania four years Returned to the Fatherland and by Request wrote a full Account of the Voyage Across the Sea and the Redemptioner Traffic.

> "Amerika, O neues Heimath land!
>   Du Land der Freiheit, Land voll Licht und Wonne!
> Sei uns gegrüsst du gastlich holder Strand,
>   Sei uns gegrüsst du goldene Freiheits-Sonne."

> "They came, oft wronged beneath the mast,
>   Or, when escaped the dreaded wave,
> How many wept their loved ones cast
>   For burial, in an ocean grave."

THE term Redemptioner had its origin in a peculiar system of voluntary servitude, recognized by law and by custom, under which a freedman entered into a contract with another person, to serve the latter for a stipulated time and at a stipulated price, for moneys paid to him or for his benefit, before the service was entered upon. Through the fulfillment of this contract apprenticeship or servitude, the servitor was said to redeem himself, hence the name of REDEMPTIONER given to those who entered into such agreements.

There were two kinds of Redemptioners, and the distinction should be borne in mind. The first were the so-called "indentured servants" who made specific contracts before setting sail, to serve a term of years to masters ; the second, known sometimes as "free willers," were without money, but anxious to emigrate, therefore agreed with the ship-masters to sell themselves and their families on their arrival, for the captain's advantage, and thus repay the cost of their transportation.[108]

The historian Gordon very clearly and fully sets forth the character of still another class of immigrants. He says : "A part of the emigration to the Colonies was composed of servants, who were of two classes. The first and larger, poor and oppressed in the land of their nativity, sometimes the victims of political changes, or religious intolerance, submitted to a temporary servitude, as the price of freedom, plenty and peace. The second, vagrants and felons, the dregs of the British populace, were cast by the mother country upon her colonies, with the most selfish disregard of the feelings she outraged. From this moral pestilence the first settlers shrunk with horror. In 1682 the Pennsylvania Council proposed to prohibit the introduction of convicts, but the evil was then prospective to them only, and no law was enacted. But an act was now passed (1722), which, though not prohibitory in terms, was such in effect. A duty of five pounds was imposed upon every convicted felon brought into the Province, and the importer was re-

---

[108] MELLICK'S *Story of an Old Farm*, p. 149.

quired to give surety for the good behavior of the convict for one year; and to render these provisions effectual, the owner or master was bound under a penalty of twenty pounds, to render, on oath, or affirmation, within twenty-four hours after the arrival of the vessel, an account to the collector of the names of the servants and passengers. But such account was not required when bond was given conditioned for the reëxportation of such servants within six months." [109]

The earliest direct reference to this traffic in German Redemptioners which I have found, appears in the work of Eickhoff [110] who cites a letter written in 1728 by several persons at that time, which fully bears out the existence of the trade in German Redemptioners at that period. The letter states that two persons, Oswald Siegfried and Peter Siegfried had informed them (the writers) for the second time from the city of Amsterdam, that there was a certain broker in that city, who would carry emigrants to Pennsylvania, even when they were unable to pay for their passage, if they could manage to scrape together only half the passage money; and those who had nothing at all, if they were in a condition to perform manual labor when they

---

[109] GORDON'S *History of Pennsylvania*, p. 189.

[110] " Das diese art der Passagierbeförderung etwa im Jahr 1728 ihren Anfang nahm, laszt sich nach einem Schreiben von Heinrich Kundig, Michael Krabiel und David Kaufmann an ihre mennonitischen Glaubensgenossen in Amsterdam (Marz 1738) vermuthen, worin Jene erzöhlen, sie hätten Allen von der Auswanderung nach Pennsylvanian abgerathen, welche kein Geld hätten, um die Überfahrt selbst zu bezahlen, oder Freunde in Pennsylvanien, die dies thäten. ' Nun hat uns aber Oswald Siegfried und Peter Siegfried zum 2 mal aus Amsterdam geschrieben, dass einer gewissen Kauffman in Amsterdam habe, der de leit nach Benselfania führen wil, wenn sie schon die Fracht nicht haben, wenn sie nur durch einander die halbe Fracht ausmachen Können; wenn auch leit seien, die nichts haben, wenn sie nur im Stant seien, dass sie arbeiten Können, werden auch mit genommen. Missen davor arbeiten, bis sie 7½ Bischtolen abverdient haben.' "

arrived. They would be obliged to labor upon their arrival until their passage money amounting to 7½ pistoles (about $30) had been earned.[111]

In my attempt to make this sketch as complete as possible, I have carefully examined all the sources of information that were accessible or of which I was cognizant. Many writers have touched upon the Redemptioners with more or less fullness but it was a German visitor to Pennsylvania to whom we are indebted for the fullest, and as I believe a most trustworthy account of the man-traffic which this is an attempt to describe. I refer to the little volume written by Gottlieb Mittelberger.[112] Without any attempt at fine writing he tells what he saw and had personal knowledge of. His narrative, in addition to bearing inherent evidences of reliability, is further fortified and supported by the concurrent testimony of numerous other writers. In fact, his veracity has never been questioned so far as I am aware, and the student of this period of our history will of necessity have to go to him when the era under review is discussed. He declares at the outset that he " carefully inquired into the condition of the country; and what I describe here, I have partly experienced myself, and partly heard from trustworthy people who were familiar with the circumstances."

Mittelberger was a native of Wurtemburg. He came to this country in 1750 and returned to Germany in 1754. He was an organist and came over in charge of an organ which was intended for Philadelphia. He served as the

---

[111] ANTON EICKHOFF, *In Der Neuen Heimath*, p. 142.

[112] " *Gottlieb Mittelberger's Reise nach Pennsylvanien im Jahre 1750 und Rückreise nach Teutschland im Jahr 1754. Enthaltend nicht nur eine Beschreibung des Landes nach seinem gegenwärtigen Zustande, sondern auch eine ausführliche Nachricht von den unglückseligen und betrübten Umständen der meisten Teutschen, die in dieses Landgezogen sind und dahin ziehen. Frankfurt und Leipzig 1756.*"

organist of the Augustus Church at the Trappe, and as a schoolmaster during his nearly four years' stay in Pennsylvania. His services in both capacities were so highly appreciated that, when he left, the church authorities gave him a most flattering testimonial.[113]

The account which Gottlieb Mittelberger gives of his voyage to Pennsylvania and of his return to Germany four years later is the fullest known to me of a complete trip from the heart of the Fatherland to the sea, the voyage across the ocean, the trials and sufferings of that eventful period and the further events that waited on such as came penniless and dependent and who had already in Holland entered into contracts to serve some master until all their passage charges and the food they had consumed were paid for.

Mittelberger did not come as a Redemptioner; his was a business trip; he pursued his profession of organist for four years and then returned to Germany. But, as was most natural in a man of his kind and tender nature, he thoroughly sympathized with his poor countrymen in their time of adversity, and, being in daily touch with them and all that was going on in Philadelphia, no man was better acquainted with the wrongs put upon them and of the trials they were compelled to encounter. He was moved by all this, and by the appeals of his Philadelphia acquaintances, to tell the story of what he had seen and heard, upon his return to Germany, and out of the promise he then made we have his book.

It must always be borne in mind that Mittelberger's aim was to dissuade his countrymen from emigrating, and that

---

[113] A most excellent translation of this book has recently been made by Mr. Carl Theo. Eben, and published by John Jos. McVey, of Philadelphia, who has kindly permitted me to make use of the translation for my present purposes.

he puts the worst construction on the evils to be met and encountered possible, as if it was necessary to make his statements even worse than the reality!

There are some few minor inaccuracies in it, and occasionally a statement he had from hearsay is exaggerated, but there are no intentional errors, and the general truthfulness of his narrative is unquestioned. He was not friendly to this immigration of his countrymen. It is true, he gives a most flattering account of the fertility and productiveness of the country and of the ease with which a living can be made there, but when he deals with the long voyage, the unpleasant events connected with it, its fatalities and losses, he is anxious that the people shall remain at home, and he says he believes they will after they have read what he has written, because such a journey with most involves a loss of property, liberty and peace; with some a loss of life and even of the salvation of their souls, this latter because of the lack of religious opportunities in the new home.

MITTELBERGER'S NARRATIVE.

"This journey from the Palatinate to Pennsylvania," he says, "lasts from the beginning of May until the end of October, fully half a year, amid such hardships as no one is able to describe adequately. The cause is because the Rhine boats from Heilbronn to Holland have to pass by 36 custom houses, at all of which the ships are examined, which is done when it suits the convenience of the customhouse officials. In the meantime, the ships with the people are detained long, so that the passengers have to spend much money. The trip down the Rhine alone lasts four, five and even six weeks.

"When the ships and the people reach Holland, they

are detained there likewise five or six weeks.   Because things are very dear there, the poor people have to spend nearly all they have during that time. * * * Both in Rotterdam and Amsterdam the people are packed densely,

CASTLE IN THE PALATINATE.

like herrings, so to say, in the large sea vessels.   One person receives a place scarcely two feet wide and six feet long in the beadstead, while many a ship carries four to six hundred souls ; not to mention the innumerable implements, tools, provisions, water barrels and other things which likewise occupy much space.

"On account of contrary winds it sometimes takes the ships two, three and four weeks to make the trip from Holland to Cowes (on the isle of Weight, on the South coast of England).   But when the wind is good they get

(A) PENNSYLVANIA-GERMAN STOVE PLATE. HAROLD DIFFENDERFFER, PHOTO.

(B) FAMILY BAKE-OVEN. J. F. SACHSE, PHOTO.

there in eight days or sooner. Every thing is examined at the custom house and the duties paid, and ships are sometimes detained eight, ten and fourteen days before their cargoes are completed. During this delay every one is compelled to spend his last money and to consume the little stock of provisions which had been reserved for the ocean voyage ; so that most passengers, finding themselves on the ocean where they are in still greater need of them, suffer greatly from hunger and want.

"When the ships have for the last time weighed their anchors at Cowes, the real misery begins, for from there the ships, unless they have good winds must often sail eight, nine, ten or twelve weeks before they reach Philadelphia. But with the best wind the voyage lasts seven weeks.

" During the voyage there is on board these ships terrible misery, stench, fumes, horror, vomiting, many kinds of sicknesses, fever, dysentery, headache, heat, constipation, boils, scurvy, cancer mouth-rot and the like, all of which come from old and sharply salted food and meat, also from very bad and foul water so that many die miserably.

" Add to this, want of provisions, hunger, thirst, cold, heat, dampness, anxiety, want, afflictions and lamentations, together with other troubles such as lice which abound so plentifully, especially on sick people, that they can be scraped off the body. The misery reaches the climax when a gale rages for two or three days and nights, so that every one believes that the ship will go to the bottom with all the human beings on board. * * *

" Among the healthy, impatience sometimes grows so great and cruel that one curses the other or himself, and the day of his birth, and sometimes come near killing each other. Misery and malice join each other, so that they cheat and rob one another. One always reproaches the other for persuading him to undertake the journey. Frequently children cry out against their parents, husbands against their wives and wives against their husbands, brothers and sisters, friends and acquaintances against each other. But most against the soul-traffickers,—(the Newlanders).

" Many sigh and cry : ' Oh, that I were at home again, and if I had to lie in my pig sty ! ' Or they say : ' O God, if I only had a piece of good bread, or a good fresh drop of water.' Many people whimper, and sigh and cry piteously for their homes ; most of them get homesick. Many hundred people necessarily die and perish in such misery, and must be cast into the sea, which drives their relatives, or those who persuaded them to undertake the journey, to such despair that it is almost impossible to pacify and console them. In a word, the sighing and crying and lamenting on board the ship continues night and day, so as to cause the hearts even of the most hardened to bleed when they hear it. * * *

" Children from one to seven years rarely survive the voyage ; and many a time parents are compelled to see their children miserably suffer and die from hunger, thirst and sickness, and then see them cast into the water. I witnessed such misery in no less than thirty-two children in our ship, all of whom were thrown into the sea. * * *

" Often a father is separated by death from his wife and children, or mothers from their little children, or even both parents from their children ; and sometimes entire families die in quick succession ; so that often many dead persons lie in the berths besides the living ones, especially when contagious diseases have broken out on the ship. * * * That most of the people get sick is not surprising, because, in addition to all other trials and hardships, warm food is served only three times a week, the rations being very poor and very small. These meals can hardly be eaten on account of being so unclean. The water which is served out on the ships is often very black, thick and full of worms, so that one cannot drink it without loathing, even with the greatest thirst. O surely, one would often give much money at sea for a piece of good bread, or a drink of good water, if it could only be had. I myself experienced that sufficiently, I am sorry to say. Toward the end we were compelled to eat the ship's biscuit which had been spoiled long ago; though in a whole biscuit there was scarcely a piece the size of a dollar that had not been full of red worms and spiders nests. Great hunger and thirst force us to eat and drink everything; but many do so at the risk of their lives. * * *

" At length, when after a long and tedious voyage, the ships come in sight of land, so that the promontories can be seen, which the people were so eager and anxious to see, all creep from below to the deck to see the land from afar, and they weep for joy, and pray and sing, thanking and praising God. The sight of the land makes the people on board the ship, especially the sick and the half dead, alive again, so that their hearts leap within them; they shout and rejoice, and are content to bear their misery in patience, in the hope that they may soon reach the land in safety. But alas!

" When the ships have landed at Philadelphia after their long voyage no one is permitted to leave them except those who pay for their passage or can give good security; the others who cannot pay must remain on board the ships till they are purchased, and are released from the ships by their purchasers. The sick always fare the worst, for the healthy are naturally preferred and purchased first; and so the sick and wretched must often remain on board in front of the city for two or three weeks, and frequently die, whereas many a one if he could pay his debt and was permitted to leave the ship immediately, might recover.

" Before I describe how this traffic in human flesh is conducted, I must mention how much the journey to Pennsylvania costs. A person over ten years pays for the passage from Rotterdam to Philadelphia, £10. Children from five to ten years pay half price, £5. All children under five years are free. For these prices the passengers are conveyed to Philadelphia, and as long as they are at sea provided with food, though with very poor food, as has been shown.

" But this is only the sea passage; the other costs on land, from home to Rotterdam, including the passage on the Rhine, are at least $35, no matter how economically one may live. No account is here made of extraordinary contingencies. I may safely assert that with the greatest economy, many passengers have spent $176 from home to Philadelphia.

" The sale of human beings in the market on board the ship is carried on thus : Every day Englishmen, Dutchmen and high German people come from the city of Philadelphia and other places, some from a great distance, say sixty, ninety, and one hundred and twenty miles away, and go on board the newly arrived ship that has brought and offers for sale passengers from Europe, and select among the healthy persons such as they deem suitable for their business, and bargain with them how long they will serve for their passage money, for which most of them are still in debt. When they have come to an agreement, it happens that adult persons bind themselves in writing to serve three, four, five or six years for the amount due by them, according to their age and strength. But very young people, from ten to fifteen years, must serve until they are twenty-one years old.

"Many persons must sell and trade away their children like so many head of cattle; for if their children take the debt upon themselves, the parents can leave the ship free and unrestrained; but as the parents often do not know where and to what people their children are going, it often happens that such parents and children, after leaving the ship do not see each other again for years, perhaps no more in all their lives.

STRAW BASKET FOR BAKING BREAD, AND SCRAPER.

"When people arrive who cannot make themselves free, but have children under five years of age, they cannot free themselves by them; for such children must be given to somebody without compensation to be brought up, and they must serve for their bringing up till they are twenty-one years old. Children from five to ten years, who pay half price for their passage, must likewise serve for it until they are twenty-one years old; they cannot, therefore, redeem their parents by taking the debt of the latter upon themselves. But children above ten years can take part of their parents' debts upon themselves.

"A woman must stand for her husband if he arrives sick, and in like manner a man for his sick wife, and take the debt upon herself or himself, and thus serve five or six years not alone for his or her own debt, but also for that of the sick husband or wife. But if both are sick, such persons are sent from the ship to the hospital, but not until it appears probable that they will find no purchasers. As soon as they are well again they must serve for their passage, or pay if they have means.

" It often happens that whole families, husband, wife and children, are separated by being sold to different purchasers, especially when they have not paid any part of their passage money.

" When a husband or wife has died at sea, after the ship has completed more than half her trip, the survivor must pay or serve not only for himself or herself, but also for the deceased.[114]

" When both parents died after the voyage was more than half completed, their children, especially when they are young and have nothing to pawn or pay, must stand for their own and their parents' passage, and serve till they are twenty-one years old. When one has served his or her term, he or she is entitled to a new suit of clothes at parting and if it has been so stipulated, a man gets in addition a horse and a woman a cow.

" When a servant has an opportunity to marry in this country, he or she must pay for each year he or she would still have to serve, £5 or £6. But many a one who has thus purchased and paid for his bride, has subsequently repented of his bargain, so that he would gladly have returned his dear ware and lost his money in addition.

" If a servant in this country runs away from his master who has treated him harshly, he cannot get far. Good provision has been made for such cases so that a runaway is soon recovered. He who detains or returns a deserter receives a good reward.

---

[114] Less than half the voyage having been made when a passenger died, there was no claim for passage money.

"If such a runaway has been away from his master a single day, he must serve an entire week for it; if absent a week, then a month, and for a month, half a year. But if the master does not care to keep the runaway when he gets him back, he may sell him for as many years as he has still to serve."

It must not be supposed that the scenes and events described in the foregoing quotations from Mittelberger were everyday occurrences, at least so far as the sufferings, sickness and deaths at sea are concerned. They did occur, but he takes especial pains to represent everything at its worst. Many a ship came over in good condition, with no unusual sickness on board, and under the charge of humane ship captains. But so far as the sale and disposal of the passengers upon their arrival was concerned, that was an unvarying affair. It was, however, just what many of these people were aware of, and may be said to have bargained for, before they stepped on shipboard to come here, and they had only themselves to blame for the after-misery it entailed. It is not to be doubted that by far the greater number of these people were misled and deceived by the Newlanders, and were ill prepared for the voyage besides, so that only disappointment, with many of the miseries rehearsed by Mittelberger, were realized by them on the voyage and when they arrived.

The following passage from Löher is interesting: "The Germans, who for so many years were hired out to pay costs of transportation, are called 'Servants' (Knechte) or Redemptioners (Käuflinge). When they serve with English people, their language soon becomes one of mixed English and German. (A notable proof of this fact is supplied by Pastor Brunholtz, of the Lutheran

Church, who recorded the following in his diary : " On March 25, 1745, a man called on me and requested me to go to Chester, and preach to the Germans there. * * * On the morning of June 30 I went to Chester, which is about 16 miles from Philadelphia. The Germans here, who for the most part are ' servants,' as they are called, employed by English people, and so speaking a mixture of German and English."[115]) In the country they are usually well treated and cared for, especially when good fortune so wills it that they become inmates of a German household. If one of the latter secures an entire family, the man is generally occupied in field labor, and also carries on his trade if he has one, sometimes on his own account and at others on that of his master. It was allowed him to have a few head of cattle. The wife was generally a housemaid and a caretaker of children, while her own little ones were assigned to all kinds of light work. The servitude finally came to an end when the boy reached the age of 21 and the girl that of 18 years. They might not get married without the consent of their masters. A runaway was compelled to serve an additional week for each day's absence and six months for each week's absence, and could, what was otherwise unlawful, be sold to another person for the period of his unexpired service.

" When the term of service was over, a thrifty servant had saved quite a sum and secured a home for himself, for land was cheap.[116] Perhaps more than one-third of the original German immigrants and their descendants who are so well-to-do now, began life in this humble way. Their sons were already notable persons at the time of the Revolution. An Act of Parliament passed in 1756,

---

[115] MANN'S *Hallische Nachrichten*, Eng. Ed., p. 162.
[116] He could take up fifty acres of land at a nominal rent.

allowed servants, with the consent of their masters, to become soldiers. Many of these immigrants who brought
considerable amounts of gold with them, hired themselves
for a time until they should become acquainted with the
country and people. The German and English-Irish Redemptioners came mostly to Pennsylvania; the English to
Virginia, and the statistics of that State show that annually
about 1,500 Redemptioners arrived there. In later times
the service of these people became still more liberal. I have
spoken to many householders and schoolmasters who were
told by their fathers how they had been persuaded to come
to America, but who, after serving half a year of their time,
ran away. It was difficult to find a runaway from the settlements in the depths of the forest." [117]

[117] LÖHER'S *Die Deutschen in Amerika*, p. 82.

CHAPTER IV.

The Newlanders or Soul-Sellers.—Men who made a Business of sending Redemptioners to Pennsylvania.—How their Nefarious Traffic was carried on in the Fatherland.—Letters from Pastor Muhlenberg and Others.

> " Yet here sits peace ; and rest sits here.
>   These wide-boughed oaks, they house wise men—
> The student and the sage austere ;
>   And men of wondrous thought and ken.
> Here men of God in holy guise
>   Invoke the peace of Paradise."

SEAL OF GERMANTOWN.

BEFORE this influx of persons willing to sell their personal services to pay the expenses of their transportation had been long in operation, the possibilities of turning it to profitable account were considered by seafaring and other men, but more especially by a class of sharpers who, having come to this country with a full knowledge of the desire of so many of their countrymen in Germany also to migrate, availed themselves of that fact, and of the circumstances surrounding it, to make money out of it.

These man-traffickers or Seelen-Hendler, as the elder Saur denominated them, were known to the Dutch as "Zeilverkoopers," that is, soul-sellers, but among the Germans themselves more generally as Newlanders. These pestiferous fellows associated and entered into agreements with sea captains, merchants and ship owners to handle this immigrant traffic. They were almost without exception persons who had left their country for their country's good, had come to Pennsylvania as mere adventurers and, after taking in the situation thoroughly, adopted schemes of rascality whereby they might defraud their more honest and unsuspecting countrymen.

Of themselves they could not carry out their nefarious plans, but wherever such rogues are found still others will be ready to aid and abet them in their schemes. These base coparceners were found in ship masters, ship owners and commission merchants, on both sides of the Atlantic. The Newlanders went up and down the Rhine and the adjacent country, well dressed, pretending to be prosperous merchants in Philadelphia, and used all their powers of persuasion to induce the humble peasantry to dispose of their small belongings and embark for the land of promise.[118] They commonly received a commission of seven dollars per head for every immigrant they could bring to the ship owner for embarcation, and a free passage for the Newlander himself besides. When two, three,

---

[118] "Many Newlanders boast that they are rich merchants in Pennsylvania, that they sail in their own ships, and own houses in Germantown. Others are dressed in costly clothes, wearing wigs and ruffles to make an imposing appearance."—SAUR'S *German paper*, October 16, 1749.

four and five hundred souls embarked on a single vessel, it will readily be seen what a profitable business it was that these scoundrels were engaged in. Being so lucrative, it is little wonder that so many followed it. We are told that in the year 1749 alone, upwards of one hundred and thirty were engaged in it.[119] Sometimes, however, these precious scoundrels got their deserts. Here and there a German prince was to be found who was well acquainted with the nefarious character of these men, and the disreputable business they were engaged in. They retained an affection for their subjects even though the latter were leaving the Fatherland by hundreds and thousands. When, therefore, these Newlanders made themselves especially obnoxious some of them were seized, imprisoned and put to hauling dirt on the streets and other menial occupations.[120]

HENRY MELCHOIR MUHLENBERG'S ACCOUNT.

Pastor H. M. Muhlenberg, who was ever solicitous for the well-being of his misguided and maltreated countrymen, as was to be expected, also pays his respects to these Newlanders. In a letter written to a friend in Halle, in 1763, he says concerning them: "I cannot forbear making some remarks touching *Newlanders*, in order to caution our German countrymen. I do not speak of such as return to Germany for their patrimony, or to collect money for others, who reside here, and who sometimes use the

[119] Es sind dieses Jahr, 130 Neulaender drussen.—CHRISTOPHER SAUR'S *Pennsylvania Berichte*, September 16, 1749.

[120] So haben verschiedene Herrn im Reiche beschlossen dass die boese Neulaender, oder seelen-verkaeufer, anhalten und verhindern wollen dass ihre unter thanen sollen aus ihren Reiche nicht gekauft werden von den Rotterdamer Kaufleuten. Zu dem ende haben die Herrn im Reiche etliche solcher Neulaender in Gefaengnisse gesetzt in schul-karren geschlossen und dreck fahren lassen.—SAUR'S *Pennsylvania Berichte*, December 1, 1754.

WITMER'S BRIDGE ACROSS THE CONESTOGA RIVER. BUILT 1800.

money collected to purchase merchandise, which they sell in our markets. This is a lawful transaction. * * * In speaking of the Newlanders I mean such as are not disposed to support themselves honestly. I mean those who solicit powers of attorney to collect money in Germany for others, they having none to collect for themselves—who are a the same time in the service of others—urging upon Germans, till they prevail upon them, by means fair or foul, to forsake their *Vaterland* and immigrate to the New World. The usual course pursued by them is, first to seek the acquaintance of merchants in Holland, from whom they receive free passage, also a stipulated sum of money, for every family or unmarried person, they can prevail on to leave their homes for Holland. To accomplish their mission successfully, they resort to various artifices. As a studied prelude to the tragedy, they appear gorgeously attired, make an imposing display with their watches, using every means to create the impression that they are persons of immense wealth.

" Thus the credulous are often deceived, become anxious to emigrate and live in so prosperous and rich a country as Pennsylvania. By these plausible representations and glowing descriptions of America, the impression is made that in Pennsylvania the Elysian fields are to be found— that every desirable vegetable grows spontaneously; hills and mountains are pregnant with unalloyed gold and sil-

---

[121] Witmer's Bridge, one of the oldest and most picturesque of the stone bridges in Pennsylvania, spans the Conestoga river a short distance beyond the eastern limits of Lancaster city. A safe crossing over this stream was much needed to accommodate the great volume of traffic carried on between Philadelphia and the interior of the State. Its erection is due to the energy and enterprise of a single person of German descent, Mr. Abraham Witmer, who with his own resources undertook the task of construction in 1799, and completed it in 1800. The bridge is in a perfect state of preservation to-day and accommodates a heavy business traffic.

ver ; that the fountains gush copious and ceaseless streams
of milk and honey. The Newlanders aver that in Pennsylvania the menial servant becomes the independent lord ;
the spinster the perfect lady ; the laborious husband soon
plays nobleman at ease ; the plodding care-worn peasant
and the toiling mechanic are created Lord Barons. * * *
Many are naturally disposed to improve their temporal
condition, consequently they desire to live in such a country.
In Europe the country is overburdened with people—the
labor of the poorer class is not in demand—the taxes are
enormous—the service to the lords of the manor intolerable. Under such circumstances, the Newlander easily
prevails with many to leave their hearths and homes. In
haste the Germans convert their effects into money, honestly pay their debts, if they have any. The balance of
the money is placed into the hands of the Newlander for
safe keeping. Finally they enter upon their exodus from
home. The expenses of the Rhine passage are charged
to their account. On their arrival in Holland, if detained
there, Dutch merchants advance the poorer classes some
money, which is added to the bill for contingencies. The
several sums with a poll tax [122] and ocean fare, swell the
amount enormously. Before immigrants embark they
must sign articles of agreement written in English, and
the Newlanders persuade the people that they are their impartial friends to see that they have justice done them.
The more human freight the ship captains can crowd into
a ship the more profitable it is for them, if they do not die
on the way, otherwise they may lose by it. For that reason
the ships are kept clean and all kinds of precautions are
taken to keep the passengers in good health, and to bring
them to market in good condition. In former years they

---

[122] This is an allusion to the tax levied on foreigners.

were not so careful, and allowed many to die. When parents died on ship board leaving children behind them the captains and Newlanders acted as guardians of the children, and took what property was left by the parents so that when the children reached the shore, they were sold to pay their and their parents' passage money. Children un-

AUTOGRAPH ENTRY OF REV. H. M. MUHLENBERG IN TRAPPE RECORDS, 1742.

der six are gratuitously disposed of. The chests and goods of the deceased are sold; the money thus realized squares the account. Such heaven-abhorrent deception, led to the formation of an association in Philadelphia to assist as far as was possible, and protect them in their right. So soon as the ships in Holland are fully freighted they set sail. The hardships that must be encountered are made lighter through the sweet hope that they speedily reach the new world and attain their longed for Paradise.

"Finally the ship reaches Philadelphia, where merchants and ship owners receive the bills of freight and articles of agreement subscribed by the immigrants. Before debarking, passengers are examined by a medical officer, whether they are free from contagious diseases. If all is right the immigrants are marched to the Court House to take the oath of fealty to the King of Great Britain; after which they are taken back to the ship. Public notice is then given that German passengers will be sold for their freight. Those having means to pay are allowed to leave the vessel. To the less fortunate—*unbemittelte*—without means, the ship is a mart. Purchasers make their selections, agree afterwards with their preëmpted servants for a stipulated period of service. Young and unmarried persons of both sexes are sold first and their future condition depends much on their master's disposition, situation and rank in society. Married people, widows, and the infirm are dull sale. If they have children these are sold, and the parents' fare charged to the children's account, and the children are consequently obliged to serve a longer time. Children are in this way not infrequently separated forever from their parents. Some children are sold to English masters and in this way forget their mother tongue. By having their children sold, parents are allowed to leave the ship. Still, their condition is unenviable; they are destitute, poorly clad, the infirmities of age often weighing them down, making them appear as if they had emerged from a sepulchre.

"Many of them are compelled through their poverty, to beg their bread from door to door from their German countrymen. The English usually close their doors against them, through fear of infectious diseases. These things cause one's heart to bleed, to see and hear fellow mortals, who had been persuaded to leave a Christian country, lamenting, weeping, wringing their hands in sad despair, because of their misery, and the dispersion of their children. Little did the parents anticipate such things.

" Some having become exasperated beyond measure, invoke the angry elements of heaven and conjure up the denizens of hell, to crush to atoms the Newlanders, merchants in Holland and ship owners who so grossly deceived them. As those cannot hear the denunciations of their victims, they are of course not moved to compassion. Many of the Newlanders, who both hear and see these things, only laugh at their victims, giving them the taunting comfort which the priests of old gave to Judas Iscariot—
' what is that to us, see thou to it.' The children of poor parents, if kept in hardship, learning that because of the non-sale of father or mother they have to serve the longer, often became incensed, yea even embittered against their own parents." [123]

The immigrants that met with the readiest sale and brought the highest prices were mechanics and laboring men. That was the kind of labor most in demand both in city and country. Of course, when these conditions were united with good health and youth, or early middle age, the servant was not long in finding a purchaser and master. Old men and women were not desired, because their days of greatest usefulness were behind them.

There were Newlanders who had still other men or agents under them, engaged in this nefarious practice. Dr. Ernest Otto Hopp, of Germany, in his book on this German slavery in this country, tells of one Heerbrand who achieved unusual notoriety as a procurer of ignorant Germans for America. He had a considerable number of men in his pay who were continually procuring victims, kidnapping beggars and vagrants who had no connections, paying two florins for every one delivered to him. He was also a ship captain and is said to have alone brought six hundred of these people to America.

---

[123] *Hallische Nachrichten*, pp. 997-1012.

Ship captains had a lien on their passengers until the ships' charges were paid, and Professor Kalm in his travels tells that when he reached Philadelphia in September, 1748, on the ship *Mary*, upon going on shore with the captain, the latter turned to his mate and charged him " not to let any one of the twenty-three Germans and their families go out of the vessel unless he paid for his passage, or some one else did it for him." [124]

Gottlieb Mittelberger also pays his respects to these rascals in his usual vigorous and off-hand manner. After saying that the large emigration to America is due to the persuasions and deceptions practiced by the Newlanders, he says :

" These men-thieves inveigle people of every rank and profession, among them many soldiers, scholars, artists and mechanics. They rob the princes and lords of their subjects and take them to Rotterdam or Amsterdam to be sold there. They receive there from their merchants for every person of ten years and over 3 florins or a ducat ; whereas the merchants get in Philadelphia 60, 70 or 80 florins for such a person, in proportion as said person has incurred more or less debts during the voyage. When such a Newlander has collected a ' transport,' and if it does not suit him to accompany them to America, he stays behind, passes the winter in Holland or elsewhere ; in the spring he again obtains money in advance for emigrants from his merchants, goes to Germany again, pretending that he had come from Pennsylvania with the intention of purchasing all sorts of merchandise which he was going to take there.

" Frequently these Newlanders say that they had received powers of attorney from some countrymen or from

---

[124] PETER KALM'S *Travels in America.*

En

Resa

Til

Norra AMERICA,

På

Kongl. Swenska Wetenskaps
Academiens Befallning,

Och

Publici kostnad,

Förrättad

Af

PEHR KALM,

Oeconomiæ Professor i Åbo, samt Ledamot af
Kongl. Swenska Wetenskaps-Academien.

Tom. II.

Med Kongl. Maj:ts Allernådigste Privilegio.

STOCKHOLM,
Tryckt på LARS SALVII kostnad, 1756.

FAC-SIMILE OF TITLE-PAGE OF PETER KALM'S TRAVELS IN
NORTH AMERICA.

the authorities of Pennsylvania to obtain legacies or inheritances for these countrymen; and that they would avail themselves of this good and sure opportunity to take their friends, brothers or sisters, or even their parents with them; and it has often happened that such old people followed them, trusting to the persuasion of these Newlanders that they would be better provided for.

"Such old people they seek to get away with them in order to entice other people to follow them. Thus they have seduced many away who said if such and such relatives of theirs went to America, they would risk it too. These men-thieves resort to various tricks, never forgetting to display their money before the poor people, but which is nothing else but a bait from Holland, and accursed blood-money.

"When these men-thieves persuade persons of rank, such as nobles, learned or skilled people who cannot pay

their passage and cannot give security, these are treated just like ordinary poor people, and must remain on board the ship till some one comes and buys them from the captain, and when they are released at last from the ship, they must serve their lords and masters, by whom

LESSER SEAL OF PROVINCE
(Used by Supreme Court).

they have been bought, like common day-laborers. Their rank, skill and learning avail them nothing, for here none but laborers and mechanics are wanted. But the worst is that such people, who are not accustomed to work, are treated to blows and cuffs, like cattle, till they have learned the hard work. Many a one, on finding himself thus shamefully deceived by the Newlanders, has shortened his own life, or has given way to despair, so that he could not be helped, or has run away, only to fare worse afterwards than before.

" It often happens that the merchants in Holland make a secret contract with their captains and the Newlanders, to the effect that the latter must take the ships with their human freight to another place in America, and not to Pennsylvania where these people want to go, if they think they can elsewhere find a better market for them. Many a one who has a good friend or acquaintance, or a relative in Pennsylvania to whose helping care he has trusted, finds himself thus grievously disappointed in consequence of such infamous deception, being separated from friends whom he will never see again in this or in that country. Thus emigrants are compelled in Holland to submit to the wind and to the captain's will, because they cannot know at sea where the ship is steered to. But all this is the fault of the Newlander and of some unscrupulous dealers in human flesh in Holland.

" Many people who go to Philadelphia, entrust their money, which they have brought with them from their homes, to these Newlanders, but these thieves often remain in Holland with the money, or sail from there with another ship to another English colony, so that the poor defrauded people, when they reach the country, have no other choice but to serve or sell their children, if they have any, only to get away from the ship.

" The following remarkable case may serve as an example. In 1753 a noble lady, N. V., came with her two half grown daughters and a young son to Philadelphia. On the trip down the Rhine she entrusted more than 1,000 rix-dollars to a Newlander who was well known to her. But when the ship on which the lady had taken passage, started from Holland, this villain remained behind with the money; in consequence of which the lady found herself in such want and distress that her two daughters were compelled to serve. In the following spring this poor lady sent her son to Holland to search for the embezzler of her money, but at the time of my departure, in 1754, nothing had as yet been heard of him, and it was even rumored that the young gentleman had died during his voyage."[125]

It is not easy to tell of all the hardships, indignities and injustices that were practiced upon these people, not always, it is true, but often. Many to whom they were indentured were wholly unscrupulous, and intent upon getting everything possible out of them, no matter what the terms of the indentures were. When possible such papers were treated as if they did not exist. They were kept beyond the time of service agreed upon. They were not sent to school according to promise, and although both German and English were to be taught them, only the latter language was employed. Sometimes they were restrained from attending church. Hard masters there were who often treated them cruelly, requiring labor at their hands which they were not bound to perform. The avarice of the masters frequently kept them from providing the necessary sustenance and clothing for their helpless servants.[126]

---

[125] MITTELBERGER'S *Reise nach Pennsylvanian,* pp. 38–41.

[126]" Die Berschwerungen armer Knecht sind mannichfaltig. Oft wollen die Meister ihre verbundenen Knecht über die zeit behalten. Oft versagen sie ihnen den in Fall, dass sie als Kinder verbunden wurden, mit ausgehaltenen unterricht. Oft geben sie denselben nur im Englischen wenn er auch im Deutschen ausgedungen war. Oft halten sie sie von ihrem Gottesdienste zurreck. Oft behandeln sie dieselben mit Wuth und Grans amkeit. Oft weisen sie ihnen Arbeit an dazu sie nicht verpflichtet waren. Oft verbietet ihnen der Geiz den gehoerigen unterhalt und Kleidung zurechen."— PROF. KUNZE'S *Rede vor der Deutschen Gesellschaft zu Philadelphia,* 1782.

CHAPTER V.

"Ein armer Wand'rer bin ich hier,
　Und oftmals Schwer die Noth ;
Oft weh und einsam ist es mir—
　Denn Wieb und Kind sind tod !
So singe ich das Trauerlied—
　Und Sehnsucht drück't mich sehr,
Und in mei'm Hertz schläft Weib und Kind,
　Wie Perlen tief i'm Meer !"

ARMS OF ROTTERDAM.

THE Redemptioners never had a more sincere, able or faithful friend than Christopher Saur the elder, the famous Germantown printer and publisher. He was one of the most prominent of all the Germans in the Province during many years. A godly man, his heart was alive to the wrongs and indignities that were heaped upon so many of his unfortunate countrymen. His presence in or near the city of Philadelphia made him acquainted from day to day with what was going on among these unfortunate people. As the publisher of a German newspaper, he took occasion to

(199)

keep this human traffic and everything connected with it before the public in the columns of his paper, *Der Hoch Deutsche Pennsylvanische Berichte.* Almost every number during the seasons of arrival, had paragraphs relating to the coming of vessels, the condition of the immigrants, their treatment, their wrongs and of much else which he no doubt hoped would have a salutary effect upon the public conscience, and in that way lead to the amelioration of the hard conditions under which they voyaged and their treatment upon their arrival.

Not only as throwing much light on various phases of the Redemptioner traffic, but also as showing Saur's unwearied assiduity in stirring up the public to better the condition of the German Redemptioner immigrants, a series of extracts from his newspaper are here given, and also some from *The American Weekly Mercury*, an English newspaper.[127]

From *The American Weekly Mercury*, Philadelphia, September 1, 1720:

" On the 30 (arrived) the ship *Laurel* John Coppel, from Leverpool and Cork with *240 odd Palatinate Passengers* come here to settle."

The above is the earliest record of any ship carrying Palatines I have met. Additional interest attaches to its arrival as it is most probably the vessel on which the well-known clergyman, Rev. J. Ph. Boehm, came to this country, August 30, 1720.

The first public notice of the Redemptioner traffic that

---

[127] I am under many obligations to my learned and courteous antiquarian friend, Prof. W. J. Hinke, of the Ursinus School of Theology, for valuable aid along this line of my researches.

DOMESTIC INDUSTRIES.

MILK CELLAR AND SPRING.   SHED FOR FRUIT DRYING (SCHNITZ-HOUSE).

I have found is in *The American Weekly Mercury*, published in Philadelphia in 1722 ; it reads as follows :

" Thomas Denham to his good country friends adviseth : That he has some likely servants to dispose of. One hundred Palatines for five years, at £10 a head."

From *The American Weekly Mercury*, November 7, 1728 :

" Those Palatines who have hitherto neglected to pay for their passages in the ship *James Goodwill*, are to take notice that if they do not pay me on board of the said ship, or to Charles Reid of Philadelphia the sum from them respectively due, the 20th day of this Instant November, they will be proceeded against according to Law by David Crocket."

From *The American Weekly Mercury*, November 7, 1728 :

" Just arrived from London, in the ship *Borden*, William Harbert, Commander, a parcel of young likely *men servants*, consisting of Husbandmen, Joyners, Shoemakers, Weavers, Smiths, Brick-makers, Bricklayers, Sawyers, Taylers, Stay-Makers, Butchers, Chair makers, and several other trades, and are to be sold very reasonable either for ready money, wheat Bread, or Flour, by Edward Hoone, in Philadelphia."

As the above ship is not listed among those enumerated in Rupp's *Thirty Thousand Names* nor among those in Vol. XVII. of the second series of *Pennsylvania Archives* it is most probable that they were Irish, Scotch and English immigrants who, as has already been stated, were compelled to pass through all the conditions of servitude imposed upon the Germans, and who came under like impoverished circumstances, but not to be registered.

From *The American Weekly Mercury*, February 18, 1729:

" Lately arrived from London, a parcel of very likely English Servants, men and women, several of the men Tradesmen; to be sold reasonable and Time allowed for payment. By Charles Read of Philadelphia, or Capt. John Ball, on board his ship, at *Anthony Millkinson's Wharf.*"

From *The American Weekly Mercury*, May 22, 1729:
" There is just arrived from Scotland, a parcel of choice *Scotch Servants;* Taylors, Weavers, Shoemakers and ploughmen, some for five and others for seven years; Imported by James Coults, they are on board a sloop lying opposite to the *Market Street Wharf*, where there is a boat constantly attending to carry any one on board that wants to see them.

" N. B. The said James Coults is to be spoke with, at Andrew Bradford's, at the sign of the Bible, in Second Street."

From *The American Weekly Mercury*, May 22, 1729:
" Just arrived from London in the ship *Providence*, Capt. Jonathan Clarke, a parcel of very likely *servants*, most

Tradesmen, to be sold on reasonable Terms; the ship now lies at Mr. *Lawrence's Wharf*, where either the Master or the said Lawrence are to be spoke with."

From *The American Weekly Mercury*, August 28, 1729.
" Lately arrived from Plymouth in the ship *John and Anne*, Thomas Warcut, Master, a parcel of likely *servants*

on board the said ship, to be sold reasonable for money or country produce; credit given if required.

"The above named ship is now lying at *William Fishbourn's Wharf* and will be ready to sail for Plymouth in three weeks after."

From *The Pennsylvania Gazette*, June, 1742:

"To be sold. A likely Servant Woman, having three years and a half to serve. She is a good spinner."

From *Der Hoch Deutsche Pennsylvanische Berichte*, Philadelphia, February 16, 1745:

"We have heard of the ship *Argyle*, Captain Stettman, from Rotterdam for Philadelphia, with Germans. It was one hundred hours distant from England when it met two Spanish war ships which put the Captain and some passengers on a Holland ship by which they were put on shore in England. Another ship, the *H. Andra*, Captain Braum, bound for Philadelphia with 300 Germans, who reached Charleston, Carolina; some of the passengers have arrived in Philadelphia who each had still three doubloons to pay; others reached New York who had money and some of these are still expected here. It seems that while the ship is again being loaded it is convenient for them to journey here. These people say the Captain offered in case they would sign a new contract, he would convey them to Charleston within four days; but in case they refused then they must travel eight weeks more to Philadelphia. But if they insist in going direct to that city he would let them go hungry, he not having enough food to feed them.

"Still another ship with Germans bound for Philadelphia, was already in the Delaware but went back and entered the Susquehanna and so reached Maryland where the ship will again be loaded.

" Another ship reached Philadelphia with 400 Germans and it is said not many over 50 remain alive. They received their bread ration every two weeks and many ate in 4, 5 and 6 days what should have done them 15 days. And when they get no cooked food for 8 days their bread was all so much the sooner; and when they had to wait 3 days over the three weeks, those without money became enfeebled, and those who had money could get plenty of flour from the captain, at three pence sterling per pound and a quart bottle of wine for seven thalers. A certain man whose wife was nearly famished bought every day meal and wine for her and their children, thus kept them alive: another man who had eaten all his week's bread asked the captain for a little bread, but in vain. He then came to the captain and requested the latter to throw them overboard at once rather than allow them to die by inches. He brought his meal sack to the captain and asked him to put a small quantity into it: the captain took the bag, put in some sand and stones and returned it to the man. The latter shed some tears, laid down and died, together with his wife. The living had as much to pay as before for the bread that should have been given to the dead. When such people have no Christian love or mercy on each other, we may well ask if there is no justice in this bepraised land, and we will be answered, Yes, but he who does not know the road thither, must pay dearly for his experience. After having fasted long, no man is ready to bell the cat. Should Cain return to earth in our time and interview a good lawyer, with gold enough, he would be able to prove he had not even seen Abel."

From *The Pennsylvania Berichte*, May 16, 1748:
" Robert and Amos Strettle, of Philadelphia, announce

Der
Hoch-Deutsch

Pensylvanische Geschicht-Schreiber,

Oder:

Sammlung

Wichtiger Nachrichten, aus dem Natur- und Kirchen-Reich.

Erstes Stück. Augusti 20/ 1739.

Geneigter Leser

Unter andern Abgöttern, denen die grobe und subtile Welt der sogenannten Christen dienet, ist nicht der Geringste der Vorwitz. Curiosität und Begierde gerne offt was neues hen, in Hoffnung es werde nicht ohne einigen Nutzen, wenigst der Aufwertung und des Aufschauens bey einigen, die es lesen, schaffen. Auch möchten wohl künfftig, einige Anmerckungen und der Zeit dienliche Sagen ernstlichen Gemüthern zum Nachden-

FAC-SIMILE OF PART OF FIRST PAGE OF CHRISTOPH SAUR'S PAPER, THE FIRST PERMANENT GERMAN PAPER PUBLISHED IN AMERICA.

that their contracts with their debtors expire on June 30, and all the Germans who came to Philadelphia from Rotterdam on their ship and have not paid their passage money will be legally proceeded against unless they pay by that time."

From *The Pennsylvania Berichte*, Philadelphia, August 1, 1749:

"A letter has been received in Germantown, written in the beginning of August, 1749, in Virginia, in which two potters say they sailed from Rotterdam for Philadelphia. Their company contracted with the Captain of the ship to pay ten doubloons for their passage, but he deceived them and carried them all to Virginia, and sold them for five years. They ask whether there is no help for them, as they never entered into such a contract. It appears the ship belonged to the Captain and was not consigned to any agent in Philadelphia."

From *The Pennsylvania Berichte*, Germantown, November 16, 1749:

"The ships on which so many persons had put their chests, and which were so long in coming over, arrived on the 9 and 11 of the present month in Philadelphia. We hear that many of these chests were broken open. It is customary that when a ship captain receives goods and wares for delivery, he must turn them over to the owner as he receives them when the freight is paid, and what is lacking must be made good by him. But the Germans pay and must pay when their chests are robbed or when famished with hunger, even though their contracts are expressly to the contrary."

From *The Pennsylvania Berichte*, December 1, 1749:
"It is well known that after ships arrive in Philadelphia

with Newlanders, there is always a new crop of spurious twenty-shilling Philadelphia bills in circulation, dated August 10, 1739."

From *The Pennsylvania Berichte*, Germantown, July 16, 1750:

" During the past summer Abraham Bär, of Madedeche, took with him on his trip to Rotterdam, two beggar boys who bound themselves to serve seven years for their passage money. When they reached here they learned that they could not be made to serve longer than 4 years or until the age of 21 years."

From *The Pennsylvania Berichte*, No. 123, August 16, 1750:

" Six ships with Irish servants have arrived at Philadelphia, and two ships with German Newcomers. Some say 18 more are on their way here ; others say 24 and still others 10,000 persons."

From *The Pennsylvania Berichte*, Germantown, December 16, 1750:

" Capt. Hasselwood has arrived from Holland with the latest ship that brought Germans. It is the fourteenth that has come laden with Germans this year. 4,317 have registered in the Court House. (The last one mutinied against the captain and all the chests of the salesmen and themselves are under arrest.) Besides these, 1,000 servants and passengers arrived from Ireland and England."

From *The Pennsylvania Berichte*, Germantown, June 16, 1752:

" On the 5th of the present month a ship with a few Germans reached Philadelphia. It is a year since they left Germany and they were five months in reaching the Delaware, which being frozen, they sailed for the island of Antiqua in the West Indies. They suffered much from lack

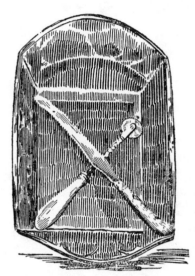

of food and from scurvy, from which many died, among the latter being the captain himself. Out of 200 passengers only 19 survived, besides the helmsman and two sailors. It is said they were Suabians and it became a second nature to them to use an oath to every second word, and they wished to each other that thunder and lightning would strike them. The kind of religion these people have is not known, but they use a hundred thousand cuss words."

BREAD TRAY, KNIFE AND PIE CRUST SCORER.

From *The Pennsylvania Berichte,* Boston, September 25, 1752:

" On last Tuesday a ship arrived from Holland with 300 Germans, men, women and children. Some of them will settle in Germantown, and the rest in the eastern part of the Province. There were 40 births on board during the voyage. Among the mechanics and artists were a great many glass workers, and a factory will be established for them as soon as possible."

From *The Pennsylvania Berichte,* New York, October 16, 1752:

"During the past week came Captain Pikeman with Palatines."

From *The Pennsylvania Berichte*, October 16, 1752 :
"From a letter received from Charleston, South Carolina, we learn that a vessel reached that harbor after a voyage of 18 weeks' duration. The people were all suffering from hunger and thirst. Another vessel that came from Rotterdam by way of Liverpool, also arrived with a cargo of Palatines, all of whom were fresh and well. When the Captains are stingy and save the money that should be used in buying provisions, the poor passengers die of starvation, while their friends must pay for their deaths. If however the Captains are liberal and buy sufficient food, then it is just to pay for the food."

From *The Pennsylvania Berichte*, Germantown, December 1, 1752 :
"While tyrannical Sea Captains for many years past kept the poor German immigrants in such a plight, that many of them died, the Government of the Province passed a law that when the newly arrived Germans made complaint hereafter, that they were not allowed the room on shipboard that was contracted for, nor the food agreed upon, the Captain should pay a fine of ten pounds. But nevertheless we hear that although the poor people almost died of hunger : when they reached the river Delaware they were informed by the Newlanders that visitors would arrive and would ask them whether they had room enough, and sufficient to eat, then they should all exclaim Yes! yes! but if they complained, they would not be allowed to land under four weeks' time. When the passengers are therefore tired of the sea and ship and of the want

of food, all who were able to do so called out, Yes! yes.
If they complained after they landed, concerning a lack
of food and space, then there was no help for them.   The
tyrannical captains would rather spend a hundred pounds
among Newlanders and visitors than a thousand pounds
in fines."

From *The Pennsylvania Berichte*, March 1, 1753:
" Captain Hyman Thompson, being about to return to
Europe, all those who came over on his Ship, and are still
indebted to him, are notified that the accounts have been
placed in the hands of Mrs. Carl and Alexander Stedmann.
If they do not come forward promptly they will be legally
proceeded against and put into the costs."

From *The Pennsylvania Berichte*, September 16, 1755:
" Many Redemptioners having joined the army in Philadelphia, they will again be delivered to their former masters.   They are sharply questioned whether they are
servants, but when they declare they are not, when they
really are, they are whipped."

From *The Pennsylvania Berichte*, Germantown, February 16, 1756:
" We have heard during the past fall that a ship with
Germans was driven on the coast of France and many were
drowned.   The rest were taken to England and sent over
in a merchant vessel to this country, and it is known that
they were five months on the sea, when the ship sprung
a leak which could not be found, compelling all on board
to labor at the pumps for seven days and nights.   At last
they were overtaken by a ship bound for Charleston, when
the Captain of the latter took off sixteen families with the

necessary provisions and nothing else, soon after which the ship went down while the rescued ones reached Carolina."

From *The Pennsylvania Berichte*, Philadelphia, August 16, 1756:
" A ship having arrived from Ireland with servants, some artisans, those interested can call on Thomas Gardens, at Mr. Parnell's wharf, or on the Captain Nathanael Ambler on the ship. They are Irish."

From *The Pennsylvania Staatsbote*, November 9, 1764:
"German Arrivals.
" To-day the ship Boston, Captain Mathem Carr, arrived from Rotterdam, with several hundred Germans. Among them are all kinds of mechanics, day laborers and young people, men as well as women, and boys and girls. All those who desire to procure such servants are requested to call on David Rundle, on Front Street."

From *The Pennsylvania Staatsbote*, December 14, 1773:
" To be sold. A Dutch Apprentice lad, who has five years and three months to serve; he has been brought up to the tailor's business. Can work well."

From *The Pennsylvania Staatsbote*, January 18, 1774:
"German People.
" There are still 50 or 60 German persons newly arrived from Germany. They can be found with the widow Kriderin, at the sign of the Golden Swan. Among them are two Schoolmasters, Mechanics, Farmers, also young children as well as boys and girls. They are desirous of serving for their passage money."

From *The Pennsylvania Staatsbote*, April 25, 1785 :
"For sale, a bound German maid-servant. She is a strong, fresh and sound person, and is not sold because of any defect, but only because she is unsuited to the work she is engaged in. She understands all kinds of farm labor, is very affable and suitable for a hotel. She still has five years to serve."

Not only farmers and mechanics were among these people, but students and schoolmasters also came into this work-market. Pastor Kunze tells us that he himself had this experience : A student who arrived was secured, and with his help a Latin school was started.[128] In 1793 the elders of the Lutheran and Reformed church at Hamburg, Berks county, secured a schoolmaster, John Friedrich Schock, who served them three years and four months, in consideration of having his passage money paid, and receiving the customary outfit (gebräuchlichen Freiheits Kleidung) at the end of his term of service.

As an example of the manner in which the arrivals of ships bringing German passengers whose passage money was unpaid, was brought to public attention, I quote the following announcement from *Bradford's Journal* for September 29, 1773 :

"GERMAN PASSENGERS.

"Just arrived in the ship *Britannia*, James Peter, Master. A number of healthy GERMAN PASSENGERS, chiefly young people, whose freights are to be paid to *Joshua Fisher* and Sons, or to the Master on board the Ship lying off the draw-bridge."

128 *Hallische Nachrichten*, p. 1477.

PENNSYLVANIA-GERMAN FARM LIFE.

MAKING CIDER FOR HOME USE.

From Rupp's collection of names I find this ship had reached Philadelphia eleven days before the advertisement appeared in the newspaper. A reasonable inference is that at that particular time the Redemptioner market was not as brisk as it might have been, and that special efforts were necessary to work off the human cargo. The above-named firm seems to have been largely engaged in the business of bringing over German immigrants.

Here is a partial list of the passengers on the already named ship *Britannia*, prepared in the office of Messrs. Joshua Fisher & Sons, showing the amount of the passage money due by each, as well as some additional expenses incurred by them on the voyage, most probably for provisions, which were never over-abundant and generally insufficient.

Andreas Keym	£26.7
Lena Bekker, his wife	22.2
Expense 16 days	1.12
	£50.1
Hendrick Soueau	£20.15
Dorothea, his wife	20.11
Expenses	1.12
	42.18
John Frederick Camerloo	£23.15
Anna, his wife	22.1
Expenses	1.12
	£47.8
Simon Martz	
Ann, his wife	
Anna Margaretta, daughter	
Expenses	£ 2.8

Augustinus Hess £19.1
Maria, wife............................ .... 18.19
Anna Margtta daughter 19.4
Expenses.. .... 2.8
                                                         ─────
                                                         £59.12

Jacob Schott ⎱
Anna, wife   ⎰ £17.1
Expenses...................... .... 1.12
                                                         ─────
                                                         18.13

Christopher Schever ⎱
Anna, wife   ⎰ £50.7
.... 1.12
                                                         ─────
                                                         £51.19

John George Kunkell ⎞
Anna, wife   ⎬ £41.5
Catherina, daughter ⎠
Expenses.. 3.4
                                                         ─────
                                                         £44.9

Jacob Steyheler £19.19
Catharina, wife 17.18
Expenses.. .... 1.12
                                                         ─────
                                                         £39.9

Bernard Schmit   ⎞
Margaretta, wife   ⎬ £61.5
Turgen, son   ⎬
Catharina, daughter ⎠
Expenses.. 3.4
                                                         ─────
                                                         £64.9

Andreas Otto ⎱
Sophi, wife ⎰ ·······································£41.7
Expenses.. 1.12
                                                         ─────
                                                         £42.19

John Danl. Roth ⎱
Anna, wife   ⎰ ·······································£49.8
Expenses.. 1.12
                                                         ─────
                                                         £51.

Jacob Wanner }
Maria wife }..£20.15
Expensse 1.12
                                                   ————
                                                   £22.7

Daniel Spees }
Anna, wife }..£38.17
Expenses.. 1.12
                                                   ————
                                                   £40.9

Christian Habert }
Anna Maria, wife }..£43.4
Expenses.. 1.12
                                                   ————
                                                   £44.16

Daniel Spees Jr. }
Anna, wife }..£36.17
Expenses.. 1.12
                                                   ————
                                                   £38.9

Andreas Kirch }
Anna Maria, wife }.. £44.9
Maria Elizabeth }
Expenses.. 2.8
                                                   ————
                                                   £46.17

Jacob Twytser }
Johanna Barbara, wife }..£42.7
Expenses.. 1.12
                                                   ————
                                                   £43.19

Conrad Foltz }
Susanna, wife }..£51.
Maria, daughter }
Expenses.. 2.8
                                                   ————
                                                   £53.8

William Schwartz }
Anna Maria, wife }..£35.16
Expenses.. 1.12
                                                   ————
                                                   £37.8

Christian Nell ....£20.
Expenses.. .16
                                                   ————
                                                   £20.16

Johann Jeremiah Snell £24.19
Expenses.................... .... .16
                                                                    —————
                                                                    £25.15

Gerrett Benengé...£23.11
Expenses .... .16
                                                                    —————
                                                                    £24.7

Anty. Guerin £21. 3.6
Expenses.. .16.
                                                                    —————
                                                                    £21.19.6

Pierie Mullott...£21.
Expenses.. .16
                                                                    —————
                                                                    £21.16

Gertuna Vogelsand [129] £17.18
                                                                    .16
                                                                    —————
                                                                    £18.14

[129] The original of the foregoing interesting document is among the manuscript collections of the Historical Society of Pennsylvania. Rupp, in his
Thirty Thousand Names, gives the names of the passengers on the *Britannia,*
but not all of them. This list gives additional ones.

ROACH TRAP, BÜGELEISEN AND BREI-PFANNE.

CHAPTER VI.

REDEMPTIONERS OR INDENTURED SERVANTS NOT ALL GER-
MAN. — IRELAND, WALES, SCOTLAND AND ENGLAND CON-
TRIBUTED LARGE NUMBERS TO CARRY ON THE WORK OF
COMMONWEALTH-BUILDING IN PENNSYLVANIA.

> "Be this my home till some fair star
>   Stoops earthward and shall beckon me ;
> For surely Godland lies not far
>   From these green heights and this great sea,
> My friend, my lover, trend this way
>   Not far along lies Arcady."

AN EPHRATA SYMBOL.

WHILE, of course, un-
der the general title
of Redemptioners, I have reference mainly to those of German birth, these people were
composed of nearly every
other nationality that contributed material to the upbuilding of the American com-
monwealths. Such being the
case, and while, when we
find reference to indentured
servants and Redemptioners
in many authors, the refer-
ence, where no direct distinction is made, is to Germans. I
have deemed it quite germane to the subject to devote a few

(217)

paragraphs to those of other nationalities, to the Irish, who, after the Germans, were the most numerous, the English, the Scotch and the Welsh.   There was no legal distinction between any of them prior to the registry law of 1727. The Germans only were required to take the oath of allegiance, that not being required of the others who were already subjects of the British crown.

Furthermore, in the early days of the history of Pennsylvania and the three Lower Counties of New Castle, Kent and Sussex, many of the indentured servants came over as already such, having been either in the service of well-to-do masters at home, or, having been taken into such service there to supply the needed labor on the lands which their masters had already bought from the Proprietary. Once here, all the other conditions were applicable to them as to those from foreign countries.   They received the same outfit upon the completion of their term of service, and were equally entitled to take up fifty acres of land at a nominal annual rental.

Such being the state of the case, the indentured servants, whatever their nationality, naturally fall into the same category and may be considered together.   A further reason for so doing is found in the fact that those writers who have dealt with the general question, have given their attention almost exclusively to those who came from Germany, while the rest have barely received mention and in most cases have been passed by without any reference whatever.

So greatly was the value of colonists regarded by Penn, that when he prepared his frame of laws in England, in 1682, a section was given to the manner in which these persons should be registered, treated and otherwise cared for.   Special advantages were offered to such as should bring along servants. Both the master and the servant were entitled to fifty acres of land upon the conclusion of the latter's term of service, upon special conditions. The servant under the conditions imposed was not necessarily a menial. His standing might be as good as his master's and some were sent here to take charge of the property of owners who remained behind. William Penn himself sent over about a score of such indentured servants, the list of which is still extant.

The result was that during the first decade or two after Penn's acquisition of the Province, a large number of these people were brought over. Evidently, all who could bring servants did so. Either the arrivals were not all registered as the law provided, or else the registry books have been lost. James Claypole was appointed register in 1686 and a registry book in his handwriting is still extant, covering a period of about three years, which in a measure reveals the extent to which these indentured servants were brought into the Province at that time. A few extracts are here quoted from the book.

" Came in the ship Endeavour of London. George Thorp M.ᵣ Richard Hough, of Maxfield in Cheshire husbandman, (Servants) Fran. Hough, Jam: Sutton, Tho. Woodhouse, Mary Woodhouse.

" In ditto shipp: Fran: Stanfield & Grace his wife late of Garton in Cheshire Husbandman. (children) Jam: Mary, Sarah, Eliz: Grace (and) Hannah Stanfield. (Servants) Dan: Browne, Theo: Maxsey, Isa: Broohesby, Rob. Sidbotham, John Smith, Rob.ᵗ Bryan, Wᵐ Rudway, Tho. Sidbotham.

" John Maddock, in ditto shipp. Servants, George Phillips Ralph Duckard.

" The Providence of Scarborough Rob.ᵗ Hopper M.ᵣ Griffith Owen & his wife Sarah and their sone Rob.ᵗ & 2 daughters Sarah & Elenor & 7 servants named Thos. Armes, John Ball 4 years, Robert Lort for 8 years, Alexander Edwards; Jeane, Bridget & Eliza Watts 3 years.

" Henry Baker & Margaret his wife & their Daughters Rachell, Rebecca, Phebey & Hester and Nathan & Samuel their sones. Mary Becket & 10 servts named John Slidell for 4 years, Hen: Slidell 4 yeʳˢ, James Yeates 5 yeⁿ, Jno Hurst 4 yeʳˢ, Tho: ffisher 4 yeʳˢ, John Steadman 4 years, Thos. Candy for Joseph Feoror 4 yeⁿ, Deborah Booth 4 yrs. Joshua Lert 4 years.

" The Bristoll Merchant John Stephens Commander Arrived here the 10ᵗʰ of 9ᵗʰ Month 1685.

" The passengers names are as followeth viz :

" *Jasper Farmer, Senior, his Family* (names given).

" Jasper Farmer Junior's family (names given).

" *Their Servants are as followeth viz.:*

" Ioone Daly, Philip Mayow and Helen his wife, John Mayow, John Whitlce, Nicholas Whitloe, George Fisher, Arthur Smith, Thomas Alferry, Henry Wells, Robert Wilkinson, Elizabeth Mayow, Martha Mayow, Sara Burke, Shebe Orevan, Andrew Walbridge.

" In the Lion of Leverpoole.

"Joseph Fisher & Elizabeth Fisher his wife late of Stillorgin near Dublin in Ireland, Yeoman, born in Elton in Chesire in old England. (Children) Moses, Joseph, Mary, and Marth Fisher.

Servants.	Time to Serve.	Payment in Money.	Acres of Land.
Edward Lancaster..........	4	£4.10	50
W. Robertson..............	4	—	50
Ed. Doyle.........	4	—	50
Ben: Cilft..............	4	—	50

Servants.	Time to Serve.	Payment in Money.	Acres of Land.
Tho: Tearewood..........	4	—	50
Robert Kilcarth.............	8	—	50
Peter Long.................	2	6.	50
Phill Packer.................	4	—	50
Wm. Conduit...............	4	3.	50
Mary Toole.................	4	3.	50
Elez: Johnson..............	4		50[130]

REDEMPTIONERS IN DELAWARE.

The Duke of York made provision for the holding of indentured servants in his Colony of Delaware, in 1676. Under the law of September 22d of that year servants were not permitted to give or sell any commodity whatever during their term of service. All were compelled to work at their callings the whole day, with intervals for food and rest. Runaways could be seized and brought back. If cruelly treated by master or mistress, servants could lodge complaint, and if lamed or an eye struck out, they were to be at once freed and due recompense made. If, however, servants complained against their owners without cause, or were unable to prove their case, they were " enjoyned to serve three Months time extraordinary (Gratis) for every such ondue Complaint." No servants except slaves could be assigned over to other masters " by themselves, Executors or Administrators for above the Space of one year, unless for good reasons offered." Finally the law said, " All Servants who have served Dilligently; and faithfully to the benefit of their Masters or Dames five or Seaven yeares, shall not be Sent empty away, and if any have proved unfaithful or negligent in their Service, notwithstanding the good usage of their Masters,

---

[130] *Penna. Magazine of History and Biography*, Vol. VIII., pp. 328–335.

This Indenture MADE the *thirteenth* Day of *May* in the Year of our Lord one thouſand, ſeven hundred and *eighty-four* BETWEEN *Alexander Beard Brougham* in the *County of Antrim* taylor by *Consent of his ſiſter* of the one Part, and *John Dickey of Cullybackey* of the other Part, WITNESSETH, that the ſaid *Alexander Beard* doth hereby covenant, promiſe and grant, to and with the ſaid *John Dickey — his* ——Executors, Adminiſtrators and Aſſigns, from the Day of the Date hereof until the firſt and next Arrival at *Philadelphia* ——in America, and after for and during the Term of *three* ——Years to ſerve in ſuch Service and Employment as the ſaid *John Dickey* —— or *his* Aſſigns ſhall there employ *him* according to the Cuſtom of the Country in the like Kind. In Conſideration whereof the ſaid *Mr. John Dickey* —— doth hereby covenant and grant to and with the ſaid *Alexander Beard* —— to pay for *his* Paſſage, and to find allow *him* Meat, Drink, Apparel and Lodging, with other Neceſſaries, during the ſaid Term; and at the End of the ſaid Term to pay unto *him* the uſual Allowance, according to the Cuſtom of the Country in the like Kind. IN WITNESS whereof the Parties above-mentioned to theſe Indentures have interchangeably put their Hands and Seals, the Day and Year firſt above written.

Signed, Sealed, and Delivered,
in the Preſence of

Esther Dullarn
John Wier

Alex^r Beard

John Dickey

they shall not be dismist till they have made satisfaction according to the Judgment of the Constable and Overseers of the parish where they dwell." [131]

IRISH REDEMPTIONERS.

Almost every writer who has dealt with the Provincial period of our history has had something to say about this servant slavery among the German immigrants, and yet it is rare to find allusions to the Irish servants who either came voluntarily or were sent over, who were also disposed of in precisely the same way, and who were as eminently deserving of the name of "Redemptioners" as any passengers that ever came from the Rhine country. The only distinction I have been able to find between the German and Irish trade is that those who came from the German provinces, while for the most part poor and needy, were nevertheless honest peasants and handicraftsmen, who were not expatriated for any crimes, but who voluntarily forsook their homes to better themselves in Pennsylvania; while, on the other hand, those who came from Ireland did but rarely come of their own free will, were not honorable and industrious members of the body politic, but on the contrary, were largely composed of the criminal classes whom it was deemed desirable to get out of the country, and who were hurried on ship-board by any and every expedient that would accomplish that purpose.

The fact that they were called "Servants" by those who shipped them here, and by those who purchased or hired them, instead of "Redemptioners," as in the case of the Germans, has no significance whatever. The process in both cases was precisely alike. The further fact that fewer of these "Servants" came from Ireland than Ger-

---

[131] *Duke of York's Book of Laws,* 1676–1682, pp. 37–38.

many, and the additional one that they were already citizens of Great Britain and, therefore, not so likely to attract attention, has apparently kept their coming and their conditional servitude out of general sight.

This sending of jailbirds and promiscuous malefactors was not a new idea when put into practice in Pennsylvania.

Irish indentured servants had the reputation of being incorrigible runaways.[132] Franklin's *Pennsylvania Gazette* in almost every issue for many years contained advertisements about runaway servants.

REDEMPTIONERS IN VIRGINIA.

"Conditional servitude under indentures or covenants, had from the first existed in Virginia. The servant stood to his master in the relation of a debtor, bound to discharge the costs of emigration by the entire employment of his powers for the benefit of his creditor. Oppression early ensued: men who had been transported into Virginia at an expense of eight or ten pounds, were sometimes sold for forty, fifty, or even threescore pounds. The supply of white servants became a regular business; and a class of men, nic-named 'spirits,' used to delude young persons, servants and idlers, into embarking for America, as to a land of spontaneous plenty. White servants came to be a usual article of traffic. They were sold in England to be transported, and in Virginia were resold to the highest bidder; like negroes, they were to be purchased on shipboard, as men buy horses at a fair. In 1672, the average price in the colonies, where five years of service were due, was about ten pounds; while a negro was worth twenty or twenty-five pounds. So usual was this manner of dealing in Englishmen, that not the Scots only, who were taken

---

[132] JOHN RUSSELL YOUNG'S *Memorial History of Philadelphia.*

on the battlefield of Dunbar, were sent into involuntary servitude in New England, but the royalist prisoners of the battle of Worcester; and the leaders in the insurrection of Penruddoc, in spite of the remonstrances of Haselrig and Henry Vane, were shipped to America. At the corresponding period, in Ireland the crowded exportation of Irish Catholics was a frequent event, and was attended by aggravations hardly inferior to the atrocities of the African slave trade. In 1685, when nearly a thousand of the prisoners, condemned for participating in the insurrection of Monmouth, were sentenced to transportation, men of influence at court, with rival importunity, scrambled for the convicted insurgents as a merchantable commodity." [133]

It is a curious fact that during the administration of Governor Thomas, 1740-1747, the enlisting of indentured or bought servants—Redemptioners—as soldiers, was permitted to be put into execution, England being then at war with Spain. It was an innovation and injurious to many. John Wright, an old and most worthy Lancaster county magistrate and member of the Assembly having denounced the practice, was dismissed from his office. Proud says: "The number of bought and indentured servants who were thus taken from their masters, as appears by the printed votes in the Assembly, were about 276, whose masters were compensated by the Assembly for their loss sustained thereby, to the amount of about £2,588." [134]

IN IRELAND ALSO.

While it appears there were agents in England and Ireland engaged in the business of hunting up immigrants for

---

[133] BANCROFT'S *History of the United States.* Boston Ed., 10 vols. Vol. I., pp. 175-176.
[134] PROUD'S *History of Pennsylvania*, Vol. II., p. 220.

sale and service in Pennsylvania, and that these dealers in human poverty were as base and unscrupulous as the New-landers who zigzagged across Germany on the same mission, it is nevertheless an established fact that it was an authorized business, recognized by law as well as sanctioned by custom, and that a number of honorable men, of excellent standing in their respective communities on both sides of the water were engaged in this servant traffic, for servants these people were called and not redemptioners.

ONE OF THE CLOISTER BUILDINGS AT EPHRATA.

Mr. Benjamin Marshall was a Philadelphia merchant, shipper and importer. His father was the celebrated diarist Chistopher Marshall, of Revolutionary memory, a born Irishman, but a true and unswerving supporter of the patriot cause. I present several letters written by Benjamin Marshall to his business correspondents in Ireland, which throw much light on this part of my subject and are of genuine historical value. The first one is as follows:

> "Philadelphia, November 9, 1765.
> "To Barney Egan:
> "Should thee have a mind (to send) a Vessel this Way, about 100 Men and Boys Servants with as many passengers as could be got, so as to be here by the Middle

or Latter end of May, I think might answer well. Stout, able Laboring men & Tradesmen out of the Country with Young Boys & Lads answers best. Women are so troublesome (that) it would be best to send few or none, as there is often so many Drawbacks on them. This I mention should thee have any intention of sending a Vessel this way for any thing."

Mr. Marshall was seemingly desirous that a ship-load of Irish Servants should be consigned to his house in the spring of 1766; so to make sure of it he wrote another letter on the same day to another Irish correspondent as follows:

"Philadelphia, November 9, 1765.

" To Thomas Murphy :

" The chief articles that answer here from Ireland which can be brought are Linnens, (which ought to go to Liverpool to receive the Bounty) Beef, Butter, Men, Women & Boys Servants the less Women the better as they are very troublesome, and the best time for Servants is about the month of May."

A year later Mr. Marshall again writes to the correspondent first named, the following letter :

"Philadelphia, June 7th, 1766.

" To Barney Egan, Esq. :

" Irish servants will be very dull such numbers have already arrived from Different parts & many more expected, that I believe it will be over done, especially as several Dutch vessels are expected here, which will always command the Market. Captain Power I believe has near sold all his, he being pretty early." [135]

---

[135] *Pennsylvania Magazine of History and Biography*, Vol. XX., pp. 210–212.

The fact is, this traffic was profitable all around. We have seen how the agent made it pay in securing the immigrants; how the ship masters coined money out of it in a number of ways, most of which were disreputable, and, finally, how even respectable merchants on this side of the water were prompt to take a hand in disposing of these cargoes of human beings for the money that was in the business: for when has money failed to carry the day?

I have found in a very long letter written in October, 1725, by Robert Parke, from Chester township in Delaware county, to Mary Valentine, in Ireland, the following interesting passage, which throws much light on the subject of indentured servants: the writer recommended that his old friend might indenture some of his children if he had not sufficient means to pay all the passage money.

"I desire thee may tell my old friend Samuel Thornton that he could give so much Credit to my words & find no Iffs nor ands in my Letter that in Plain terms he could not do better than Come here, for both his & his wife's trade are very good here, the best way for him to do is to pay what money he Can Conveniently Spare at that Side & Engage himself to Pay the rest at this side & when he Comes here if he Can get no friend to lay down the money for him, when it Comes to the worst, he may hire out 2 or 3 Children & I wod have him Cloath his family as well as his Small Ability will allow, thee may tell him what things are proper to bring with him both for his Sea Store & for his Use in this Country. I wod have him Procure 3 or 4 Lusty Servants & Agree to pay their passage at this Side he might sell 2 & pay the others passage with the money. * * * " [136]

[136] *Pennsylvania Magazine of History and Biography*, Vol. V., p. 357.

ROCKING MEAT CHOPPER, SHEEP SHEARS, ETC.

DOMESTIC UTENSILS.

A KITCHEN OUTFIT.

The following letters from the then British Consul in Philadelphia, are of exceeding interest. They show not only that this traffic was still active at the time they were written, but give actual figures indicating that while the arrival of German Redemptioners had greatly declined, those from Ireland were pouring in more numerously than ever.

" Philadelphia, September 22, 1789.

" To the Duke of Leeds :

" * * * Few indentured servants have arrived since the Peace 'till the present year,—In the course of which many hundreds have arrived in the Delaware from Ireland alone and more are expected. Some have been imported into Maryland but not in so great a proportion as into Pennsylvania. The trade is a lucrative one and will be pursued eagerly unless proper obstacles are thrown in the way which I humbly presume may be done upon principles perfectly consistent with the (English) constitution ; having in view so humane a purpose as the providing for the convenience and comfort of the unwary emigrants so often seduced from their country by the force of artful and false suggestions. * * * They pass the term of their servitude and when that expires they for the most part continue laborers for years in the neighborhood where they have served, having no immediate means to enable them to settle lands[137] or to enable them to migrate to a distant country ; the mere temporary loss of labor of this description of people is an object of great consequence to any country, but when it is considered that few of them ever return to their native land, the importance of their loss is immensely aggravated.   " P. Bond."

---

[137] This is a mistake ; they could take up fifty acres of land, as has already been stated, at a rent of one cent per acre, annually, if they so desired.

"Philadelphia, November 10, 1789.

"To the Duke of Leeds:

"* * * The migration hither since the Peace, my Lord, have been much greater from Ireland than from all other parts of Europe. Of 25,716 passengers (Redemptioners and Servants) imported into Pennsylvania since the Peace, 1,893 only were Germans, the rest consisting of Irish and some few Scotch. Of these (2,176) imported during the present year, 114 only were Germans. An almost total stop has been lately put to the migration hither from the Palatinate and other parts of Germany, so that the few who now come hither from that country, get into Holland by stealth and embark at Amsterdam and Rotterdam, and these are very ordinary people. * * * As to the condition and treatment of these people, many were crowded into small vessels destitute of proper room and accommodations, and abridged of the proper allowance of food. They suffered greatly and contagious diseases were often introduced into the Province by them. The terms, too, of paying the passage money were frequently departed from: passengers who embarked as Redemptioners were hurried from on ship board before the limited time for their redemption was expired, and before their friends could have notice of their arrival to interpose their relief and rescue them from servitude." [138]

Phenias Bond was the British Consul at Philadelphia during 1787–1788 and 1789. He was born in Philadelphia in 1749 and was the son of Dr. Phineas Bond and Wilhelmina Moore, and a nephew of the distinguished Dr. Thomas Bond, of the University of Pennsylvania. His royalistic tendencies during the Revolution resulted in his

---

[138] *Annual Report of the American Historical Association*, 1896, Vol. I., pp. 619–620.

arrest as a public enemy, but he was subsequently released on parole. From his private and public stations he was certainly acquainted with the situation.[139]

James Logan did not look with a kindly eye on the arrival of any nationality save Englishmen. This dislike seems to have extended to the Irish, albeit he himself was Irish born. In the Logan MSS are found frequent allusions expressive of this frame of mind. In 1725 he says : " There are so many as one hundred thousand acres of land, possessed by persons, (including Germans), who resolutely set down and improved it without any right to it," and he is much at a loss

MYSTIC SEAL OF THE EPHRATA BRETHRRN.

to determine how to dispossess them. In 1729 he expresses himself as glad to find that Parliament is about to take measures to prevent the too free immigration to this country. In that year the twenty-shilling tax on every servant arriving was laid but even that was evaded by the captain of a ship arriving from Dublin, who landed one hundred convicts and papists at Burlington, thus escaping the tax. It looks, he says, as if Ireland is to send all her inhabitants hither, for last week not less than six ships arrived, and every day two or three arrive also. The common fear is, that if they continue to come, they will make themselves proprietors of the province. It is strange, he says, that they thus crowd where they are not wanted.

---

[139] I am indebted to S. M. Sener, Esq., for having drawn my attention to the above valuable letters.

But, besides, convicts are imported thither.[140]   The Indians
themselves were alarmed at the swarms of strangers, and
he was afraid of a breach between them, for the Irish were
very rough to them.

In 1730 he returns to the same subject and complains
of the Scotch-Irish, " who were acting in a very disorderly
manner and possessing themselves of Conestoga Manor,
fifteen thousand acres, being the best land in Lancaster
county.   In doing this by force, they alleged that it was
against the laws of God and nature, that so much land
should be idle, while so many Christians wanted it to labor
on, and to raise their bread." [141]

There can be no doubt that some of these German and
Irish immigrants gave the Proprietary a great deal of trouble.   They availed themselves of all the advantages they
were able to secure and very often concerned themselves
very little whether they complied with the laws of the
Province or not.   Secretary Logan more than once refers
to this matter in his correspondence.   In a letter to John
Penn, dated November 25, 1727, he says:

" We have many thousands of foreigners, mostly Pala-
tinates, so called, already in yᵉ Countrey, of whom nearly
1,500 came in this last summer;   many of them are a sur-
ley people, divers Papists amongst them, & yᵉ men generally well arm'd.   We have from the North of Ireland,
great numbers yearly, 8 or 9 Ships this last ffall discharged at Newcastle.   Both these sorts sitt frequently
down on any spott of vacant Land they can find, without
asking questions;   the last Palatines say there will be

---

[140] One Augustus Gun, of Cork, advertised in the Philadelphia papers that
he had powers from the Mayor of Cork, for many years to procure servants for
America.   (RUPP'S *History of Berks and Lebanon Counties*, p. 115.)

[141] Quoted by RUPP in his *History of Berks and Lebanon Counties*, pp.
114-115.

twice the number next year, & ye Irish say ye same of their People; last week one of these latter (ye Irish) applied to me, in the name of 400, as he said, who depended all on me, for directions where they should settle. They say the Proprietor invited People to come & settle his Countrey, that they are come for that end, & must live; both they and the Palatines pretend they would buy, but not one in twenty has anything to pay with." [142]

In 1729, John, Thomas and Richard Penn wrote to Logan as follows concerning this vexed question :

"As to the Palatines, you have often taken notice of to us, wee apprehend have Lately arrived in greater Quantities than may be consistent with the welfare of the Country, and therefore, applied ourselves to our Councill to find a proper way to prevent it, the result of which was, that an act of assembly should be got or endeavoured at, and sent us over immediately, when we would take sufficient Care to get it approved by the King. [143] With this resolution we acquainted the Govenour, by Capt String-fellow, to Maryland, the 25th Feb^ry, a Duplicate of which we have since sent by another shipp, both wch times we also enclos'd Letters for thee; but as to any other people coming over who are the subjects of the British Crown, we can't Conceive it anyways practicable to prohibit it : but supposing they are natives of Ireland & Roman Catholicks, they ought not to settle till they have taken the proper Oaths to the King, & Promis'd Obedience to the Laws of the Country, and, indeed, we Can't Conceive it unreasonable that if they are Inclinable to settle, THEY SHOULD BE OBLIG'D TO SETTLE, EITHER BACKWARDS TO

---

[142] *Pennsylvania Archives:* Second Series, Vol. VII., pp. 96–97.

[143] All laws passed by the Provincial Assembly were subject to the approval of the Crown. Frequently action on them was delayed for long periods, and sometimes they were not acted on at all.

234   *The Pennsylvania-German Society.*

This *INDENTURE* Witnesseth that

John Spelman a Shoemaker

doth Voluntarily put *him* self Servant *to Hugh Lyle Master of the Ship Harmony*

to serve the said *Hugh Lyle*
and his Assigns, for and during the full Space, Time and Term of *three 1/2* Years from the first Day of the said *John's* arrival in *Baltimore* – in the United States of AMERICA, during which Time or Term the said Master or his Assigns shall and will find and supply the said *John* with sufficient Meat, Drink, Apparel, Lodging and all other necessaries befitting such a Servant; and at the end and expiration of said Term, the said *John* to be made Free, and receive according to the Custom of the Country. Provided neverthelefs, and these Prefents are on this Condition, that if the said *John* shall pay the said *Hugh Lyle* or his Assigns *ten Pounds British £ in twenty one* Days after *his* arrival *he* shall be Free, and the above Indenture and every Claufe therein, absolutely Void and of no Effect. In Witnefs whereof the said Parties have hereunto interchangeably put their Hands and Seals the *16th* Day of *Feb'y* in the Year of our Lord, One Thousand Seven Hundred and Eighty *four* in the Presence of the Right Worshipful *Richard Kellett Esq'* Mayor of the City of Cork

A REDEMPTIONER'S CERTIFICATE.

S<small>ASQUEHANNAH</small> <small>OR</small> <small>NORTH</small> <small>IN</small> Y<small>ˣ</small> C<small>OUNTRY</small> <small>BEYOND</small> <small>THE</small> <small>OTHER</small> settlements, *as we had mentioned before in relation to the Palatines;* but we must desire Care may be taken that they are not suffered to settle towards Maryland, on any account."[144]

Just as the Ubii, a German tribe was moved to the banks of the Rhine by the Romans, that they might serve as a guard and outpost against invaders,[145] so did the Government of Penn also try to settle them on the frontiers as a guard against the incursions of the Red men.

Further light is thrown on this interesting question by an original manuscript in the collection of the Historical Society of Pennsylvania. It is "A List of Serv<small>ts</small> Indented on Board the Pennsylvania Packet Capt. Peter Osborne for Philadelphia the 15<small>th</small> day of March, 1775. Coming from a British port, it is of course not mentioned by Rupp nor in Volume XVII. of the second series of State Archives. It gives a list of thirty-seven names of tradesmen, evidently all English, Scotch or Irish, with the amount due the ship owner and the sums for which they were sold, as well as the names of the buyers. This list is too long to be given here, but we will quote a few items:

Benj. Boswell, Baker,	Due £21.4	Sold for £18.		
John Haynes, Hair Dresser,	"	22.4	" "	20.
John Thomas, Smith,	"	26.4	" "	20.
William Avery, Taylor,	"	21.4	" "	20.
W<small>m</small> Edwards, Painter,	"	36.4	" "	20.
W<small>m</small> Chase, Cordwainer,	"	23.4	" "	19.
James Vanlone, Watchfinisher,	"	17.5	" "	21.
W<small>m</small> Longwood, Groom,	"	23.4	" "	20.
Geo. Warren, Labourer,	"	14.7	" "	24.
John Longan, Husbandman,	"	19.5	" "	19.
W<small>m</small> Mitchell, Stone Mason,	"	21.4	" "	20.

[144] *Pennsylvania Archives:* Second Series, Vol. VII., pp. 131–132.
[145] T<small>ACITUS</small>, *Germania*, C. 28.

We here get a glimpse at the sums these servants were sold for, and find that in a majority of cases the amount was less than the cost incurred by their passage across the ocean.

Just how this traffic was profitable to the ship-master or the broker, is not evident from the meager revelations furnished by the paper itself. The explanation probably is that there was a large profit on the extra charges always set against each immigrant, and that a reduction of a few pounds could well be made on each one sold and still leave a handsome surplus on the investment. From other sources we learn that when a passenger died, leaving no

RAZOR CASE, RAZOR AND LANCET.

relative behind to look after his possessions, his chest—and a great oaken chest was the almost invariable accompaniment of the German immigrant—was seized by the ship-master and all its contents appropriated. Even when young children were left by the deceased, their rights were often ignored and whatever of value there may have been was confiscated in the rough, sailor-like fashion of the times, without the slightest regard for the rights of these unprotected and helpless ones. The heart often sinks at the recital of these inhuman proceedings practiced because there were none to protest or defend.

It deserves to be stated that many who came here and were well to do, bringing their servants along, often lost the standing in the community they at first held. They were unable to maintain their old social standing against the democratic spirit which even then prevailed, and in many instances their humble servitors, the Redemptioners, taught to labor in the stern school of adversity, prospered, and in the second and third generations, by their thrift and industry, took the places once held by their old masters.

ARMS OF CITY OF LONDON.

STREET SCENE IN OLD GERMANTOWN.

CHAPTER VII.

CHRISTOPHER SAUR'S NOTABLE LETTERS TO GOVERNOR
MORRIS, PLEADING FOR LEGISLATION LOOKING TO THE
BETTER PROTECTION OF GERMAN IMMIGRANTS IN GENERAL
AND THE GERMAN REDEMPTIONERS IN PARTICULAR.

> " They, wandering here, made barren forests bloom,
>   And the new soil a happier robe assume :
>   They planned no schemes that virtue disapproves.
>   They robbed no Indian of his native groves,
>   But, just to all, beheld their tribes increase,
>   Did what they could to bind the world in peace,
>   And, far retreating from a selfish band,
>   Bade Freedom flourish in this foreign land."

SEAL OF WILLIAM PENN.

CHRISTOPHER SAUR did not confine his efforts for rendering aid to his countrymen to the columns of his wide-awake newspaper. Nor did he confine his energy and activity to words alone. He went among the newly arrived Redemptioners and rendered whatever material assistance was in his power. In certain cases he gave money to relieve their necessities ; in others he

(238)

saw that they were cared for when such care was required, and in still others, the sick and starving wretches were taken to his own home and those of his friends to be cared for and nursed back to health there.   If they died, he saw that they received Christian burial.

But, while ever on the alert to render assistance of this practical kind, he was at work in still other ways, his efforts all being directed towards the end so near his loyal German nature.   His name will always be revered by Pennsylvania-Germans for his unselfish work in the interest of his countrymen, and the two letters in their behalf, addressed to Governor Morris, alone constitute a monument to his memory as enduring as brass or the pyramids of Egypt.   They are here given in grateful memory of his excellent service in the cause of humanity.

CHRISTOPHER SAUR'S FIRST LETTER TO GOVERNOR
MORRIS ON THE TRIALS AND WRONGS OF
THE EARLY GERMAN IMMIGRANTS.

" Germantown, Pa., March 15th, 1755.
" Honored and Beloved Sir :—

" Confidence in your wisdom and clemency made me so free as to write this letter to you.   I would not have it that anybody should know of these private lines, otherwise it would have become me to get a hand able to write in a proper manner and style to a person as your station requireth.

"It is now thirty years since I came to this Province, out of a country where no liberty of conscience was, nor humanity reigned in the house of my then country lord, and where all the people are owned with their bodies to the lord there, and are obliged to work for him six days in every week, viz. : three days with a horse, and three days with a hoe, shovel or spade; or if he cannot come himself, he must send somebody in his place. And when I came to this Province and found everything to the contrary from where I came from, I wrote largely to all my friends and acquaintances of the civil and religious liberty, privileges, etc. and of the goodness I have heard and seen, and my letters were printed and reprinted and provoked many a thousand people to come to this Province, and many thanked the Lord for it, and desired their friends also to come here.

" Some years the price was five pistoles per head freight, and the merchants and the captains crowded for passengers, finding more profit by passengers than by goods, etc.

" But the love for great gain caused Steadman to lodge the poor passengers like herrings, and as too many had not room between decks, he kept abundance of them upon deck; and sailing to the *Southward*, where the people were at once out of their climate, and for the want of water and room, became sick and died very fast, in such a manner that in one year no less than two thousand were buried in the seas and in Philadelphia. Steadman at that time bought a license in Holland that no captain or merchant could load any as long as he had not two thousand loaded. This murderous trade made my heart ache, especially, when I heard that there was more profit by their death than by carrying them alive. I thought of my provoking letters being partly the cause of so many people's deaths. I wrote to the magistrate at Rotterdam, and immediately the *"Monopolium"* was taken from John Steadman.

" Our Legislature was also petitioned, and a law was made as good as it is, but was never executed. Mr. Spofford, an old, poor captain, was made overseer for the vessels that came loaded with passengers, whose salary came to from $200 to $300 a year, for concealing the fact that sometimes the poor people had but twelve inches place and not half bread nor water. Spofford died and our Assembly chose one Mr. Trotter who left every ship slip, although he knew that a great many people had no room at all, except in the long boat, where every man perished. There were so many complaints that many in Philadelphia and almost all in Germantown signed a petition that our Assembly might give that office to one Thomas Say, an English merchant, at Philadelphia, of whom we have the confidence that he would take no bribe for concealing what the poor people suffered; or if they will not turn Mr. Trotter out of office, to give him as assistant one Daniel Mackinett, a shopkeeper in Philadelphia, who speaks Dutch and English, who might speak with the people in their language, but in vain, except they have done what I know not.

"Among other grievances the Germans suffer is one viz: that the ignorant Germans agree fairly with merchants at Holland for seven pistoles and a half [146]; when they come to Philadelphia the merchants make them pay what they please, and take at least nine pistoles. The poor people on board are prisoners. They durst not go ashore, or have their chests delivered, except they allow in a bond or pay what they owe not; and when they go into the country, they loudly complain there, that no justice is to be had for poor strangers. They show their agreements, wherein is fairly mentioned that they are to pay seven pistoles and a half to Isaac and Zacharay Hoke, at Rotterdam, or their order at Philadelphia, etc. This is so much practiced,

---

[146] SAUR here means the price for carrying immigrants from Rotterdam to Philadelphia.

that of at least 2,000 or 3,000 pounds in each year the country is wronged. It was much desired that among wholesome laws, such a one may be made that when vessels arrive, a commissioner might be appointed to inspect their and agreement and judge if 7½ pistoles make not seven and a half. Some of the Assemblymen were asked whether there was no remedy? They answered, ' The law is such that what is above forty shillings must be decided at court, and every one must make his own cause appear

Francis Daniel Pastorius.

good and stand a trial.' A very poor comfort for two or three thousand wronged people, to live at the discretion of their merchants. They so long to go ashore, and fill once their belly, that they submit and pay what is demanded; and some are sighing, some are cursing, and some believe that their case differs very little from such as fall into the hands of highwaymen who present a pistol upon their breast and are desired to give whatever the highwaymen pleaseth; and who can hinder them thinking so? I, myself, thought a commission could be ordered in only such cases, but I observed that our assembly has more a mind to prevent the importation of such passengers than to do justice to them; and seeing that your honor is not of the same mind, and intends to alter the said bill, I find myself obliged to let your Honor know the main points, without which nothing will be done to the purpose.

"I was surprised to see the title of the bill, which, in my opinion, is not the will of the crown, nor of the proprietors; neither is it the will of the Lord, who gives an open way that the poor and distressed, the afflicted, and any people

INTERIOR OF AN OLD BORING-MILL ON THE TULPEHOCKEN. HERE RIFLE BARRELS WERE MADE DURING THE REVOLUTION.

PENNSYLVANIA-GERMAN ENTERPRISE.

THE PENNSYLVANIA-GERMAN SOCIETY.

may come to a place where there is room for them; and if there is no room for any more, there is land enough in our neighborhood, as there are eight or nine counties of Dutch (German) people in Virginia, where many out of Pennsylvania are removed to. Methinks it will be proper to let them come, and let justice be done them. The order of the Lord is such: 'Defend the poor and fatherless; do justice to the afflicted and needy, deliver the poor and needy, and rid them out of the land of the wicked.'— Ps. 82.

" Beloved sir, you are certainly a servant of the Lord our God, and I do believe you are willing to do what lies in your power; but I am ready to think, that as you left the bill to your councillors, you will not be so fully informed of the worst of the grievances, as one of them has a great share of the interest. If these are not looked particularly into, that which is the most complained of viz: that the captains often hurry them away without an agreement, or the agreement is not signed, or, if a fair agreement is written, signed or sealed, it will not be performed, and they must pay whatever they please; and when the people's chests are put in stores until they go and fetch money by their friends, and pay for what they agreed upon, and much more, and demand their chest, they will find it opened and plundered of part or all; or the chest is not at all to be found wherefore they have paid, and no justice for them, because they have no English tongue, and no money to go to law with such as they are; and that we have no such an officer as will, or can speak with the people but will rather take pay for concealing their grievances—and who will speak to such an one, as it stands?

" The law is, that ' a man may get security as good as he can.' But when merchants BIND some other people together, whose families were obliged to die, and who are famished for want, and as a prisoner at the vessel is retained and forced to bind himself—one for two or three, who are greatly indebted and who, perhaps, pays his own debt while the others can't—he is freed to go out of the country, and will go rather than go to prison; and if poor widows are bound for others much in debt, who will marry such a one? Must she not go sorrowful most of her lifetime?

EARLY COFFEE MILL.

"Formerly, our Assembly has bought a house on an island in the river Delaware, where healthy people will soon become sick. This house might do very well in contagious distempers, but if a place were allowed on a healthy, dry ground—where, by a collection, the Germans might build a house, with convenient places, and stoves for winter, etc.; it would be better for the people in common sickness where their friends might attend them and take care of them. They would do better than to perish under the merciless hands of these merchants; for life is sweet.

"Beloved sir, I am old and infirm, bending with my staff to the grave, and will be gone by and by, and hope that your Honor will not take it amiss to have recommended to you the helpless. We beg and desire in our prayers that the Lord may protect you from all evil, and from all encroachments, and if we do the like unto them that are in poor condition and danger, we may expect the Lord will do so to us accordingly; but, if we do to the contrary, how can we expect the Lord's protection over us? For He promises to measure to us as we do measure.

"I conclude with a hearty desire that the Lord will give your Honor wisdom and patience, that your administration may be blessed, and in His time give you the reward of a good, true and faithful servant, and I remain your humble servant,

"Christoph Saur,
"Printer in Germantown."

For some reason, Governor Morris, who was on bad terms with the House, did not regard the proposed bill favorably although he had recommended such a measure himself in a message to the House on December 12th of the previous year.[147] This angered the Assembly who sent him a sharp message on May 15, 1755, part of which is here given. "* * * The grevious Calamities we were then threatened with, the melancholy Spectacle of the Distress of so many of our Fellow Creatures perishing for Want of Change of Apparel, Room, and other necessaries on board their Ships, and after being landed among Us the extreme Danger of the Benevolent and the Charitable exposed them to in approaching those unhappy Sufferers, together with the Governor's own Recommendation, gave Us Reason to hope that he might be at Liberty and that his own Inclinations would have induced him to have passed such a Bill as might prevent the like for the future, but we are under the greatest Concern to find Ourselves disappointed in these our reasonable Expectations.

---

[147] *Colonial Records*, Vol. VI., p. 190.

"By our Charters and the Laws of this Province the whole Legislative Power is vested in the Governor and the Representatives of the People; and as we know of no other Negative upon our Bills but what the Governor himself has, we could wish he had been pleased to exercise his own Judgment upon this our Bill without referring the Consideration of it to a Committee of his Council most of them Such, as We are informed, *who are or have lately been concerned in the Importations, the Abuses of which this bill was designed to regulate and redress.*

"The German Importations were at first and for a considerable Time of such as were Families of Substance and industrious, sober, People, who constantly brought with them their Chests and Apparel and other Necessaries for so long a voyage. But these we apprehend have for some time past been shipped on board other vessels in order to leave more Room for crowding their unhappy Passengers in greater Numbers, and to secure the Freights of such as might perish during the voyage, which experience has convinced us must be the Case of very many where such Numbers (as have been lately imported in each Vessel) are crowded together without Change of Raiment or any other Means of Keeping themselves sweet and clean. But this Provision the Governor has been pleased to throw out of our Bill; and yet we think it so essentially necessary that the Want of it must necessarily poisen the Air those unhappy Passengers breathe on Shipboard, and spread it wherever they land to infect the Country which receives them, especially as the Governor has likewise altered the Provision We had made by the Advice of the Physicians for accommodating them with more Room and Air upon their Arrival here.

"We have reason to believe that the Importations of

CONTINENTAL CURRENCY PRINTED AT EPHRATA.
Fac-simile of an uncut sheet, by Julius F. Sachse.

Germans have been for some Time composed of a great Mixture of the Refuse of their People and that the very Gaols have contributed to the Supplies We are burdened with. But as there are many of more Substance and better Character, We thought it reasonable to hinder the Importer from obliging such as had no connections with one another to become jointly bound for their respective Freights or Passages; but the Governor has thought fit to alter this also in such a manner as to elude the good Purposes intended by the Act, by which means those who are of more Substance are involved in the Contracts and Debts of Others, and the Merchants secured at the Expence of the Country where they are necessitated and do become very frequently Beggars from Door to Door, to the great Injury of the Inhabitants, and the Increase and Propogation of the Distempers they have brought among us. Many who have indented themselves for the Payment of their Passages have frequently been afflicted with such frequent and loathesome Diseases at the time as have rendered them altogether unfit for the Services they had contracted to perform, for which we had provided a remedy by the Bill; but the Governor has thought fit to strike it out and leave Us exposed to this grevious Imposition without a Remedy," etc.

It was this action on the part of the Governor Morris that called out Christopher Saur's second letter, which is also given.

Two months later this staunch and steady friend of his countrymen, whose wrongs were daily brought under his notice, again wrote to Governor Morris on this subject, as follows :

" Germantown, Pa., May 12, 1755.
''*Honored and Beloved Sir:*
"Although I do believe with sincerity, that you have

at this time serious and troublesome business enough, nevertheless, my confidence in your wisdom makes me to write the following defective lines, whereby I desire not so much as a farthing of profit for myself.

" When I heard last that the Assembly adjourned, I was desirous to know what was done concerning the Dutch bill and was told that your Honor have consented to all points, except that the German passengers need not have their chests along with them ; and because you was busy with more needful business, it was not ended.   I was sorry for it, and thought, either your Honor has not good counsellers or you cant think of the consequences, otherwise you could not insist on this point.   Therefore I hope you will not take it amiss to be informed of the case, and of some of the consequences, viz. :—The crown of England found it profitable to peopling the American colonies ; and for the encouragement thereof, the coming and transportation of German Protestants was indulged, and orders were given to the officers at the customhouses in the parts of England, not to be sharp with the vessels of German passengers—knowing that the populating of the British colonies will, in time become, profit more than the trifles of duty at the customhouses would import in the present time. This the merchants and importers experienced.

" They filled the vessels with passengers and as much of the merchant's goods as they thought fit, and left the passengers' chests &c behind, and sometimes they loaded vessels wholly with Palatines' chests.   But the poor people depended upon their chests, wherein was some provision, such as they were used to, as dried-apples, pears, plums, mustard, medicines, vinegar, brandy, gammons, butter, clothing, shirts and other necessary linens, money and whatever they brought with them ; and when their chests

were left behind, or were shipped in some other vessel they
had lack of nourishment. When not sufficient provision
was shipped for the passengers, and they had nothing
themselves, they famished and died. When they arrived
alive, they had no money to buy bread,
nor anything to sell. If they would spare
clothes, they had no clothes nor shirt to
strip themselves, nor were they able to
cleanse themselves of lice and nastiness.
If they were taken into houses, trusting
on their effects and money, when it
comes, it was either left behind, or robbed and plundered by the sailors behind
or in the vessels. If such a vessel arrived before them, it was searched by
the merchants' boys, &c., and their best
effects all taken out, and no remedy for
it, and this last mentioned practice, that
people's chests are opened and their best
effects taken out, is not only a practice
this twenty five, twenty, ten or five
years, or sometime only; but it is the
common custom and daily complaints to
the week last past; when a pious man,
living with me, had his chest broken open
and three fine shirts and a flute taken out.
The lock was broken to pieces and the
lid of the chest split with iron and
chisels. Such, my dear Sir, is the case,
and if your honor will countenance the
mentioned practices, the consequences

CLOCK OF THE PRO-
VINCIAL PERIOD.

will be, that the vessels with passengers will be filled with
merchant's goods, wine, &c., as much as possible, and at

the King's custom they will call it passengers' drink, and
necessaries for the people, then household goods, &c., which
will be called free of duty. And if they please to load the
vessels only with chests of passengers and what lies under
them, that will be called also free of duty at the customhouses; and as there are no owners of the chests with
them, and no bill of loading is ever given, nor will be
given, the chests will be freely opened and plundered by
the sailors and others, and what is left will be searched
in the stores by the merchants' boys and their friends and
acquaintances. Thus, by the consequence, the King will
be cheated, and the smugglers and store boys will be glad
of your upholding and encouraging this, their profitable
business; but the poor sufferers will sigh or carry a re-
venge in their bosoms, according as they are godly or un-
godly, that such thievery and robbery is maintained.

"If such a merchant should lose thirty, forty, fifty or
ten thousand pounds, he may have some yet to spend and
to spare, and has friends, but if a poor man's chest is left
behind, or plundered either at sea or in the stores he has
lost all he has. If a rich man's store, or house, or chest
is broken open and robbed or plundered there is abundance
of noise about it; but if 1,000 poor men's property is taken
from them, in the manner mentioned, there is not a word to
be said.

"If I were ordered to print advertisements of people
who lost their chests, by leaving them behind against their
will, or whose chests were opened and plundered at sea,
when they were sent after them in other vessels, or whose
were opened and plundered in the stores of Philadelphia—should come and receive their value for it, (not four
fold) but only single or half; your honor would be wondering
of a swarm from more than two or three thousand people.

But as such is not to be expected, it must be referred to
the decision of the great, great, long, long day, where
certainly an impartial judgment will be seen, and the last
farthing must be paid, whereas in this present time, such
poor sufferers has, and will have no better answer than is
commonly given: 'Can you prove who has opened and
stolen out of your chest?' or 'Have you a bill of loading?' this has been the practice by some of the merchants
of Philadelphia, and if it must continue longer, the Lord
our God must compare that city to her sister Sodom, as he
said: 'Behold this was the iniquity of Sodom: pride,
fullness of bread and abundance of idleness was in her.
Neither did she strengthen the hand of the poor and needy
(Ezekiel, 16:40) but rather weakened the hand of the
poor and needy' (18:2)."

* * * * * * * * *

In a postscript, as if he could not write too often or too
forcibly of the wrongs of these poor people, he adds, con-
veying a threat:

"The Lord bless our good King and all his faithful
ministers, and your Honor, and protect the city of Philadelphia and country from all incursions and attempts of
enemies. But if you should insist against a remedy for
the poor Germans' grievances—although no remedy is to
be had for that which is past—and an attempt of enemies
should ensue before the city of Philadelphia, you will certainly find the Germans faithful to the English nation; as
you might have seen how industrious they are to serve the
King and government, for the protection of their substance, life and liberties. But, as there are many and
many thousands who have suffered injustice of their merchants at Philadelphia, it would not be prudent to call on
them all for assistance, as there are certainly many wicked

among the Germans; which, if they should find themselves overpowered by the French, I would not be bound
for their behaviour, that they would not make reprisals on
them that picked their chests and forced them to pay what
they owed not! and hindered yet the remedy for others.
No! if they were all Englishmen who suffered so much, I
would much less be bound for their good behaviour.

"Pray sir do not look upon this as a trifle; for there are
many Germans, who have been wealthy people are many
Germans, who have lost sixty, eighty, one, two, three,
four hundred to a thousand pounds' worth, by leaving their
chests behind, or were deprived and robbed in the stores,
of their substance, and are obliged now to live poor, with
grief. If you do scruple the truth of this assertion, let
them be called in the newspaper, with hopes for reme-
dies, and your Honor will believe me; but if the Dutch
(German) nation should hear that no regard is for them,
and no justice to be obtained, it will be utterly in vain to
offer them free schools—especially as they are to be reg-
ulated and inspected by one who is not respected in all
this Province.

"I hope your Honor will pardon my scribbling; as it has
no other aim than a needful redressing of the multitude of
grievances of the poor people, and for the preserving of
their lives and property, and that the Germans may be ad-
hered to the friendship of the English nation, and for securing the honor of your Excellency, and not for a farthing
for your humble servant.

                                "Christopher Saur,
                                "Printer of Germantown."

It will be noted that both the Assembly and Saur averred
that some of the members of the Governor's Council were
engaged in this most disreputable business, and it may be

that the influence of these interested persons was at the bottom of his rejection of the measures proposed to remedy these evils. On the day following the delivery of the message of the House to the Governor, the latter replied with equal acerbity. He briefly gives his reasons for his action in the matter, but they are lame and unsatisfactory, strengthening the belief that he was trying to take care of his friends.

It is said of the elder Christopher Saur that "on learning from time to time that a vessel containing passengers had arrived in Philadelphia from Germany, he and his neighbors gathered vehicles and hastened to the landing place, whence those of the newcomers who were ill, were taken to his house, which for the time being was turned into a hospital, and there they were treated medically, nursed and supported by him until they became convalescent and able to earn their own living." [148]

[148] CHARLES G. SAUER'S *Address at Memorial Services at the Church of the Brethren*, at Germantown, January 1, 1899.

AN OLD GERMANTOWN LANDMARK.

OLD ROBERT'S MILL, NEAR GERMANTOWN.

CHAPTER VIII.

THE MORTALITY THAT SOMETIMES CAME UPON THE IMMI-
GRANTS ON SHIP-BOARD.—ORGANIZATION OF THE GERMAN
SOCIETY OF PENNSYLVANIA, AND ITS EXCELLENT WORK.—
LANDS ASSIGNED TO REDEMPTIONERS AT THE END OF THEIR
TERMS OF SERVICE, ON EASY TERMS.

"Er ward in engen Koje Kalt,
Kam nie zurück zum Port.
Man hat ihn auf ein Brett geschnallt,
Und warf ihn über Bord."

"Dem bieten grane Eltern noch
Zum letztenmal die Hand ;
Den Koser Bruder, Schwester, Freund ;
Und alles schweigt, und alles weint,
Todtbloss von uns gewandt."

ARMS OF THE PALATINATE.[149]

IN a general way, the mortality among the immigrants resulting from the crowded condition of the ships, the bad character of the provisions and water and frequently from the scant supply of the same, the length of the voyage and other causes, has al-

[149] The arms, or *wappen*, of the Palatinate is an imposing piece of heraldic art, sufficient, one would think, to do honor to a land a thousand times the size

(256)

ready been alluded to. But it is only when we come down to an actual presentation of the records that have reached our day, that we get a correct idea of the appalling character of the death rate upon which the German settlements in Pennsylvania were built. Doubtless something beyond the ordinary was seen in the migration from Europe to other portions of the American continent, but as that migration was more circumscribed in its numbers and the rapidity of its inflow, so also was the death rate attending it on a minor scale. It is surprising that the reality, as it became known in the Fatherland, did not hold back the multitudes anxious to come over. Perhaps the ebb and flow, as we now know it, greater in some years, and then again greatly diminished in others, may be accounted for by the fears that came upon the intending immigrants as letters from friends gradually drifted back to the old home. Some

---

of the Palatinate. Even the shield of Achilles, as pictured by Homer, was not more elaborate or picturesque. Its manifold armorial divisions arose out of the numerous changes and acquisitions to the original fief. I subjoin a description of it in German, without venturing on a translation.

Das Kurpfälsichen wappen bestehet aus zusam mengebrunden ovalrunden Schilden. Der 1. ist quadrirt mit einem Mittelschilde, welcher im Schwartzen Felde einem goldenen rothgeprouren Löwen, wegen der Pfaltz am Rhein hat. Das 1. Quartier des Haupt-Schilders ist vom Silber und Blau, Schraggeweckt, wegen Baiern ; in 2. goldenen ist ein Schwazer gekrärter Löwe, wegen Julich : im 3. bauen ein silbernes Schildchen, aus dem 8. goldene Stabe im Kreis gesetzt, heroorgehen, wegen Cleve ; im 4. silbernen is ein rother Löwe, mit einer blauen Krone, wegen Berg. Der 2. Hauptschild ist quergetheilt. In der abern Hälfte, in goldenem Felde, ist vorn ein Schwarzer Querbalken, wegen der Grafschaft Mors ; hintem im blauen, 3. goldene Kreuzchen, über einem dreyfachen grünen Hügel, wegen Bergen op Zoom. Die untere Hälfte ist 3 mal in die Länge getheilt. Im vordersten silbernen Felde ist ein Blauer Löwe, wegen Veldenz ; im mittlern goldenen ein von Silber und Roth, zu 4. Reihen geschackter Querbalken, wegen der Graffschaft Mark, im hintersten silbernen sind 3 rothe Sparren, wegen Ravensburg. Der 3te rothe Hauptschild enthält den goldenen Reichsapfel, wegen des Erztruchsestenamts. Diese 3. Hauptschilde werden von dem Kurhute bedeckt, und von der Kelte des St. Georgen und St. Hubertordens und des goldenen Bliesses umgeben ; und von 2. Löwen gehalten.

of them must have been of a character to daunt the courage of even the stout-hearted dwellers along the Rhine. We only know that these people continued to pour into the province for more than a century in spite of all the drawbacks that were presenting themselves during all that time.

Although the first large colony of German immigrants to cross the ocean, and that suffered excessive losses on the voyage, did not come to Pennsylvania, it nevertheless deserves special mention here, because it was the largest single body of colonists that ever reached America, and because many of its members eventually found their way into the valleys of the Swatara and Tulpeh ocken. It was the colony sent to the State of New York at the request of Governor Hunter, who happened to be in England when the great German Exodus to London occurred, in 1709. Even the members of this early colony were redemptioners, in fact if not in name. They contracted to repay the British government the expenses incurred in sending them over. They were called "Servants to the Crown." After they had discharged their obligations, they were to receive five pounds each and every family forty acres of land.

Three thousand and more of these people were embarked in midwinter for New York. The exact date is unknown. It was probably some time during the month of January, 1710. The diarist Luttrell says, under date of December 28, 1709, "Colonel Hunter designs, next week to embark for his government at New York, and most of the Palatines remaining here goe with him to people that colony." Conrad Weiser, who was among them, wrote at a late period of his life that "About Christmas-day (1709) we embarked, and ten ship loads with about 4,000 souls were sent to America." Weiser was a lad of thirteen years at the time, and wrote from recollection many years after. As he was wrong in the number who set sail, so he no doubt was as to the time of embarcation. These 3,000 persons of both sexes and all ages were crowded into ten ships. No official register of them is known. The vessels were small and as about 300 persons were crowded into each one, the voyage was a dreary one. By the middle of June seven of the ships had made land; the latest did not arrive until near the close of July—a five months' voyage, and one, the *Herbert*, did not come at all, having been cast ashore on Long Island and lost. The deaths during the voyage were "above 470," writes Governor Hunter, but other authorities place them at a far higher

number. Conrad Weiser, in his old age and without actual data for his estimate, places the loss at 1,700, which is much too high. The best authorities place the number at 859, showing a mortality of more than 25 per cent. Boehme states that "Of some families neither parents nor children survive." Eighty are said to have died on a single ship,

SEAL OF GERMAN-
TOWN.

with most of the living ill. It deserves also to be stated that the children of these maltreated immigrants were by order of Governor Hunter apprenticed among the colonists, which act was bitterly resented by the parents. It was one of the first of the long series of wrongs that befell them. It was no doubt the sorrowful experience of these ten shiploads of Germans that thereafter turned all the immigrants towards Pennsylvania. But one more ship with Palatines went to New York, and that was in 1772. It is even possible this ship was carried out of its course and made port at New York instead of Philadelphia.

Christopher Saur in his first letter to Governor Morris asserts that in a single year two thousand German immigrants found ocean burial while on their way to Pennsylvania.

Caspar Wistar wrote in 1732 : " Last year a ship was twenty-four weeks at sea, and of the 150 passengers on board thereof, more than 100 died of hunger and privation, and the survivors were imprisoned and compelled to pay the entire passage-money for themselves and the deceased. In this year 10 ships arrived in Philadelphia with 5,000 passengers. One ship was seventeen weeks at sea and about 60 passengers thereof died."

Christopher Saur in 1758 estimated that 2,000 of the passengers on the fifteen ships that arrived that year, died during the voyage.

Johann Heinrich Keppele, who afterwards became the first president of the German Society of Pennsylvania, says in his diary that of the 312½ passengers on board the ship in which he came over, 250 died during the voyage.

But it must not be supposed that all ships carrying immigrants encountered the appalling losses we have mentioned. In 1748 I find this in Saur's paper : " Seven ships loaded with German immigrants left Rotterdam ; of these three have arrived in Philadelphia, making the passage from port to port in 31 days, all fresh and well so far as we know. They were also humanely treated on the voyage."

A ship that left Europe in December, 1738, with 400 Palatines, was wrecked on the coast of Block Island. All save 105 had previously died and fifteen of those who landed also died after landing, making a loss of seventy-seven per cent.

A vessel that reached the port of Philadelphia in 1745, landed only 50 survivors out of a total of 400 souls that had sailed away from Europe. In this case starvation was the principal cause of the appalling mortality.

In 1754, the sexton of the Stranger's Burying Ground in Philadelphia, testified under oath that he had buried 253 Palatines up to November 14th, to which " six or eight more should be added." It seems the diseases contracted on ship-board followed them long after they reached Philadelphia.[150]

In February, 1745, Saur said in his newspaper : " Another ship arrived in Philadelphia with Germans. It is said she left port with 400 souls and that there are now not many more than 50 left alive."

" On the 26th of December, 1738, a ship of three hundred tons was wrecked on Block

AN OLD TAR BUCKET, SUCH AS WAS ALWAYS CARRIED BY THE CONESTOGA WAGONS.

Island, near the coast of the State of Rhode Island. This ship sailed from Rotterdam in August, 1738, last from Cowes, England. John Wanton, the Governor of Rhode Island, sent Mr. Peter Bouse, and others, from Newport, to Block Island, to see how matters were. On the 19th of January, 1739, they returned to Newport, R. I., reporting that the ship was commanded by Capt. Geo. Long, that he died on the inward passage, and that the mate then took

---

[150] *Colonial Records*, Vol. VI., p. 173.

charge of the ship which had sailed from Rotterdam with 400 Palatines, destined for Philadelphia, that an exceedingly malignant fever and flux had prevailed among them, only 105 landing at Block Island, and that by death the number had been further reduced to 90. The chief reason alleged for this great mortality was the bad condition of the water taken in at Rotterdam. It was filled in casks that before had contained white and red wine. The greater part of the goods of the Palatines was lost." [151]

It may be stated in this connection that the ship *Welcome*, on which Penn came over in the fall of 1683, was of 300 tons. The small-pox broke out on board and proved fatal to nearly one-third of those on board. [152]

FORMATION OF THE GERMAN SOCIETY.

Despite all the efforts made by private individuals, and the various enactments of the Provincial Assembly, effectual and permanent relief was not destined to come in that way. It was not until a united, influential and determined body of men formed themselves into a corporation and set to work at the task before them with a will, that the dawn at last began to break. It was on Christmas day in 1764 that a number of the most influential German residents in Philadelphia met in the Lutheran School House, on Cherry street and organized the " German Society of Pennsylvania." It was legally incorporated on September 20, 1787, but it did not wait for that legal recognition to begin its work. Its first president was Johann Heinrich Keppele, an opulent and influential merchant of Philadelphia. His efficiency in conducting the affairs of the Society was so clearly recognized that he was annually reëlected to the Presidency for a period of seventeen years.

---

[151] *Pennsylvania Gazette*, February 8, 1739.
[152] WATSON'S *Annals of Philadelphia*, Vol. I., p. 15.

HENRY KEPPELE.

No time was lost in beginning the work mapped out, to do away with the manifold abuses that attended the immigration of Germans, to succor the sick and to lend substantial aid to the needy and deserving. The Assembly was at once taken in hand and certain reforms demanded. The matter came up before that body on January 11, 1765, and an act in nine sections, prepared by the Society, was laid before it, in which the rights of immigrants were provided for while on the sea, and safeguarded after their landing. Objections were at once made by prominent merchants who had previously driven a very profitable trade in Redemptioners, and who saw in the passage of the proposed act an end to their iniquitous but profitable traffic; but it was enacted into a law despite their protests. Governor John Penn, however, refused to sign the act because it was presented to him on the last day of the session. It has been suspected that his principal reason was that he was unwilling to give offense to his many influential English friends whose revenues it was certain would be interfered with.

SEAL OF THE GERMAN
SOCIETY OF PENN-
SYLVANIA.

But the German Society meant business and was not to be turned down by a single rebuff, from whatever source. During the following summer another bill was brought forward, modifying the former one in some particulars. This one was also passed and this time the Governor's signature was added, May 18, 1765. All immigrants who had complaints to make were invited to present them to the Society, which in turn became the champion of these oppressed people. In 1785 it succeeded in procuring legislation providing for the establishment of a Bureau of Registration, and the appointment of an official who could speak both the German and English languages. Previously the newcomers had been haled before the Mayors of the city, to take the necessary oaths ; yet Seidensticker tells us that from 1700 to 1800 there were only two Mayors of Philadelphia who could speak the German language. For a time, this active and unceasing energy put an end to the most serious complaints, but later they again came to the front, and in 1818 still another act, and a more strict and exacting one, was passed, after which these long-continued wrongs finally disappeared.

The Society was of much assistance in a financial way to the needy immigrants, aiding thousands to better their condition, and on the whole did an untold amount of good. It solicited outside contributions but most of the money expended was contributed by the members themselves. It supplied bread, meat and other good and fresh food to the needy ones, but sometimes the need was even greater than the Society's means would allow. It sent the sick to special houses and appealed to the authorities whenever an injustice was brought to its notice. But the Society frequently had its own troubles with those whom it tried to succor. Its generous deeds sometimes failed to satisfy the wishes and expectations of the newcomers. They looked for more. They expected that the Society would also clear the rough land for them and hand it over to them according to the terms of their contracts with the Newlanders, which was of course an impossibility. Some also insisted that the Society should buy their time, clothe and keep all the old, poor, infirm and sick, and give them a decent burial when dead.[153]

---

[153] See MUHLENBERG'S letter in *Hallische Nachrichten*, p. 998.

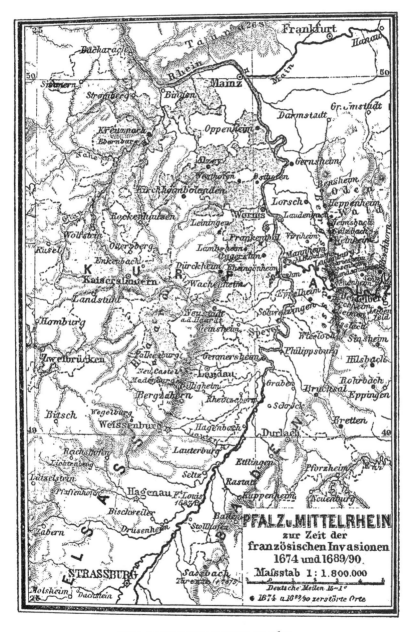

MAP OF THE PALATINATE IN 1690.

Able men presided over the destinies of the Society. The elder Muhlenberg took a warm interest in it and had advised its organization in the *Hallische Nachrichten*. Two of his sons were among its presidents; General Peter Muhlenberg in 1788 and also from 1801 to 1807 and his brother Frederick Augustus Muhlenberg from 1789 to 1797, at the same time that he was serving as Speaker of the Federal House of Representatives. The Society has continued its good work down to our own time. It has not only a fine Society Hall, but an excellent library and a very considerable endowment.

Friedrich Kapp gives a single example out of the hundreds of cases in which the German Society interfered in the interests of persons and families and saw justice done them. It is the case of one George Martin, who, for himself, his wife and five children, two of whom were under five years of age and who under the regular custom should be counted as one full freight, contracted with the captain of the ship *Minerva* to be carried to Pennsylvania for the sum of £9 per head, or £54 for all charges. He advanced forty guilders in Rotterdam, or about $16.66. Martin died on the passage across the ocean. When the rest of the family reached Philadelphia, the three eldest sons were each sold by the captain to five years' service for £30, or £90 in all; the remaining two children under five years of age were disposed of for £10 for the two, in all £100 to pay the £58 agreed upon in the contract. But that was not all; the forty-six-year-old widow was also sold to five years of servitude for £22. The Society secured the widow's release, but she made no objection to the children paying the passage money in the manner indicated.[154]

At the present hour steamship companies are doing

---

[154] FRIEDRICH KAPP, *Die Deutschen im Staate New York*, p. 219.

just what the individual ship owners did one hundred and fifty years ago.   They have their regular agents in Italy, Austria, Germany and Poland, who are painting the old pictures over again, holding up the old attractions and, often in ways far from reputable, securing emigrants to fill their coffers.   In this way we can easily account for the 500,000 persons who have come to this country during the present year.   Before the Chinese exclusion law was passed, thousands of those people were brought here by syndicates and their services sold to those who would have them.   The Padrone system which prevails among the Italian immigrants of the poorer classes is also little else than a revival of the old-time methods that prevailed in the goodly Province of Pennsylvania during the period under consideration.   As practiced now it is shorn of its worst features by the humanity of the times, but the underlying principles are not widely different.

LAND PROVIDED FOR REDEMPTIONERS.

At some time, and somewhere, either by written page or verbal declaration, it was decreed that bond servants should receive at the expiration of their term of service, fifty acres of land from the Proprietary Government at the exceedingly low annual quit rent of two shillings, or about one cent per acre.   Nothing in the various regulations and laws prescribed for the government of the Province was more generous and wise than that.   It was designed to give the newly freed man an opportunity with every other immigrant to get a good start in life.   It cast behind what the man had previously been and recognized him as a free man, entitled to all the rights and privileges of full citizenship.   His quit rent was to be only one-half that which his former master was required to pay. In short, the fullest opportunity was given him to repair his fortunes if his industry and thrift so inclined him.

But all my researches to trace the origin of this practice of bestowing these fifty acres of land upon bond servants, have been unavailing. There are many allusions to it scattered throughout the laws regulating the affairs of the Province, as well as among more recent writers, but it is always alluded to as an already existing law. The original decree or place of record is nowhere revealed. For in-

GOURD FOR SEINE FLOAT.

stance, in Penn's "Conditions and Concessions" the seventh section reads as follows : "That for every *Fifty* Acres that shall be allotted to a Servant at the End of his Service, his Quitrent shall be *Two Shillings per Annum*, and the Master or Owner of the Servant, when he shall take up the other *Fifty* Acres, his Quitrent shall be *Four Shillings* by the Year, or if the Master of the Servant (by reason in the Indentures he is so obliged to do) allot out to the Servant *Fifty* Acres in his own Division, the said Master shall have on Demand allotted to him from the Governor, the *One Hundred* Acres at the chief Rent of *Six Shillings per Annum*." [155]   Grahame

---

[155] "Certain Conditions and Concessions agreed upon by William Penn, Proprietary and Governor of the Province of Pennsylvania, and those who are the Adventurers and Purchasers in the same Province, the Eleventh of July, One Thousand Six Hundred and Eighty One."

makes an emphatic declaration about such a law in a paragraph discussing this very article in the "Conditions and Concessions." [156]

Benjamin Furley, the English Quaker and a life-long friend of Penn, whose principal agent he was for the sale of lands in the newly acquired Province, in a letter to a friend sets forth under date of March 6, 1684, certain explanations concerning the conditions granted to settlers. Among other things he has a paragraph relative to

RENTERS.

"To those who have enough money to pay the expense of their passage as well for themselves as for their wives, children, and servants, but upon their arrival have no more money with which to buy lands, the Governor gives full liberty for themselves, their wives, children and servants who are not under the age of sixteen years, whether male or female, each to take fifty acres at an annual rent in perpetuity of an English *dernier* for each acre, which is less than a Dutch *sol*. It will be rented to them and to their children in perpetuity the same as if they had bought the said land. For the children and servants after the term of their service will have expired, in order to encourage them to serve faithfully their fathers and masters, the Governor gives them full liberty for themselves and their heirs in perpetuity, to take for each 50 acres, paying only a little annual rent of two English shillings (Escalins) for 50 acres, which is less than a farthing for each acre. And they and

---

[156] "To the constitutional frame was appended a code of 40 conditional laws. Among them it proclaimed that the rank and rights of freemen of the Province should accrue to all purchasers of a hundred acres of land : to all servants or bondsmen who at the expiration of their engagements should cultivate the quota of land (50 acres) allotted to them by law." (GRAHAME'S *History of Pennsylvania*, pp. 333-334.)

their fathers and masters will be regarded as true citizens. They will have the right of suffrage not only for the election of Magistrates of the place where they live but also for that of the members of the Council of the Province and the General Assembly, which two bodies joined with the Governor are the Sovereignty, and what is much more they may be chosen to exercise some office, if the community of the place where they live considers them capable of it, no matter what their nationality or religion." [157]

It will be seen from the foregoing that these 50 acres of land which were allotted to Redemptioners at the conclusion of their term of service, were not an absolute gift or donation by the Proprietors, as so many writers seem to think, but were rented to them on more reasonable terms than to their masters. I have nowhere found whether other equally favorable concessions were made when the Redemptioner purchased his 50 acres outright or when he after a while preferred exclusive ownership in preference to the payment of quit-rent. Doubtless, in the latter case, he came in on the same footing as any other original purchaser. A recent history ventures upon the following explanation: "The land secured by settlers and servants who had worked out their term of years, was granted in fee under favor which came directly or indirectly from the crown." [158] To the average reader that must appear like an explanation that does not explain, and is incorrect in addition. The regulation did not convey an absolute title to land. It was granted under a reservation and not in fee simple. Every student knows that all the laws passed in the Province were subject to revision by the crown, and

---

[157] See article by Judge S. W. PENNYPACKER in *Pennsylvania Magazine of History and Biography*, Vol. VI., pp. 320–321.

[158] SCHARF & WESTCOTT'S *History of Philadelphia*, Vol. I., p. 134.

therefore whatever law or custom, to be legal, must have received the royal assent. What is much more to the point is when and where that concession to indentured servants was first proclaimed and put upon record. It seems unreasonable that there was no legal authorization of the practice.

ADDENDA.

Long after the foregoing remarks and speculations concerning the time and place where the custom of allowing indentured servitors to take up 50 acres of land at a nominal quit-rent had been written, and after the chapter in which they appear had been printed, I had the good fortune to find the authorization that had so long eluded my search.

On March 4, 1681, King Charles signed the document which gave to William Penn the Province of Pennsylvania. Very soon thereafter Penn wrote an account of his new possessions from the best information he then had. It was printed in a folio pamphlet of ten pages, entitled: " Some ACCOUNT *of the* PROVINCE *of* PENNSILVANIA *in* AMERICA; *Lately Granted under the Great Seal of* ENGLAND *to* WILLIAM PENN, ETC. *Together with Priviledges and Powers necessary to the well-governing thereof. Made publick for the Information of such as are or may be disposed to Transport themselves or Servants into those Parts. London: Printed, and Sold by Benjamin Clark Bookseller in George-Yard Lombard-Street, 1681.*" The title of the tract in fac-simile will be found on page 272.

In this scarce and valuable little tract Penn sets forth the " Conditions " under which he was disposed to colonize his new Province. Condition No. III. reads as follows:

SOME

ACCOUNT

OF THE

PROVINCE

OF

PENNSILVANIA

IN

AMERICA;

Lately Granted under the Great Seal

OF

ENGLAND

TO

William Penn, &c.

Together with Priviledges and Powers necef-
fary to the well-governing thereof.

Made publick for the Information of fuch as are or may be
difpofed to Tranfport themfelves or Servants
into thofe Parts.

LONDON: Printed, and Sold by *Benjamin Clark*
Bookfeller in *George-Yard Lombard-ftreet,* 1681.
PENN'S FIRST PAMPHLET ON HIS AMERICAN POSSESSIONS.

" My conditions will relate to three sorts of people : 1st. Those that will buy : 2dly. Those that take up land upon rent : 3dly. Servants. To the first, the shares I sell shall be certain as to number of acres ; that is to say, every one shall contain five thousand acres, free from any Indian incumbrance, the price a hundred pounds and for the quit-rent but one English shilling or the value of it yearly for a hundred acres ; and the said quit-rent not to begin to be paid till 1684. To the second sort, that take up land upon rent, they shall have liberty so to do paying yearly one penny per acre, not exceeding two hundred acres.—To the third sort, to wit, servants that are carried over, fifty acres shall be allowed to the master for every head, AND FIFTY ACRES TO EVERY SERVANT WHEN THEIR TIME IS EXPIRED. And because some engaged with me that may not be disposed to go, it were very advisable for every three adventurers to send an overseer with their servants, which would well pay the cost."

COAT-OF-ARMS OF GEORGE ROSS, SIGNER OF THE DECLARATION OF INDEPENDENCE, FROM LANCASTER, PA.

THE OLD MARKET SQUARE AT GERMANTOWN.

CHAPTER IX.

The Traffic in Redemptioners as Carried on in the
Neighboring Colonies—Men Kidnapped in the Streets
of London and Deported—Prisoners of War sent to
America and sold into Bondage in Cromwell's Time.

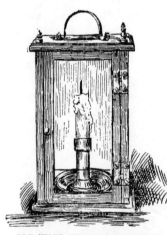

OLD-TIME WOODEN LANTERN.

" God's blessing on the Fatherland,
    And all beneath her dome ;
And also on the newer land
    We now have made our home."

" Ein dichter Kreis von Lieben steht,
    Ihr Brüder, um uns her ;
Uns Knüpft so manches theuere Band
An unser deutsches Vaterland,
Drum fällt der Abschied schwer."

WHILE my discussion
of this question has
special reference to the Province of Pennsylvania, the
trade had so ramified into the
neighboring regions to the
south of us, that a brief glance
at what prevailed there will
assist us in understanding the situation at our own doors.
In fact we may be said to have taken it from them, because

it prevailed there many years before it developed in Pennsylvania. It prevailed in Virginia from an early period, and when Lord Baltimore established his government in his new Province of Maryland, he was prompt to recognize the same system in order to more rapidly secure colonists. In the beginning the term of service there was fixed at five years. In 1638 the Maryland Assembly passed an act reducing it to four years, which remained in force until 1715, when it was amended by fixing the period of service for servants above the age of twenty-five years, at five years; those between the age of eighteen and twenty-five years, at six years; those between fifteen and eighteen at seven years, while all below fifteen years were compelled to remain with their masters until they reached the age of twenty-two years. [159]

Servants in Maryland were from the first placed under the protection of the law, which no doubt threw many safeguards around them, preventing impositions in many cases, and securing them justice from hard and inhuman masters. Either by law or by custom the practice grew up of rewarding these servants at the expiration of their time of service, as we find in 1637 one of these servants entitled to " one cap or hat, one new cloth or frieze suit, one shirt, one pair of shoes and stockings, one axe, one broad and one narrow hoe, fifty acres of land and three barrels of corn " out of the estate of his deceased master.[160] There, as in Pennsylvania, the way to preferment was open to man and master alike. There as here many of these Redemptioners became in time prosperous, prominent people. No stigma was attached to this temporary ser-

---

[159] LOUIS P. HENNIGHAUSEN, *The Redemptioners and the German Society of Maryland*, pp. 1–2.

[160] LOUIS P. HENNIGHAUSEN, Case quoted from *Maryland Archives*, 1637.

vitude, and intermarriages between masters and their female servants were not infrequent, nor between servants and members of the master's household.   But these people could not select their masters.   They were compelled to serve those who paid the sums due the ship captain or ship owner.   Indeed their lot was often during its duration actually harder than that of the negro slaves, for it was to the owner's interests to take care of his slaves, who were his all their lives, while the indentured servants remained with him for a few years only.   There were consequently as many complaints there as in Pennsylvania.

We must not lose sight of the fact, however, that for many years these Redemptioners were almost exclusively of English and Irish birth.   It was not so easy to deal with them as with foreigners.   They sent their complaints to England, and measures were taken there to prevent the abuses complained of.   The press even took up the refrain and the letters sent home appeared in the newspapers, ac-

Wm Markham

companied by warnings against entering into these contracts.   It was not until the institution was in full career in Penn's province that it began there.   The first Germans who reached Maryland in considerable numbers were such as migrated out of Pennsylvania.   Lancaster county lay on the Maryland border, and the migrating instinct soon took them to Baltimore, Harford, Frederick and the western counties.   As these people made themselves homes and became prosperous, they needed labor for their fields and naturally enough preferred their own countrymen.   The

Newlanders, however, were just as willing to send their ship-loads of human freight to Baltimore as to Philadelphia, and it was not long before ships began to arrive in the former port even as they were doing at the latter. While Pennsylvania, in 1765, at the instigation of the German Society newly formed in the State, passed laws for the protection of these immigrants, nothing of the kind was done in Maryland until a long time afterwards. The Maryland newspapers of the period teem with notices of the arrivals of immigrant ships and offerings for sale of the passengers, just as did those of Philadelphia. Here are a few examples :

From the *Baltimore American*, February 8, 1817—

"GERMAN Redemptioners.

" The Dutch ship *Jungfrau Johanna*, Capt. H. H. Bleeker, has arrived off Annapolis, from Amsterdam with a number of passengers, principally farmers and mechanics of all sorts, and several fine young boys and girls, whose time will be disposed of. Mr. Bolte, ship broker of Baltimore, will attend on board at Annapolis, to whom those who wish to supply themselves with good servants, will please apply ; also to Capt. Bleeker on board."

Two weeks later this appeared in the same paper :

" That a few entire families are still on board the *Johanna* to be hired."

Here is another :

"For Sale or Hire.

" A German Redemptioner, for the term of two years.

He is a stout, healthy man, and well acquainted with farming, wagon driving and the management of horses.   For further particulars apply to

"C. R. GREEN, Auctioneer."

Redemptioners.

THERE ſtill remain on board the ſhip Aurora, from Amſterdam, about 18 paſſengers, amongſt whom are,

Servant girls, gardeners, butchers, maſons, ſugar bakers, bread bakers, 1 ſhoemaker, 1 ſilver ſmith, 1 leather dreſſer, 1 tobacconiſt, 1 paſtry cook, and ſome a little acquainted with waiting on families, as well as farming and tending horſes, &c. They are all in good health. Any perſon, deſirous of being accommodated in the above branch es will pleaſe ſpeedily to apply to

Captain JOHN BOWLES,
in the ſtream, off Fell's-Point;
Who offers for Sale,

80 Iron-bound Water Caſks
1 cheſt elegant Fowling Pieces, ſingle and double barrelled
15,000 Dutch Brick, and
Sundry ſhips Proviſions.
July 14.   d7t eq4t

SHIPMASTER'S ADVERTISEMENT OF REDEMPTIONERS.

On April 11th we have this:

"GERMAN REDEMPTIONER—$30 REWARD.

"Absconded from the Subscriber on Sunday, the 5th inst., a German Redemptioner, who arrived here in November last, by name Maurice Schumacher, about 30 years of age, 5 feet 9 inches, well proportioned, good countenance, but rather pale in complexion, short hair, has a very genteel suit of clothes, by trade a cabinet maker, but has been employed by me in the making of brushes. He is a good German scholar, understands

French and Latin, an excellent workman, speaks English imperfectly. $30 Reward if lodged in jail.

"Jos. M. Stapleton,
"Brush Maker,
"139 Baltimore Street."

On March 3d a reward is offered for the capture of a German Redemptioner, a tailor who took French leave from Washington.

On March 11th a reward of $30 is offered for the capture of a German Redemptioner, a bricklayer.

As late as April 7th of the same year, 1817, I find our old friend, the *Johanna*, which, arriving on February 8th, had not yet disposed of her living cargo, as the following advertisement shows :

"GERMAN REDEMPTION-
ERS.

"The Dutch ship *Johanna*, Captain H. H. Bleeker, has arrived before this City, and lies now in the cove of Wiegman's Wharf; there are on board, desirous of

THE PRICE OF A "DUTCH BOYE."

binding themselves, for their passage, the following single
men : Two capital blacksmiths, a rope maker, a carrier, a
smart apothecary, a tailor, a good man to cook, several
young men as waiters, etc.   Among those with families are
gardeners, weavers, a stonemason, a miller, a baker, a
sugar baker, farmers and other professions, etc."
Two months in port and not all sold yet!
One more extract from the *Baltimore American* and I
am done.   It is this, in the issue of February 7, 1817, a
winter of extraordinary severity in that latitude :

" A ship with upward of 300 German men, women and
children has arrived off Annapolis, where she is detained
by ice.   These people have been fifteen weeks on board
and are short of provisions.   Upon making the Capes,
their bedding having become filthy, was thrown overboard.
They are now actually perishing from the cold and want
of provisions."

No bedding, few provisions, with the thermometer rang-
ing from five degrees above to four below zero.   Surely
the Maryland Redemptioner was tasting all the miseries
of servitude, as his Pennsylvania brother had done for
three-quarters of a century previously.

In answer to a strong newspaper appeal made by a
German descendant, a meeting of Germans and descendants of Germans was called on February 13, 1817, to form
a society to protect and assist, so far as was possible, the
German immigrants.   That action resulted in the formation of the German Society of Maryland.   The membership was composed of the best and most prominent men in
the State, and it at once went to work with an energy and
determination that promised good results.   The captain of
the *Johanna* was prosecuted for illegal practices and for
appropriating to his own use the effects of dead passengers.
The sick on board were sent to hospitals.

John Penn

In 1818 the Society was instrumental in securing the passage of an act by the Maryland Assembly consisting of numerous sections in which provision was made to do away with the evils which had hitherto prevailed in the importation, sale and treatment of Redemptioners of German and Swiss ancestry. Every one of the disgraceful practices which formerly obtained was done away with. The Society took care that this excellent law was strictly enforced and in a few years the bringing over of Redemptioners became so unprofitable that the very name disappeared from the records. Upon one occasion—it was in March, 1819—a ship, the *Vrouw Elizabeth*, reached Baltimore with a number of immigrants, who before embarking had subscribed to the usual conditions. But when they reached this country, they refused to comply with their agreements. The officers of the Society refused to countenance this action and wrote them a letter in which they said that as the Captain of the ship had treated them with the utmost kindness, they must comply with their contracts and that the Society would not countenance their attempt to evade their honest obligations. Herein the Society manifested its desire to deal fairly with Shipmasters as well as with the poor people they brought over.[161]

It deserves to be stated that, in addition to the large number of Germans who went to Maryland from Pennsylvania, there was also considerable immigration into that State through the port of Annapolis. From the entries at that city we learn the fact that from 1752 to 1755, 1,060 German immigrants arrived there; in 1752, 150; in 1753, 460; and in 1755, 450. They are spoken of as Palatines.[162]

[161] I desire to express my acknowledgment for many of the foregoing facts relating to the Redemptioners of Maryland, to the excellent little work of LOUIS P. HENNIGHAUSEN, Esq., to which I have already referred.

[162] *Publications of the Society for the History of the Germans in Maryland*, for 1890-1891, pp. 18-19.

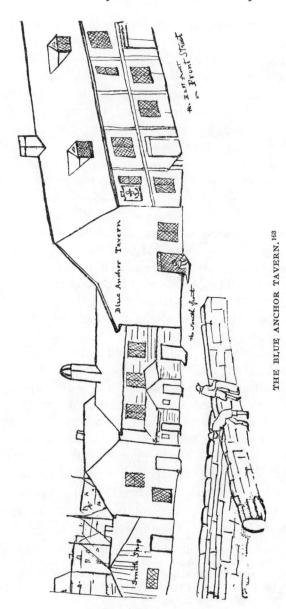

THE BLUE ANCHOR TAVERN.[163]

"No public records were kept of the contracts entered into abroad by the Redemptioners (of Maryland) nor of the time of the expiration of their service. The Redemptioners were not furnished with duplicates of their contracts. They could be, and sometimes were, mortgaged, hired out for a shorter period, sold and transferred like chattel by their masters. (*Maryland Archives,* 1637–50, pp. 132–486.) The Redemptioners, belonging to the poor and most of them to the ignorant class, it is apparent that under these circumstances were at a great disadvantage against rapacious masters, who kept them in servitude after the expiration of their true contract time, claiming their services for a longer period.

"As the number of slaves increased in the colony, and labor became despised, the Redemptioner lost caste and the respect which is accorded to working people in non-slave-holding communities. He was in many respects treated like the black slave. He could neither purchase nor sell anything without the permission of the master. If

---

163 One of the historical buildings of early Philadelphia was "The Blue Anchor Tavern." It was built at the confluence of Dock Creek with the Delaware. This creek was formed by several springs leading out of the swampy ground near its mouth. The tavern was built by George Griest. It stood on what is now the southwest corner of South and Ninth streets. The river bank in front of it was low and sandy and elsewhere high and precipitous. Penn left the ship *Welcome* on which he had come over, at Upland, now Chester, and came up the river in a boat, landing at "The Blue Anchor." Tradition assigns to it the honor of being the first house built in Philadelphia. It was small in size, having fronts on both Front and Dock streets, with ceilings 8½ feet high. While it looked like a brick house it in reality was framed of wood with bricks filled in. The tavern, from its favored locality, was a noted place for business. All small vessels made their landing there. There was a public ferry across Dock Creek at the tavern, Dock Creek being then navigable for small craft. Griest, the first landlord, was a Quaker, as were his successors, Reese Price, Peter Howard and Benjamin Humphries. Proud says the house was not quite finished at the time of Penn's arrival in November, 1682. Later the tavern went by the name of "The Boatswain and Call." It was torn down in 1828. (See WATSON'S *Annals of Philadelphia.*)

caught ten miles away from home, without the written permission of his master, he was liable to be taken up as a runaway and severely punished. The person who harbored a runaway was fined 500 pounds of tobacco for each twenty-four hours, and to be whipped if unable to pay the fine. There was a standing reward of 200 pounds of tobacco for capturing runaways, and the Indians received for every captured runaway they turned in a ' match coat.' For every day's absence from work ten days were added to his time of servitude. The master had a right to whip his Redemptioner for any real or imaginary offense, which must have been a very difficult matter to determine, for offenses may be multiplied. The laws also provided for his protection. For excessively cruel punishment the master could be fined and the Redemptioner set free. I presume in most cases this was only effective when the Redemptioner had influential friends who would take up his case." [164]

The System in New York.

New York had a similar system, although, owing to the fact that the many large landed estates owned by the Patroons, were worked by free tenant farmers, the number of white indentured servants was not nearly so great as in Pennsylvania. The character of this labor was, however, the same as in Pennsylvania and Maryland. They consisted of convicts sent from England and Ireland, of the miserably poor who were kidnapped and sold into servitude, and of Redemptioners who were disposed of on their arrival, as in Pennsylvania, to pay the cost of transportation and other expenses.[165] It is elsewhere stated in these

---

[164] Louis P. Hennighausen, *The Redemptioners*, pp. 5–6.
[165] See John Fiske's *Dutch and Quaker Colonies in America*, Vol. II., p. 286.

At a Council at the Court House, Saturday the eighth of September 1753.

Present

Joshua Maddox Esquire.

The Foreigners whose names are underwritten, imported in the Ship St Michael, Thomas Ellis commander from Hamburgh but last from Cowes did this day take the usual Qualifications.

No 62

Johann Benedicktus Breittenfeld
Friedrich Heinrich Hern
[---] Herst
Andereas + Lindner
Harmen in [---]
[---] Schäfer
[---] Hann Hohn
John Henry + Ratiler
J Henry + Grootjor
Johann [---] Morgen
Hans Henry + Fete
Johann Erich Reider
Johan Friedrich Bachr
Johann Henry X Saxe
Christian Wilhelm Töll
Johann Horper
J. George X Saxe
Johannes X Kehr
Friederich + Ranlery

Willhelm + Latink
Christian + Latinck
J Henry + Seydling
Lorentz X Shlüter
J. Friederich X Utter
J. Andereas + Vougt
G. Christoph + Warinken
J Henry + Krape
Cord Henry X Sander
J. Peter X millberg
Clas Coffen X Kröger
J. Christian + Heyl
Michael X Kind
Johan David Clein
Christoph Wegener
Hieronimus Engler
Conrad X Eichler
Ludewig [---] Töpper
H. Christoph + Gall

pages that many of the children of parents who died on
the ten ships that brought over the more than three thousand Germans to New York in 1710, were bound out to servitude by the Government authorities.

The State of New York also legislated on this perplex-
ing question, as may be seen by the following:

" AND WHEREAS, the emigration of poor persons from
Europe hath greatly conduced to the settlement of this
State, while a Colony; AND WHEREAS, doubts have arisen
tending to the discouragement of further importations of
such poor persons;—*therefore* be it further enacted, by the
authority aforesaid that every contract already made or
hereafter to be made by any infant or other person coming
from beyond the sea, executed in the presence of two witnesses and acknowledged by the servant, before any
Mayor, Recorder, Alderman or Justice of the Peace, shall
bind the party entering into the same, for such term and
for such services as shall be therein specified: And that
every assignment of the same executed before two credible
witnesses shall be effectual to transfer the same contract
for the residue of the term therein mentioned. But that
no contract shall bind any infant longer than his or her arrival to the full age of twenty-one years; excepting such
as are or shall be bound in order to raise money for the
payment of their passages, who may be bound until the
age of twenty-four years, provided the term of such service
shall not exceed four years in the whole." [166]

THE TRAFFIC IN VIRGINIA.

The early Virginia colonists were a class, who came not
to work themselves, but to live on the labor of others.

---

[166] *New York Laws*, Chapter 15. "An act concerning apprentices and Servants." Passed February 6, 1788.

This required the aid of servile labor. Negro labor was at first resorted to. That was in 1619, but as the demand was greater than the supply, other sources had to be found. Convicted criminals were sent from the mother country in large numbers. But other means were also resorted to. Men, boys and girls were kidnapped in the streets of London, hurried on ship-board and sent to the new colony, where they were indentured as servants for a term of years. The usual term of service was four years but this was only too frequently prolonged beyond that period for trivial offenses. Fiske says " their lives were in theory protected by law, but when an indentured servant came to his death from prolonged ill usage or from excessive punishment, or even from sudden violence, it was not easy to get a verdict against the master. In those days of frequent flogging, the lash was inflicted upon the indentured servant with scarcely less compunction than upon the purchased slave."[167] But the majority of the indentured white servants of Virginia, like those of Pennsylvania, were honest, well-behaved persons, who like the latter sold themselves into temporary servitude to pay the charges of transportation. The purchaser paid the ship master with the then coin of the colony, tobacco, and received his servant. There as in Pennsylvania they were known as Redemptioners, and like those in this State numbered many of excellent character. There was no let up in this importation of convicts and servants until it was terminated by the Revolutionary War. It has been variously estimated that the number of involuntary immigrants sent to America from Great Britain between 1717 and 1775 was 10,000 and during the seventeenth and eighteenth centuries 50,000.[168] Probably a ma-

[167] JOHN FISKE'S *Old Virginia and her Neighbours*, Vol. I., p. 177.

[168] *American Historical Review*, II., p. 25. See also the *Penny Cyclopedia*, Vol. XXV., p. 138.

jority of these reached Virginia.   The latter colony received more Redemptioners than any of the other colonies during the seventeeth century, but in the eighteenth, Pennsylvania was the more favored province.

There were still another class of servants who were sent to America who deserve to be mentioned in this connection.   They were prisoners of war, men who were captured by Cromwell at Dunbar and Worcester.   Some of

PASSENGER SHIP OF THE PERIOD—1750.
From a Contemporary Drawing.

these were sent to Virginia.   After the restoration of the Stuart dynasty, so many non-conformists were sold into servitude in Virginia as to lead to an insurrection in 1663, followed by legislation designed to keep all convicts out of the colony. [169]

Of the services rendered to the colony of Virginia by these indentured servants it has been said they were " the main pillar of the industrial fabric, and performed the most honorable work in establishing and sustaining it." [170]

In Virginia, as in Pennsylvania, many of these Redemptioners rose to be persons of wealth and importance in the Commonwealth, and occasionally became members of the House of Burgesses. At the same time it deserves to be very distinctly stated that the general character of the Redemptioners in Virginia was by no means equal to that of the Germans who came to Pennsylvania; nor was anything else to be expected considering the classes from whom so many sprung.

In New Jersey.

Mellick informs us that the laws of New Jersey were about like those of Pennsylvania in relation to the Redemptioners. Contiguous as the two were, with only the Delaware river between, this was to be expected. In Section 5, of the *Colonial Entry Book* of that State, occurs the following :

" The waies of obtayning these servants have beene usually by employing a sorte of men and women who make it theire profession to tempt or gaine poore or idle persons to goe to the Plantations and having persuaded or deceived them on Shipp board they receive a reward from the person who employed them."

---

[169] FISKE'S *Old Virginia and her Neighbours*, Vol. II., pp. 184–185.

[170] BRUCE'S *Economic History of Virginia*, Vol. I., p. 609.

"Many of the early settlers of Virginia reached that colony as servants, doomed according to the severe laws of that age, to temporary bondage. Some of them, even, were convicts." (BANCROFT'S *History of the United States*, Vol. II., p. 191.)

In New Jersey, under the laws, white servants could not be compelled to serve more than four years if sold or bound after attaining the age of seventeen years. Young children were held until they attained their majority. When the term of service expired the redemptioner received two suits of clothing, one falling axe, one good hoe and seven bushels of corn. The master was not allowed to inflict corporeal punishment upon his bond servant, but he could bring the case to the attention of a civil magistrate.

It is a noteworthy fact that the most popular novel published in the United States in the year 1899 has a Redemptioner for its hero, and for the most part the scene of the novel is laid in New Jersey. Another work of fiction, almost equal to the previous one mentioned in popularity, deals with a Redemptioner hero in Virginia.[171]

The colony South Carolina also received some of this Redemptioner immigration, and pretty nearly the same

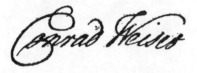

conditions and terms for taking them there, and holding them in bondage, prevailed as elsewhere.

Joshua Kocherthal in his little pamphlet, published in Frankfort in 1709, in which he strives to divert German emigration from Pennsylvania to South Carolina, says in his ninth chapter that "Special arrangements have to be made with the Captain for each half grown child. Perons too poor to pay, sometimes find proprietors willing to advance the funds, in return for which they serve the latter for some time in Carolina. The period of service, in time

---

[171] FORD'S *Janice Meredith* and JOHNSTON'S *To Have and to Hold.*

of peace, is from two to three years, but when the fare is
higher (he states it to be from five to six pounds sterling,
but the cost of a convoy and other expenses, raise it to
seven and eight pounds for every adult), the time is necessarily longer." [172]   He adds in an appendix that " an immigrant to Pennsylvania must have the ready money with
which to prepay his passage, while for one going to Carolina, this is not necessary."

---

[172] *Full and Circumstantial Report Concerning the Renowned District of Carolina in British America*, 1709.

See also DR. JACOBS' *German Emigration to America*, pp. 39-40.

THE DE LA PLAINE HOUSE, GERMANTOWN.

CHAPTER X.

ARGUMENT ATTEMPTING TO SHOW THE REDEMPTIONER
SYSTEM WAS BY NO MEANS AN UNMIXED EVIL.—THAT
MUCH GOOD CAME OUT OF IT.—THAT IN MOST RESPECTS
IT WAS PREFERABLE TO THE UNENDING ROUND OF TOIL
THAT HAD TO BE ENCOUNTERED IN THE FATHERLAND.

FRANKLIN ARMS.

"O, Rivers, with your beauty time-defying,
Flowing along our peaceful shores to-day,
Be glad you fostered them—the heroes lying
Deep in the silent clay.

"Be jubilant ye Hill-tops old and hoary—
Proud that their feet have trod your rocky
ways ;
Rejoice, ye Vales, for they have brought you
glory
And ever during praise."

ONE hundred and fifty years
are but a short period in
the history of the human race.
In the early ages of the world
that number of years would come
and go and at their close men thought and did and felt
about as at their beginning. Habits and morals were not as
now, things that change almost as regularly and frequently

(292)

as the earth's revolutions around the sun. But times have undergone a wonderful transformation during the past century and a-half. So far away is 1730 in its customs and manner of thought, that we hardly realize that it was the time in which our great-grandfathers lived, and yet in some things we seem as far removed from those days as we are from the biblical patriarchs who lived and died upon the Judean hills, thousands of years ago.

This man-traffic, which I have attempted to describe in these pages, did not at that time create the general abhorrence with which we now regard it. It was a matter of every-day business in every community. It had the

SPECIMEN OF EPHRATA DISPLAY TYPE, MADE AND USED AT THAT
PLACE PRIOR TO 1748.

endorsement, so far as we may judge from the records and the spirit of that time, of the majority of the community. It was recognized as a legitimate business by

the laws of the land.   It was in full accord with the common life of the people.   Even Sauer, Mittelberger,
Muhlenberg and the other worthies of that period who
have been referred to and liberally quoted, did not arraign
the system itself, but the numberless and almost nameless
abuses it called forth.   It was the injustice, the hardships,
the rascality, misrepresentations, methods of transportation, the crowded condition of the ships, the hunger and
starvation, the sufferings, the general horrors by which it
was accompanied, that called forth their protests.   Never,
since men have gone down to the sea in ships, have such
sufferings and iniquities been known.   Only men dead
to all the better instincts of our human nature could have
been guilty of the barbarities practiced upon these inno-
cent, helpless victims of man's inhumanity to man.

Even as I read them to-day, I cannot understand why
these men did not arise in their might and their wrath,
smite their oppressors, and cast them into the sea, even as
their own dead were thrown into the kindly waters, un-
knelled, uncoffined and unknown.   They were many and
their oppressors few ; smarting under the deceptions and
wrongs practiced upon them, their forbearance seems almost inexplicable.   Here, too, the spirit of the age played
its part.   It was an age of loyalty to lord and master.   To
them the doctrine of *jure divino* was not a mere abstrac-
tion.   It was one of the overmastering principles of their
lives.   They were respecters of authority, and to an extent that for half a century and more led to their disadvantage.   For once the divine precept of obedience to authority worked to their undoing.

We fail to understand how these poor people should have
consented to all this unutterable injustice and wrong-doing
for several generations.   If the immigrant of 1728 was

unaware of what was in store for him, the same cannot be said of those who came in 1750 and thereafter. The At-

FAC-SIMILE OF COVER ON BAILEY'S GERMAN ALMANAC.[173]

[173] The above cut is a fac-simile of the cover on an almanac—*Der Gantz Neue Berbesserte Nord-Americanische Calender. Auf das 1779ste Jahr u. f. w. Berfertigt von David Rittenhaus*,—published at Lancaster, Pa., by Francis

lantic was wide, but not so wide that letters could not reach the relatives and friends who were still in the old home. We know many of them wrote and told the horrors that had been encountered. It is true, as is elsewhere recounted, that the Newlanders even stole the letters from America, when they could, to prevent the dismal tales they told from becoming known to those for whom they were intended; but that, doubtless, was an infrequent occurrence, and possible only on favorable occasions. Why then did these people persist in coming, five and six thousand yearly, for lengthy periods? The question is difficult to answer, perhaps, and yet I venture upon an explanation.

Why do thousands of gold-seekers and other adventurers brave all the hardships of Alaskan winters to find fortunes in the Klondike? Everybody knows that not one in a score of them is successful, and yet the hegira thitherward is as active to-day as when that wealth-fever first set the gold-seekers in motion. We hear and know some are successful. The rest hope they may be. All who came to America did not score failures. Not all were penniless and needy. Those who were able to make a fair start were successful far beyond anything they could ever have attained in their old homes. The virgin lands were rich almost beyond description. In that the booklets of Penn, Pastorius, Thomas and others did not exaggerate. The situation in this particular was not overdrawn, and the lands were cheap. It is true there was hard labor and plenty of it before the settler. But he was a German, strong of will

Bailey. It possesses especial historical interest from the fact that the winged allegorical figure of Fame, seen in the upper part, holds in one of her hands a medallion portrait of Washington, while in the other she has a horn, from which a blast is blown with the legend *Des Landes Vater.* This is the first recorded instance where the designation of "Father of his Country" was given to Washington.

PENNSYLVANIA-GERMAN FARM LIFE.

A COMMUNITY CIDER-PRESS.

and limb, inured to toil and not afraid to labor every day in the year except Sundays, if the situation required such service. The seasons were on his side and he saw houses and lands, such as he never dreamed of owning, belonging to him, yielding him an abundant support and providing an inheritance for those whom he should leave behind him.

Another important condition of life came to the front with these people, to which most of them perhaps had been strangers in the old home. It was the question of food. Not only did the soil yield its abundant harvests, but the fields and the woods made no mean additions to their larder. Game of many kinds was at their command. Fur and feather and fin may almost be said to have been as much the product of their farms as wheat and corn and potatoes. Meat could be on their tables daily if they so desired. Mittelberger is very explicit on this point. He says: "Provisions are cheap in Pennsylvania. The people live well, especially on all sorts of grain, which thrives very well, because the soil is wild and fat. They have good cattle, fast horses and many bees. The sheep which are larger than the German ones, have generally two lambs a year. Hogs and poultry, especially turkeys are raised by almost everybody. Every evening many a tree is so full of chickens that the boughs bend beneath them. *Even in the humblest and poorest houses in this country* there is no meal without meat, and no one eats the bread without the butter or cheese, although the bread is as good as with us. On account of the extensive stock raising, meat is very cheap: one can buy the best beef for three kreuzers a pound." [174] He tells of poultry and eggs, fish, turtles, venison, wild pigeons, and other foods; not

---

[174] MITTELBERGER'S *Reise nach Pennsylvanian im Jahr 1754*, pp. 64-65.

to mention nuts, grapes and other fruits that were to be had in every woods for the gathering.

All these things were well known in the Fatherland. Every letter spoke of them. Such flattering tales had their effect. They came for the most part to men and women whose lines in life were hard and drawn. The struggle for existence there was all those words imply. Nowhere in Europe was it harder. It was a from-hand-to-mouth life. The food was often scant, and not of the best at that. As these letters and the various descriptions of Penn's wonderful land which were everywhere distributed by the Newlanders were read around the fireside during the bleak winters, and the ever-present scant larder forced itself upon the mind, there could be but one result.

The overmastering instinct of the race to better its condition came upon them. There are many causes that lead men to seek new homes, in distant lands, but there is one that overtops all the rest. It is the desire to better their worldly condition, the hope of material advancement, in short, it is better bread and more of it that lies at the source of nearly all the migrations of the human family. The love of gain, the desire for property and the accumulation of wealth was the great underlying principle of all colonization on the American continent. It was this all-powerful motive that crowded out all else, and led these people to brave all dangers, known and unknown, to reach this western Eden. So long as distress and danger and difficulties are in the dim distance, we fail to give them due consideration. It is only when they become a present reality, a source of trial and sorrow, that we realize the true condition of things.

These people were ready to encounter the obstacles they knew were to be met. Perhaps they underestimated their importance and character. That was something which could not be guarded against. At all events, their fears were cast behind them and that hope which springs eternal in the human breast held sway, and spurred them to take the leap in the dark which many lived to regret, and which thousands regretted while dying. No sadder tale can ever be told. It has become an imperishable page in the history of the Germans of Pennsylvania ; one that the historian reluctantly deals with, so full of sorrow and heartbreak is it.

So abominable and inhuman were the dealings of the Newlanders, shipmasters, ship-owners and most of the commission merchants with these helpless immigrants, and so sad and sorrowful the fate of many of them, that the wrath of the reader is also aroused and the denunci-ation has become universal.

BARBER'S BASIN, IN USE 150 YEARS AGO.

The same incidents are told by them all, and the worst are of course chosen for exposure ; the same tale of starvation and pestilence and death is rehearsed so that we almost insensibly reach the conclusion that from the beginning until the end, there was one long, continuous cloud over the horizon of these people, unrelieved by a single rift and un-illumined by a single ray.

Almost every writer whom I have consulted has written only in terms of unqualified condemnation of the evils that arose out of the system of bonded servants. There is however one noteworthy exception.

Elder Johannes Naas, who, next to Alexander Mack, was the most celebrated and influential member of the Taufer or Brethren church in Germany, came to this country in 1733. Shortly after his arrival he wrote a long letter to his son, Jacob Wilhelm Naas, who was living in Switzerland at the time, in which all the incidents and circumstances of his voyage are minutely detailed. The letter is well worth reading by every one who has an interest in the events I have been trying to depict. Want of space prevents its appearance here in its entirety. The concluding portion bears directly on the case of the Redemptioners, and contrary to the customary practice, the writer regards that question favorably, rather than otherwise, for which reason I quote that part of his letter.

Elder Naas' Letter.

"Now that we have safely arrived in this land and have been met by our own people in great love and friendship all the rest has been forgotten (the mishaps and hardships of the voyage) in a moment, so to speak, for the sake of the great joy we had in one another. This hardship has lasted about nineteen weeks; then it was over, wherefore be all the glory to the Highest: Amen, yea; Amen!

"For it does not rue us to have come here, and I wish with all my heart that you and your children could be with us; however, it cannot be and I must not urge you as the journey is so troublesome for people who are not able to patiently submit to everything, but often in the best there are restless minds, but if I could with the good will of God do for you children all, I assure you that I would not hesitate to take the trip once more upon me for your sake; not because one gets one's living in this land in idleness! Oh! no; this country requires diligent people, in what-

FAC-SIMILE OF EARLIEST ENTRIES IN TRAPPE CHURCH RECORDS, MARCH 8, 1729.

ever trade they may be—but then they can make a good living. There are, however, many people here, who are not particularly successful ; as it seems that if some people were in Paradise it would go badly with them. Some are to be blamed for it themselves ; for when they come to this country and see the beautiful plantations ; the number of fine cattle ; and abundance in everything ; and, knowing that they only just have come here too, then they want to have it like that at once, and will not listen to any advice but take large tracts of land with debts, borrow cattle and so forth. These must toil miserably until they get independent. Well, what shall I say, so it is in the world, where always one is better off than the other. If a person wants to be contented here, with food and shelter, he can under the blessing of God and with diligent hands get plenty of it. Our people are well off ; but some have more abundance than others, yet nobody is in want. What I heard concerning the people who do not have the money for the passage, surprised me greatly, how it goes with the young, strong people and artisans, how quickly all were gone, bricklayers, carpenters, and whatever trades they might have. Also old people who have grown children and who understand nothing but farm labor, then the child takes two freights (fare for two) upon itself, its own and that of the father or of the mother four years, and during that time it has all the clothing that is needed and in the end an entirely new outfit from head to foot, a horse or cow with a calf. Small children often pay one freight and a half until they are twenty-one years old. The people are obliged to have them taught writing and reading, and in the end to give them new clothes and present them with a horse or cow.

"There are few houses to be found in city or country

where the people are at all well off, that do not have one or two such children in them. The matter is made legal at the city hall with great earnestness. There parents and children often will be separated 10, 11, 12, 13, 14, 15, 16, 17, 18, 19, 20 hours (in distance), and for many young people it is very good that they cannot pay their own freight. These will sooner be provided for than those who have paid theirs and they can have their bread with others and soon learn the ways of the country.

" I will make an end of this and wish patience to whomsoever reads this. God be with you all. Amen.[175]

"Johannes Naas."

This is an extreme view, and not wholly a just one. The facts as they stand recorded in the works of historians and the letters of private individuals are true, and they must always be accepted as such. At the same time it must be admitted they present us with but one side of the story. Is there no other side to their picture? There are, admittedly, two sides to every narrative? Is this one of the German immigration and the indenturing of many individuals as servants for a term of years an exception? It would, indeed, be an anomalous case if it were so. But it is not. Men like Christoph Saur and Pastor Muhlenberg and Gottlieb Mittelberger embarked in this cause to right a great existing wrong, one that was daily occurring before their own eyes, and with which they were almost hourly made acquainted. It was a crime almost without a parallel in its atrocity, practiced against their countrymen and it may be, their own kith and kin. They were tireless in their efforts

---

[175] The complete letter from which the above extract is taken may be found in Dr. M. G. BRUMBAUGH'S recently published *History of the German Baptist Brethren*, pp. 108–123—a valuable addition to the early religious history of Pennsylvania.

to strike it down.   They left no stone unturned, nothing undone that would do away with this crime against humanity.   They showed it up at its worst to arouse the better part of our human nature against the evil, believing, and most truly, that in this way it could most quickly be driven out of existence.   If they saw a brighter side to the question it was not for them to reveal it.   It was the wrong against which their blows were directed.   The better and brighter side needed no defense and, therefore, none was made for it.

ONE OF THE DANGERS ENCOUNTERED BY THE EARLY SETTLERS.

And there was a brighter side just as certainly as there was a dark one.   That must, indeed, be an evil's crown of evil that is wholly and unspeakably bad and totally without redeeming features.

Let us, for a while, turn this gloomy picture to the wall and see whether we can discover something better on the other side.   Let us bear in mind, in the first place, that while many plunged heedlessly into the pitfalls laid by the soulless soul-brokers, there were—must have been—thousands of others who were not ignorant of what a servant for a term of years meant. Why did these eager thousands hurry from their homes in the Fatherland to such a fate here? We know full well how it was with a majority of them there. Born in poverty, unable to rise above the station of hewers of wood and drawers of water, they were doomed to lives of unceasing toil, with the hope of bettering their condition as remote as the distant and unheeding stars. What had even the fertile valleys of the Rhine to offer these men? Nothing, and well they knew it. Surely things could not be worse for them in America, and in this we must all agree.

It was a voluntary action on their part. They knew the consequences of their step. They were aware that a shipowner would not carry them three thousand miles across the broad ocean and feed them on the way for nothing, merely out of charity. Men do not give valuable things to every comer for nothing. They knew this indebtedness must be repaid when they reached this country by some one for they could not do it themselves. But whoever assumed the temporary burden, they knew that in the end their own strong arms must make payment. It cannot be doubted the trials of the voyage were more severe than was anticipated. For that, perhaps, they were not prepared. A healthy young man who may never have known a day's sickness in his life, little thinks the plague will smite him on ship-board; and it was the foul diseases disseminated by personal contact that more than decimated so many hopeful ship companies that sailed out of Rotterdam. It will hardly be contended that the men coming to Pennsylvania under such conditions looked forward to anything but a life of work until time wiped out the score that had been marked up against them.

It is true we read of "Servants" or "Redemptioners" who fell into the hands of hard taskmasters. No doubt this was the case. It has been the case since the days of Pharaoh and will continue to be while masters and servants exist upon the earth, and that, most probably, will be until the end of time.

But that was not the rule. I cannot bring myself to believe that they were not mostly exceptional cases.[176] It was natural that Germans already in the country and in need of help on their farms, or in whatever occupation they may have been engaged, should have preferred their own countrymen. The Germans hold together: it is one of their characteristics, and always has been. The employer preferred one who spoke his own language: who can doubt that? That he preferred one from his own dorf or locality is also certain. When such came together it could not have been difficult to strike a bargain. And having thus made their engagement, will it be doubted that the faithful service of the Redemptioner, anxious to free himself and his wife and perhaps his children also, was not appreciated by the master, his own countryman, and perhaps even an acquaintance? To doubt kind treatment from the buyer to the bought, under these conditions is to impugn German honor, German kindness, and that German sense of right which we know is always true to eternal instincts. We have reason to know that as a rule the existing conditions worked well. It was also the servitor's privilege to find another master when the one he had was not to his liking.

---

[176] "These indentured servants were not badly treated either by the Swedes or the Friends. Their usual term of service was four years, and they received a grant of land, generally fifty acres, at the expiration of the term. The system was originally contrived in Maryland in order to increase the labor of the province, and many of the bond servants were persons of good character, but without means, who sold their services for four or five years in order to secure a passage across the ocean to the new land of promise." (SCHARF & WESTCOTT'S *History of Philadelphia,* Vol. I., p. 134.)

If these men were poor, they were nevertheless honorable. It was their bounden duty to comply with their contracts. Nothing could be gained by shirking their duties, save trouble. Every one was certain that the day of deliverance would come, when he in turn would be an independent land-owner and entitled to all the rights of citizenship enjoyed by any one. He saw around him, men of standing and character in the community, who had stood on the lowest rung of the social ladder where he himself was then standing. They had attained their position by fulfilling their engagements faithfully. They were an example and their successful careers were an incentive to all who knew them, to also do as they had done. The laws of the Province made no distinction between him and those above him. He could aspire to anything or any place anyone else had attained. In addition to that, they lent him a helping hand when the hour of his freedom arrived and gave him lands, if he wanted them, on the most favorable terms. There was every incentive for a " Redemptioner " to make a man of himself if he had the will and ability to do so. And why should he not strive towards that end ? His hour, the hour so long awaited, had come at last ; the prize he had set out to reach was now within his grasp ; the day of fruition was at hand. He had worked hard, but he had done that in the Fatherland also, done it on scanty rations and without any hope of rising or in any way bettering his position. He had passed that point in his new home. He was a free man. The three, four, or five years had rolled away quickly and he was now master of the situation.

And what had others done? They had become the owners in fee simple of estates that ranged from a hundred to a thousand acres of the best and brightest lands the sun shines on to-day. They had become the owners of estates, which in Germany would have entitled them to the highest consideration. In all but name, they had in reality become what the Newlander had promised. Nowhere in all North

A CUSTOM IN THE FATHERLAND.

America was such prosperity seen. It had taken years of honest toil to accomplish this, but it had been done and now the independent owner could sit down, literally as well as figuratively, under his own vine and roof tree with the world's abundance of good things about him.

With such encouragement the " Redeemed "—no longer the " Redemptioner "— had but to go to work for himself as earnestly as he had done for him who had taken him into his family. Generally he was a man in the vigor of life, with many years of good work still in him. There was still ample time to go ahead and improve his condition. Released from the indenture that had held him, with his

earlier ambition to improve still strong within him, his lot
was a hundred fold better and more promising than it had

Kort en klaer ontwerp,

dienende tot

Een onderling Accoort,

O M

Den arbeyd / onruſt en moeye-
lijckheyt/van Alderley-hand-wercx-
luyden te verlichten

D O O R

Een onderlinge Compagnie ofte

Volck-planting(onder de protectie vande H: Mo:
Heeren Staten Generael der vereenigde Neder-lan-
den;en byſonder onder het gunſtig geſag van de
Achtbare Magiſtraten der Stad Amſtelre-
dam) aen de Zuyt-revier in Nieu-neder-land op te rechten; Beſtaende in

Land-bouwers,
Zee-varende Perſonen,
Alderhande noodige Ambachts-luyden, en Meeſters
van goede konſten en wetenſchappen.

Steunende op de voor-rechten van hare Acht-
baerheden (als hier na volgt) tot dien eynde verleent.

t'Samen geſtelt

Door Pieter Cornelisz, Plockhoy van Zierck-zee, voor hem ſelven en andere
Lief-hebbers van Nieu-neder-land.

t'Amſterdam gedruckt by Otto Barentſz. Smient, Anno 1662.

TITLE-PAGE OF PLOCKHOY'S BOOK.
Containing a Scheme for Settlement on the Delaware.[177]

---

[177] There is, perhaps, no book or tract relating to the history of Pennsylvania
that has greater interest for the student of the early history of the State than
the little book whose title-page is given in fac-simile above. It is the first description of the country written by one living there at the time, and who died

been in his old home. He felt it and he fell to work to make the most of it. German industry and German thrift still accompanied him. The greedy ship-master and the avaricious broker could not rob him of these. With them and the ready assistance that was ever forthcoming on the part of the old master and nearby acquaintances, he started out on his independent career.

The result is well known. He prospered as he deserved to do. His cattle multiplied and the soil failed not to pour forth its abundance. The days of adversity passed away. The era of prosperity took their place, and his early hopes and aspirations were realized. That was the career of thousands. Even though some had in earlier days encountered unspeakable evils, was not this rich fruition of later years infinitely better than anything that could have fallen to their lot in Germany? There they were not bound to a master by indentures, but necessity compelled them to serve him nevertheless from boyhood until incapacitated by age, when the poorhouse received their worn-out frames. He was a servant all his life without any recompense at its close, while his food in the meantime was

---

within its borders after spending most of his life there. The man was Peter Cornelius Plockhoy, a Dutchman who led a colony of Mennonites to Pennsylvania at an unknown period and settled at the Hoorn Kill, several miles below Philadelphia. After having been in existence only a few years, Governor Carr, of New York, sent an expedition up the Delaware, which broke up and dispersed the little colony. What became of Plockhoy, the founder and leader, there are no records to tell. He, however, wrote and had printed at Amsterdam, in the Dutch language, in 1662, the little tract bearing his name, in which he gives a history of his colony and its people. With the dispersion of his little colony, Plockhoy also disappeared, and it was not until 1694, when aged, blind and destitute, he, with his wife, reached the Mennonite settlement at Germantown, where kind and willing friends built him a house, planted him a garden, and where he died. There is not a more pathetic story connected with the history of our State than this one of poor Plockhoy. His little tract is of excessive rarity, the only copy in Pennsylvania being in the library of Judge Pennypacker, of Philadelphia.

See *Proceedings of the Pennsylvania-German Society*, Vol. II., p. 34.

FRANKLIN COLLEGE, 1787.

THE PENNSYLVANIA-GERMAN SOCIETY.

that of the poor laborer, poor in kind and scant in quantity. Surely, we cannot contrast such an existence with that passed by his fellow laborer, Redemptioner though he was, in the welcoming breezes of Pennsylvania.

Thousands of them achieved both fame and fortune. Often, if he was a good man and true, he married his quondam owner's daughter, and with her got back part of the riches his years of honorable servitude had helped to create. Among his own countrymen he lost no caste by reason of his service. Why should he? In the world around him one-half his fellows were working as hard as he to repay borrowed money or to pay for lands or other valuables they had purchased. He too was paying a debt voluntarily incurred and there was no disgrace attached to it.

Our early history is filled with the story of Redemptioners who grew rich by their honest toil and left honorable names to their descendants. I have at this moment an autobiographical sketch lying before me, written by one of these people. He came to the town where I was born, and for nearly half a century lived within easy speaking distance of my own home. He was well educated. He was honest and faithful. The community honored him with public office, while his enterprise, energy and thrift brought him a large estate. He founded a family and his descendants to-day are honorable and honored, the wealthiest people in the community.[178] These are things we

---

[178] So few Redemptioners, so far as I have ascertained, left records of their careers, that I am tempted to throw in the form of a note a part of what the one spoken of above says of himself. After telling of his birth at Diedelsheim, in the Palatinate, on January 16, 1750, he proceeds to relate that his father was a Lutheran clergyman and his mother the daughter of another also ; who the sponsors at his baptism were, all of which were furnished to him by his pastor when he left Germany. He then says :

"My beloved father died in the year ——, at the age of 57 : my beloved

must not forget in passing judgment upon this man traffic. Common fairness demands it. It rescued thousands from lives of poorly requited toil and placed them where their labor met with its proper reward. Instead of remaining hewers of wood and drawers of water until life's close, they were placed in conditions where the results of their

---

mother departed this life in the year 1760. Even in my tender youth, no expense and pains were spared upon my education by my parents. My father had me not only attend church and hear the word of God, but also diligently attend school. I was also sent to a Latin school from my 6th to my 13th year, that with this and an acquaintance with other necessary branches of knowledge, I might the better get along in the world. For the parental love and faithfulness I experienced, may the great God reward my parents before the throne of the Lamb in Heaven.

"After my father found me qualified to renew my baptismal covenant by a public profession of my faith, I was confirmed in the 13th year of my age, and received for the first time the Lord's Supper. Soon after I expressed my wish to learn the mercantile profession, to which my father gave his consent. I then served a four years apprenticeship in the city of Stuttgart with Mr. Barnhard Fredk. Behruger. After this I went to Heidelberg where I was in the employ of John W. Godelman for two years. From thence I went to Manitz and entered the celebrated house of John George Gontzinger.

"In order to learn more of the world and to improve my fortune, I resolved to travel to Holland, with the hope of finding employment in some large com merical house. My undertaking was unsuccessful, and this contributed to my coming to America, for as I saw no prospect of getting employment in Holland and did not wish to return to my native land, the way to America was prepared. I crossed the ocean in the ship *Minerva*, Capt. Arnold, and landed in Philadelphia on Sept. 20, 1771. I had to content myself with the circumstances in which I then was, and with the ways of the country, which it is true, were not very agreeable. I was under the necessity of hiring myself to Benjamin Davids, an inn-keeper, for three years and nine months. My situation was unpleasant, for my employment did not correspond with that to which I had been accustomed from my youth, in my fatherland. In the course of nine months my hard service ended, for with the aid of good friends, I found means in a becoming way to leave Davids, for the employ of Messrs. Miles & Wistar, where I remained three years and six months."

The foregoing narrative shows how difficult it was, even at that early day, to secure honorable, remunerative employment in the Fatherland. Here was a young man, well born, well nurtured, of good education, trained to business, and yet after serving four years at service in a mercantile house, could find no employment either in his own land or in Holland. As a last resort he came to America. His career answers my argument affirmatively that, despite his three years and nine months of unwelcome service, it was the best thing he could do. It is very certain that he never regretted it.

work went to reward themselves. Not one of all this vast multitude, could their views have been ascertained, would have preferred the old hum-drum life of the Fatherland with its many trials and few rewards to the newer life, the freer air, the more generous living and less oppressive burdens they found in the pleasant land of Pennsylvania.

THE MORRIS HOUSE IN GERMANTOWN.
Where Washington lived in 1793.

At this distant day we can hardly realize all the untoward circumstances and conditions that fell into the lives of these sons of the Fatherland—these children of misfortune and of want. It has been said man must be born somewhere; it is true, and wherever that somewhere may be, that spot, though it be the bleakest on all the earth, will live in his memory forever, and cost him many a pang ere he becomes reconciled to new conditions.

To leave home and friends and country is a trial under

even the most favorable circumstances. To leave them, penniless, with the future all doubt and uncertainty, but with a full knowledge that a life of toil, hard and unremitting, with perhaps nothing better at the end of it, is as dreary a prospect as can shadow any life.

Thousands of them, after spending many years in freeing themselves and their loved ones from the clutches of the taskmaster, had to begin life anew on their own account, in the silence and gloom of the forest. Here their remaining years were passed, generally with abundance crowning their declining years. They had at last homes and fireside comforts to leave to those who came after them. The worst for them was now over. True, they had at last attained their early hopes, but how much in mind and person had to be endured before the period of fruition arrived. How often in their hours of deepest sadness and gloom the memories of the earlier days in the old home must have forced themselves with overpowering strength upon these sons of sorrow! Only men and women deeply imbued with the consolations of religion could have survived it all without following the advice of the Hebrew prophet's wife, to curse God and die.

Out of those olden forests, out of those homes in the valleys and mountain recesses emerged men imbued with the same spirit of freedom and independence that has marked the men of German ancestry during the long ages that have come and gone since Tacitus portrayed their sturdy virtues in his imperishable pages. Centuries of suffering as well as centuries of success were needed to build and mould the German character into what we find it to-day. The crown has come after the cross. Wrong and sorrow and toil were theirs, but through them all they were true to their lineage, and now, when another century and a-half has come and gone, the proudest eulogium we can pass upon them and their work is the one we could wish succeeding generations may pronounce upon us :— they fought a good fight, they kept the faith.

> " We leave their memory to the hearts that love them ;
>   Their sacrifice shall still remembered be ;
> The very clouds shall pause in pride above them
>   Who, though in bonds, were free."

GENERAL INDEX.

ACT, regulating sale of servants, 161; regulating discharge of servants, 162; regulating the concealment of servants, 162; regulating fees charged by public officials, 163; regulating importation of criminal servants, 164.

Action of Massachusetts Legislature, 64.

Acts relative to Provincial servants, 158, 159, 160, 161.

Agriculturists, well educated, 135.

All immigrants at first called Palatines, 53.

Ambler, Capt. Nathaniel, 204.

American Historical Association, 230.

American Weekly Mercury, 200, 201, 202.

Amsterdam, experience of immigrants in, 176.

An age of loyalty to rulers and law, 294.

Annapolis, 277, 280; immigration through port of, 281.

Antigua, island of, 208.

Application for naturalization in 1721, 90.

Appropriation of £1,000 for pesthouse, in 1750, 87.

Argyle, the ship, 203.

Arms, of Sweden, 10; of Holy Roman Empire, 13; of the Printers' Guild, 14; of William Penn, 17; of George Ross, 271.

Armstrong, Captain of ship *Rachel*, 88.

Arrivals of ships in 44 years, 43.

Asking the Governor's Assistance, 6.

Asylum for distressed Protestants of the Palatinate, 115.

Attempted explanation of Immigration, 296.

Author's estimate of the German population, 100.

Autobiography of F. S., a Redemptioner—became a citizen of standing and fortune, 312.

Average tonnage of immigrant ships, 48.

BAILEY'S ALMANAC, cover of, 295.

Baltimore American quoted, 277–280.

Baltimore, Lord, derives ideas for his colony from Virginia, 150.

Bancroft's History quoted, 95, 125, 225, 287, 289.

Bär, Abraham, mentioned, 207.

Beach, Captain, of the Ship *Francis and Elizabeth*, 87.

Berichte, Saur's German newspaper, 200, 204, 205, 206, 207, 208, 209, 211, 211.

Berkeley, Bishop, in America and his prophetic vision, 75.

Berks county spoken of, 94.

Best time for making voyage, 28.

Bill for visiting infected vessels, 86.

Cromwell's prisoners sent to America and sold as Redemptioners, 119.
Cumberland county settled by Scotch-Irish, 119.

DANGERS in wait for early settlers, 304.
Dauphin county receives settlers, 92.
Deficient food and drink, 55.
Delaware, Penn's government on banks of, 142.
Desire for lands, 94.
Dickinson, Jonathan, letter by, 33.
Discomforts of voyage, 55.
Diseases contracted on voyage, 257, 258, 259, 260.
Dislike of New York, 30.
Dissension over laws concerning Redemptioners, 155.
Donegal township settled by Scotch-Irish, 133.
Dübendörffer, John and Alexander, arrive, 41.
Dunbar, Cromwell at, 288.
Dutch and German probably spoken by Penn, 16.

EARLIEST Germans left no permanent settlements, 10.
Early provincial records reasonably complete, 8.
Ebb and flow of immigration, 44.
Ebeling estimates German population of Pennsylvania, 99.
Eby, Benjamin, history quoted, 33.
Efforts, to establish a hospital in Philadelphia in 1738, 77; of immigrants to secure naturalization, 89.
Egan, Barney, letter to, by Charles Marshall, 226.
Eickhoff, earliest reference to traffic in Redemptioners, 172.

Eickhoff, Anton, quoted, 173.
Embarkation of 3,000 Germans for New York, 258.
Endeavor, name of ship, 219.
Endless chain, as applied to German land titles, 128.
English as Redemptioners, 218.
Ephrata community, mystic seal of, 231.
Errors in regard to German population, 117.
Every writer condemns traffic in Redemptioners, 299.
Excessive mortality on shipboard, 55.
Exodus, German, to England mentioned, 258.
Extent of German immigration not realized at first, 11.
Extract from Franklin's German paper, 65.
Eyers, Capt., mentioned, 37.

FAC-SIMILE of title of Penn's letters to the Society of Free traders, 35; also of Brief Account, 23; of Trappe Records, 301.
Falkner, Daniel, arrives in 1700, 20; his " Curiouse Information " Tract, 20; his continuation of Thomas' book, 111.
Families separated by sale, 182.
Favorable accounts sent home concerning Pennsylvania, 33, 240.
Few German arrivals between 1783–1789, 49.
Fiery Cross of the Highlands spoken of, 15.
Fifty acres of land allotted to Redemptioners, 267, 268, 269, 270, 271, 272.
Fifty thousand convicts sent to America, 287.